THE PROSPECT OF
NUCLEAR JIHAD IN PAKISTAN

The Prospect of Nuclear Jihad in Pakistan

Armed Forces, Islamic State, and the Threat of Chemical and Biological Terrorism

Musa Khan Jalalzai

Algora Publishing
New York

Library of Congress Cataloging-in-Publication Data —

Jalalza'i, Musa _K_han, author.
    The Prospect of nuclear jihad in Pakistan: armed forces, Islamic State, and the threat
of chemical and biological terrorism / Musa Khan Jalalzai.
        pages ; cm
    Includes bibliographical references and index.
        ISBN 978-1-62894-165-4 (soft cover: alkaline paper)—ISBN 978-1-62894-166-1
(hard cover: alkaline paper) ISBN 978-1-62894-167-8 (eBook) 1. Pakistan—Politics and
government. 2. Nuclear terrorism—Pakistan. 3. Pakistan. Army—Political activity. 4.
Civil-military relations—Pakistan. 5. Islamic fundamentalism—Pakistan. 6. Religious
militants—Pakistan. 7. IS (Organization) I. Title.
    DS389.J357 2015
    363.325'5095491—dc23
                        2015027710

Printed in the United States

Table of Contents

I am grateful to Mr. Musa Khan Jalalzai who requested me to write a foreword for his book. Mr. Jalalzai is the author of many books, and contributes articles in various newspapers, on counterterrorism and political issues. The present well-written research book that mainly focuses on Pakistan's nuclear weapons, jihadism and the exponentially growing networks of Islamic State (ISIS). After Pakistan's nuclear test in 1998, the threat of nuclear terrorism and the proliferation of nuclear weapons in South Asia gained the attention of the international community, with fears that terrorists could acquire materials and gain nuclear know-how. In this regard, the International Atomic Energy Agency (IAEA) categorized three potential nuclear security threats: theft of a nuclear weapon and material to make an improvised nuclear explosive device, and radioactive material. Terrorist groups are actively seeking nuclear weapons or material. There are more than 100 incidents of theft or misuse of nuclear material each year. Twenty-five countries now possess weapons usable nuclear material; and nuclear facilities are expanding into dangerous neighborhoods around the globe.

The entire above mentioned are possible in Pakistan as the country's armed forces have established links with Taliban, ISIS and other extremist groups, in and outside the country. However, there is speculation that extremist elements within Pakistan's armed forces may provide nuclear material to terrorist groups to use it in India; therefore, the Pakistan Atomic Energy Commission and Strategic Planning Division removed hundred of experts. The killing of Pashtun children, men, and women in Swat, Tirah, FATA and Waziristan, by the Pakistan army, caused deep ethnic divide in the country. South Asian Terrorism Portal (SATP) reported: "Pakistan has unfailingly proved to be a country, where hardcore sectarian and India-oriented Punjabi jihadists find widespread public and official support. There has been a considerable and increasing presence of at least 57 extremist and terrorist groups in Punjab alone".

Islamabad continues with its most dangerous friendships with purveyors of terror, even as it makes desperate efforts to contain some aspects of domestic terrorism. In a 15-minute-long video released in December 2014, TTP openly exposed the past misdeeds of the Pakistan Army. A senior leader of the group, Adnan Rashid, a former Pakistan Air Force officer, accused the Pakistan Army of taking a "U-turn" and labeling jihad as terrorism, and mujahedeen as terrorists, and warned: "You remember when thousands of Pakistani youth fought your proxy war in Afghanistan and in Indian Kashmir.... And then you went into the dollar game and you earned millions from the proxy war in Afghanistan and you deceived the nation in the name of jihad. The Muslims have not forgotten the bloody game you played in Indian Kashmir, exploiting youth in the name of so called freedom"...

Relations between the Pak army and terrorist organizations are not new; the army always uses these proxy groups to destabilize India and Afghanistan. Some extremists who were recruited, funded, and trained by the ISI are now fighting in India and Afghanistan. A Daily Times report claimed that Maj. Haroon Ashiq received Rs, 150,000 from known terrorist, Ilyas Kashmiri, and killed Maj. General Faisal Alavi. "Officers of the rank of major" in the intelligence agencies, with links with the Taliban and Al-Qaeda had been arrested "because they wanted to target army generals." Former Interior Minister Rehman Malik said.

In February 2015, Dawn reported Interior Minister Choudhry Nisar Ali Khan directed Secretary to coordinate with the Ministry of Foreign Affairs, to reconcile a 'national list' of proscribed organizations, as per the blacklist of the United Nations. Officials in Interior Ministry said that the number of proscribed outfits in Pakistan, reached 72, and includes 12 banned organizations. Dawn reported Interior Ministry added Harakat-ul-Jihad Islami, Harkat-ul-Mujahedeen, Falah-i-Insaniat Foundation, Ummah Tameer-i-Nau, Haji Khairullah Hajji Sattar Money Exchange, Rahat Limited, Roshan Money Exchange, Al Akhtar Trust, Al Rashid Trust, Haqqani network and Jamaatud Dawa to the list of proscribed organizations. The Punjab-based Kashmiri Islamist groups such as Harkatul Mujahedeen (HuM), and Harkatul

Jihad-i-Islami (HuJI), as well as sectarian outfits such as Lashkar-I-Jhangvi (LJ), Jaish-e-Mohammad (JeM) and Harkatul Mujahedeen al-Alami broke off from HuM, the 313 Brigade came out of the HuJI, and Al Qanun and Al Mansur came out of the largely anti-India and hitherto 'peaceful' Lashkar-e-Toiba after the commencement of the 'global war on terror'.

During the Operation Zarb-e-Azb, in North Waziristan, no single 'good' Taliban commander was arrested. Yes, the army has arrested a good number of innocent Pashtuns, and continues to prosecute them in military courts. The problem of nuclear and biological terrorism deserves special attention from the governments of Pakistan and Afghanistan, because the army of ISIS can develop a dirty bomb, in which explosives can be combined with a radioactive source, like those commonly used in hospitals or extractive industries.

The use of this weapon might have severe health effects, causing more disruption than destruction. Political and military circles in Pakistan fear that, as ISIS has already seized chemical weapons in Al Muthanna, in northern Iraq, some disgruntled retired military officers or experts in nuclear sites, might help the Pakistan chapter of the group, to deploy biological and chemical weapons. A letter from the Iraqi government to the UN warned that, the militant-captured-chemical weapons site contains 2,500 chemical rockets filled with the nerve agent Sarin.

There is a general perception that extremist organizations in South Asia could use some advanced technologies against civilian populations. If control over these weapons is weak, the possibility of theft will increase. Each state has its own approach towards the threat perception. The more recent focus on global terrorism is also now sharpening, the focus on non-proliferation activities, that do not necessarily apply at the level of the state. There are speculations that non-state actors might possibly engage in these activities. The Islamic State that controls parts of Iraq and Syria has established its network in Afghanistan and Pakistan, as the region is already dominated by violent terrorist groups. The New York Times reported that as 1,000 Turks joined the ISIS network, the CIA estimated that the group had anywhere from 20,000 to 31,500 fighters in Iraq and Syria.

The Islamic State (ISIS) is clearly winning the media war. No matter how heinous their crimes, they are still able to recruit fighters from many nations, especially, from Tunisia, Afghanistan, Pakistan, and Europe. The threat of ISIS in Pakistan and Afghanistan is also a matter of great concern. President Ashraf Ghani expressed deep concern on the emergence of the Islamic State (ISIS) in Afghanistan, and requested that as his country's army is unable to counter this threat, the US should re-examine the current troop withdrawal timetable. Afghan Ministry of Interior also confirmed the exponential networks of ISIS in Afghanistan, while in Islamabad, Pakistan's foreign Ministry warned about the ISIS threat in the country.

Pakistan's Foreign Secretary Aziz Ahmad Choudhry told the Senate Foreign Affairs Committee at Parliament House, that Islamic State was indeed a real concern. The ISIS is now demonstrating as a strong organization since the TTP, some Afghan Taliban groups; Lashkar-e-Islam and Boko Haram have joined it. There are speculations in Islamabad's establishment, that Lashkar-e-Toiba may possibly join the ISIS network as well. The international community has also expressed deep concern on the existence of ISIS in Afghanistan. The head of Canada's spy agency warned that the Islamic State (ISIS) is spreading to Libya, Pakistan and Afghanistan. "Boko Haram just pledged allegiance to ISIS; so there's also this phenomenon of ISIS spreading," the spy chief said.

The spread of ISIS in South Asia has major ramifications. During a hearing of the US Senate Foreign Relations Committee, Chairman of the Joint Chiefs of Staff said that the growth of an ISIS-affiliated organization in Afghanistan would "initially" pose a threat to the government of Afghanistan. The Islamic State manages a sophisticated extortion racket by robbing, looting, and demanding a portion of the economic resources in areas where it operates, which is similar to how some organized crime groups generate funds. The Islamic State has gained control of the Akashat Phosphate Mine and the Al-Qaim manufacturing plant, both located in Iraq's Al-Anbar province, and owned by the Iraqi's State Company for Phosphate Manufacture which produces both sulfuric acid and phosphoric acid.

Pakistan and India are hard hit victims of extremism, while nuclear terrorism is a bigger threat. However, currently, international community is considering South Asia on the brink of nuclear terrorism. The hostile attitude of India towards Pakistan, once again puts the process of peace and stability in the region at spike. India has developed various types of tactical nuclear weapons, which have threatened the security of the region. The test of Pakistan's ballistic missiles, Shaheen-III and Nasr, capable of carrying a nuclear warhead, and India's ballistic missile, Prahaar and others, complicated nuclear weapons race in South Asia. India's tactical nuclear weapons are more dangerous than Pakistan. Indian nuclear missiles like Agni-I,

Agni-III, VI and V present a bigger threat to the national security of the subcontinent. India has also launched various military and surveillance satellites to enter into an anti-satellite weapons, and ballistic missile defense race with China. The main threat of nuclear terrorism comes from Pakistan, according to western intellectual circles, where the military and intelligence establishment has close ties with terror groups.

The future of the nuclear weapons race between Pakistan and India is precarious as both states continue to develop modern tactical nuclear weapons. On October 5, 2013, the foreign secretary of Pakistan said, "We have appraised India of our concerns on terrorism. If India has apprehensions about Pakistan, then we have more apprehensions than India," he said. Experts suggested that as the situation is going to deteriorate in the region, India and Pakistan need to resume talks on all issues, including the Line of Control, and tactical nuclear weapons. They need to work with each other on these issues that could spark an abrupt nuclear war in South Asia. Notwithstanding all efforts of the international community to help secure the nuclear weapons of both states, and as nuclear facilities, and infrastructure have grown, there are concerns that security measures may not be sufficient to protect their nuclear and biological installations.

The development of nuclear missiles that could be fired from a ship or submarine would give Pakistan "second-strike" capability, if a catastrophic nuclear exchange destroyed all land-based weapons. Over the past two years, Pakistan conducted at least nine tests of various land-based ballistic or cruise missiles that it said were capable of delivering nuclear warheads. Pakistan is the fastest-growing nuclear state in the world. Pakistan wants to construct a fourth reactor and expanding its ability to reprocess the spent fuel from these reactors to obtain additional plutonium. Once all four reactors and associated reprocessing facilities are completed, Pakistan will be able to produce an estimated 10-12 bombs-worth of plutonium a year. The nuclear threat to South Asia is not just from its nuclear members, but also from its closest neighbor, China. China has huge interest and influence in the South Asian region. At contemporary International Relations, the countries that highly cause concern in South Asian security are India, Pakistan and additionally China. On 25 February 2015, researcher Ashley J. Tellis noted the confrontations between India and Pakistan:

> Pakistan's strategic weaponry is believed to be deployed in de-mated condition routinely in peacetime. Whether that posture will

apply to the newer tactical systems is unclear. Pakistan's nuclear doctrine, unlike India or China's, is centered fundamentally on first use, and it is oriented primarily towards defeating India's conventional superiority in the event of conflict. Although Pakistan's nuclear forces are intended, strictly speaking, for deterrence and not war fighting, Islamabad's emerging tactical capabilities could inadvertently push Pakistan towards the latter. The external dangers of deterrence breakdown, which could precipitate the catastrophe of Pakistani nuclear use against India, are complemented by internal dangers as well. Pakistan's internal fissures, it is often feared, could bleed into its armed forces, resulting in risks to the security of its nuclear weaponry.

Nuclear terrorism is a grave and emerging threat to international peace and security. But no such accidents have been reported so far. But claiming that Pakistan's nuclear facilities, weapons or material are more prone to theft or terrorist attacks is something which is naive on the part of authors. The Taliban terrorists have targeted Pakistan's nuclear installations time and, while the recent attacks in Karachi and at the air force aviation base in Quetta were similar to the ones that occurred in Wah, Mehran base, Sargodha and Kamra, confirmed by Southern Command Commander General Nasir Khan Janjua in his statement to journalists. He admitted that 12 terrorists were killed on the spot and 14 soldiers, including civilians, were injured during the fight in Quetta.

Noor Dahri
Independent Researcher in Counter Terrorism & Violent Extremism, Associated with International Institute for Counter Terrorism, ICT—ISRAEL

INTRODUCTION

Fires small and large, burn throughout the region. In this book, I layout the evidence, that a far greater bonfire is being set, which could engulf South Asia. One can only hope that wisdom and calm will prevail. When we talk about Pakistan's nuclear politics, its armed forces, law enforcement agencies, politicians, judiciary, and the civilian governments, only controversies, misperceptions and unmentionable things swirl in our minds, posing an unimaginable riddle. One can only conclude that not everything is going in right direction in the country; because the army, religious leaders, politicians, and the establishment perceive the export of terrorism as a profitable business for them. They run an actual business of killings and torture, through proxies in Afghanistan, India and their own country. In February 2015, former President General Pervez Musharraf told the Guardian that ISI actively cultivated the Taliban, to counter Indian action against Pakistan.

In his short interview with the newspaper, Mr. Musharraf said: "In President Karzai's times, yes, indeed, he was damaging Pakistan and therefore we were working against his interest. Obviously, we had to protect our own interest." However, he shamelessly admitted that his government had been responsible for the killings of innocent Afghan men, women and children in the Inter-Services Intelligence (ISI) constituted suicide attacks. General Musharraf said that the ISI trained the Taliban after 2001 to undermine the Karzai government dominated by India-supported non-Pashtuns. "Obviously we were looking for some groups to counter this Indian action against Pakistan," he said. However, Dr.

Muhammad Taqi (12 February 2015) also noted Mr. Musharraf's nefarious designs against the people of Afghanistan and India:

> In response to a question on why his regime signed an agreement in 2006 with the Haqqani network, General Musharraf said that as India was stabbing Pakistan in Baluchistan and the Frontier through Afghanistan, he decided to find someone who could stab them back. Musharraf said, "Do you know that Jalaluddin Haqqani was a hero for the US...we thought we could bring peace to the region through him."

In fact, when we study this kind of radicalized mindset among Pakistani generals, and their resentment towards Afghanistan, we find more controversies about the proper role of armed forces and their relationship with terrorist organizations. Pakistani merchants of menace have managed the business of fear, forced disappearance, killing, torture, and kidnapping in Afghanistan, Baluchistan, Waziristan, FATA (Federally Administered Tribal Areas) and Kashmir, and continue to promote a hostile environment in South Asia.

Afghan- and Indian-focused militants continue to operate from Pakistan territory to disrupt efforts of regional stability. Pakistan uses these proxy forces to hedge against the loss of influence in Afghanistan, and to counter India's superior military, the Pentagon told Congress, in its six-monthly report on the current situation in Afghanistan. In a letter sent to the office of Secretary of State John Kerry, Chairman of the House of Foreign Affairs Committee, Eliot Engel, sternly demanded to consider implementing travel restrictions, suspending portions of assistance, and sanctioning Pakistani officials that maintain relationships with designated terrorist groups.

The ethno-sectarian counter terrorism policy of Pakistani generals fosters dozens of networks of terrorist groups, across the Durand Line. There is speculation that the ISI supports and trains these groups to further its nefarious agenda of strategic depth in Afghanistan. The ISI has also trained terrorist groups to destabilize India and Bangladesh. The armed forces want peace in Afghanistan, but it also wants a puppet government in Kabul. They want peace with India, but at the same time understand that conducting Jihad against India is their religious duty. There are many contradictions in Pakistan's counterterrorism policy.

The army wants to remain engaged with the United States against Pakistani Taliban (TTP), but also wants to protect Afghani Taliban, and expel India from Afghanistan. The military wants a friendly relationship with Iran, but supports the Saudi backed regime in

Bahrain. This controversial policy of Pakistan's military establishment has tainted an image of the country in the eyes of international community.

In February 2014, Pakistan's civilian government announced a new counterterrorism policy after fighting against sectarian mafia groups on its soil, for more than four decades. In December 2014, the Nawaz Sharif Government announced another strategy after the killings of innocent children in the army school in Peshawar. Prime Minister Nawaz Sharif desired to settle the issue of the Taliban insurgency through negotiation, but the military establishment didn't allow him to proceed. They avenged the killing of their children, killed hundreds of innocent children in Waziristan and FATA, looted their houses, and kidnapped numerous men and women. They killed in group, looted in group, and raped women and girls in group.

On 11 February 2015, Dawn reported the revelation of 4,557 bodies of kidnapped and missing persons. The Supreme Court asked the federal government to effectively address in a coordinated manner the handling of unclaimed bodies, as well as the issue of missing persons. One after another, law officers presented the court with their reports about the number of unclaimed bodies found in their respective provinces, the highest number being in Khyber Pakhtunkhwa (KP). Realizing the grave state of affairs, the court summoned Attorney General Salman Aslam Butt, and asked him to take an interest in the matter. Dawn reported more bodies of missing persons across the country:

> The AAG of KP, Waqar Ahmed Khan, said 2,600 bodies were found in his province, of which 43 remained unidentified. He said many mutilated bodies were found in sacks. The AAG of Punjab, Razzaq A. Mirza said, 1,299 bodies were found during the period between 2013 and 2014. Of these 51 remained unidentified and they had been given to anatomy departments of different medical colleges. Sindh AAG Adnan Karim informed the court that 437 bodies were found in the province. Of these 398 were found in Karachi south. He said 94 bodies remained unidentified. Deputy Attorney General Sajid Ilyas Bhatti, representing Islamabad Capital Territory, told the court that 68 bodies were found in the capital from 2012 to 2014. He said 32 bodies remained unclaimed.

After these atrocities by the army, and its intelligence agencies against the innocent civilians, what can we expect from the Taliban, other than the attacks they carried out against the school children in Peshawar? In his first speech to the nation, Prime Minister Mian Nawaz Sharif reluctantly declared a war against terrorism and appeared indecisive on how to counter militancy and sectarianism in the presence of a Talibanized army. He developed some strategies, nevertheless, including: forming a Cabinet Committee on National Security, a Five Points Counter Terrorism Agenda, and a Counter Terrorism Force; he issued the Protection of Pakistan Ordinance, and revamped the National Counter Terrorism Authority; but faced the wrath of armed forces. He was forced to invoke article 245 of the constitution to hand over the control of Islamabad to the army. He was forced not to extend the hand of cooperation to India and Afghanistan. When he dared to invite Indian Prime Minister Narender Modi to Pakistan, the army started deprecating him on every forum.

In 2014, Mr. Nawaz Sharif was restive and tried to control the ISI and its worldwide terror network, but failed. He gave more powers to the Intelligence Bureau (IB), when Inter-Services Intelligence (ISI) failed to intercept, consecutive terror attacks on Pakistan's military and nuclear installations, and failed to maintain professional intelligence cooperation with civilian intelligence agencies, for the last four decades. This forced the Prime Minister to restructure the IB and make it more effective to meet internal and external security threats.

Consequently, the Prime Minister's office came under surveillance. He and his family members were being watched day and night. His office activities were monitored, and a deprecatory campaign against his family was promoted in the social media. In fact, the case of Mr. Sharif is not so different from the case of former President Asif Ali Zardari, who received death threats from ISI and the GHQ. He was sternly warned that an ambulance was ready to take him to the hospital; in other words, they were quite prepared to cripple or torture the President in his office.

A decade-long war between the civilian and military intelligence agencies deeply impacted their professional capabilities. They promoted their favorite sectarian groups, and sent them to Kashmir and Afghanistan. War in the FATA (Federally Administered Tribal Areas), Waziristan, Khyber Pakhtunkhwa, and Baluchistan, and their killing business in Afghanistan, resulted in widespread instability across the country.

On policy matters, there are huge differences between the civilian and the military establishment. The army is conducting its own foreign policy, managing its own businesses and industrial relations, designing its own counter terrorism strategy, and selecting its own friends and foes across the world—apart from those of the elected governments. Religious and sectarian parties also manage their own foreign policy, and counter terrorism policy, which is quite different from both the civilian and military establishments. These three foreign and counter terrorism policies are heading in opposite directions. The enemy of the army is a friend of the civilian government, and vice versa. Democratic governments want friendly relations with India and Afghanistan, while the army and the Mullahs tried to conquer Kashmir and Afghanistan, and establish their own style of Islamic state there.

In 2013, after the country's high court issued a series of rulings, holding the armed forces accountable for human rights abuses, and political meddling, the military establishment warned the civilian institutions against such campaign. Former Army Chief, Gen. (Retd) Ashfaq Parvez Kayani issued a stern warning in his statement: "As a nation, we are passing through a defining phase. We are critically looking at the mistakes made in the past, and trying to set the course for a better future." Speaking to officers at the GHQ, General Kayani said that no individual or institution had the monopoly, to decide what was right or wrong, in defining national interest, and it should emerge only through consensus. In court hearings, on forced disappearance; the court repudiated the military for the abductions and extrajudicial killings of innocent Pashtun men and women.

The issue of sectarianism within the army and intelligence agencies is also matter of great concern. There are Sunni, Shia and Tablighi brigades within the army, representing the Saudi, Iranian, Ahmadi, and Tablighi versions of Islam. The Northern Light Infantry (NLI) is composed of Sunni and Shia sectarian elements, which promotes sectarian conflicts in four provinces, including Gilgit and Baltistan. In the 1990s, Deobandi and Shia officers of the armed forces supplied weapons to both Sunni and Shia groups in Punjab, and Khyber Pakhtunkhwa provinces. On many occasions, war of words, and physical clashes between Shia and Sunni officers in military barracks, and GHQ, is often reported by insiders. The officers and soldiers turned their arms on each other, and passed secret information to their Taliban friends in the battlefield.

In Kurram Agency, once, officers of the army revolted against the shoot and kill policies of their military leaders, against the local Pashtuns, and attacked each other's barracks. Resentment against other sects, and the killings of civilians on sectarian bases, are impelling people to internal war. The issue of ethnicity and the killing of Pashtuns highlight another schism within the armed forces.

Pashtun army officers now loath Punjabi officers, and commanders, and openly discuss the extrajudicial killings of Pashtuns in Swat, Waziristan, Mohmand and Khyber Pakhtunkhwa. Some military observers link the killings of innocent school children to the internal turmoil of the armed forces. There are speculations that army is also part of this gory drama. Consequently, majority of Pashtun officers and their families have been put under strict surveillance in, and outside the military quarters. Their activities are closely monitored by the military intelligence and ISI, their telephones are tapped, and they have been confined to their barracks. Operations in Swat, Bajaur, Mohmand, Tirah, and North Waziristan, have done nothing to raise the credibility of the armed forces.

The issue of extra-judicial killing still needs to be settled as the world's human rights groups, the HRCP, and newspapers reported grim human rights violations in the country. On 16 January 2013, BBC reported that hundreds of protesters in Peshawar had displayed the bodies of at least 14 people, who they said were victims of extra-judicial killings, outside the governor's office. They were brutally killed by Pakistani intelligence agencies in FATA region.

In July 2014, to justify these and other atrocities of the armed forces, over 100 sectarian mullahs from various schools of thought, declared the army's war against Pashtuns (Zarb-i-Azb) as an Islamic jihad. The decree (fatwa) was issued after a meeting, organized by the Sunni Ulema Board. The decree referred to Verse No 33 of Surah-i-Almaidah of the Holy Quran, which says, "Crushing of the attempts to disrupt peaceful atmosphere in a Muslim state is jihad."

On 15 June 2014, Pakistani security forces abruptly announced war against the TTP in North Waziristan, bombed houses, and killed elderly men and women. This was sternly opposed by the civilian government. According to media reports, in Mir Ali district, a four-year-old Pashtun child was weeping in front of the body of his mother, while no one was allowed by the army to help the child. However, in the same area, a pregnant woman was killed by the army, while her infant son was weeping over her body helplessly. There are numerous incidents in which Pakistan's rogue army officers killed mothers in front of their children. When families from North Waziristan reached Bannu, they also found themselves abandoned, humiliated and harassed. They criticized the kill-and-kidnap policy there, claiming that civilians had suffered most.

Before the operation began, Pakistan's military protected the Haqqani Network and shifted terrorists to safe houses. Residents fleeing military attacks in North Waziristan described that the militants had already left the area. Tajik and Uzbek Taliban in North Waziristan arrived at barber shops, knowing little Pashto, "they ... utter[Ed] four words: 'mulgari (friend), machine, zero'." In Shawal Valley, in North Waziristan, the army killed 37 civilians including 20 women and 10 children. A member of the local peace council claimed his 13-year-old daughter, brother, sister-in-law, and two of their children were killed by the army.

In one of her Daily Times articles, a Pashtun woman writer, Dr. Farhat Taj, revealed atrocities, committed by the Pakistan army against the Pashtun tribe of Aash Khel in Kurram Agency:

> Recently, the Aash Khel clan clashed with the Taliban in Central Kurram during which the clan members captured a Taliban commander. Soon it turned out that the commander was actually a Major of the Pakistan Army, leading, in the garb of a Taliban commander, the group of Taliban foot soldiers, who had attacked the anti-Taliban Aash Khel clan. The Aash Khel was so angry that they decided to kill that Major. Upon this, both the Pakistan Army and the Taliban fighters jointly attacked the Aash Khel villages. This devastated their villages and rendered over 400 innocent Aash Khel men, women and children homeless and internally displaced.

On 19 December 2013, the Wall Street Journal reported the brutalities of Pakistan army:

> Residents in Pakistan's troubled North Waziristan tribal region said that dozens of civilians were killed in an army operation following a suicide attack at a checkpoint. Local residents said that more than 20 men, mostly Pashtun truck drivers, were shot dead at a restaurant, while shelling claimed several more lives, including women and children, as the army responded to the deadly attack on its nearby outpost. Localized military operations continued through the night around the town of Mir Ali.

The hotel owner, Mr. Tufail Dawar, told the Wall Street Journal that the next day, the restaurant was full of Pashtun truck drivers, when the army officers arrived and took all the drivers outside, lined them up and then shot them on heads. The killings and humiliation of women, and tribal elders prompted resentment and loathing against the military establishment of Pakistan. Several women, children, and the elderly died on their way to the settled areas of Khyber Pukhtunkhwa province, in the scorching heat, after three other provinces refused to give them entry. In the end of July 2014, the army began a house-to-house search in Miran Shah, killed women and children, and destroyed their houses.

The violent escalation of religious and ethnic conflict in Baluchistan province became more irksome as Sunni militants and the army targeted Shia Muslims. The 62-page report of the Human Rights Watch revealed heartbreaking stories about the killings of innocent Shias in Pakistan. A Baloch journalist, Mr. Ali Baloch, criticized the killing policy of Pakistan army in Baluchistan. He also raised the issue of extra-judicial killing in the province.

According the Human Rights Watch report, more than 400 Shiites were killed in 2013. In July 2014, the Baloch Republican Party held a protest in front of the United Nation office in Geneva, Switzerland, against human rights violations in Baluchistan. On 27 February 2014, the US Department of State issued Pakistan's human rights report for 2013, which broadly highlighted the forced disappearance of Balochs, and Pashtuns in the country. The report painted a frightening picture of human rights violations in Pakistan, and noted kidnappings and forced disappearances in nearly all areas of the country. Some police and security forces held prisoners incommunicado and refused to disclose their location. Human rights organizations reported that many Sindhi and Baloch nationalists were among the missing, and there were reports of disappearances during the year, in connection with the conflicts in FATA and KP.

On 27 January 2014, Asian Human Rights Commission (AHRC) reported 100 dead bodies of the killed Balochs in three mass graves in Baluchistan province. During the last ten years, hundreds of Ahmadis have been murdered for their faith and belief, and this horrifying brutality continues under the very eyes of the Government, who take no notice or action, and blatantly allow the culprits to go scot-free. The breakdown of law enforcement, continuing abuses across the country, ongoing torture and ill-treatment of Pashtuns, the disappearances of Balochs, and extrajudicial killings are matters of great concern. Sectarian groups, including those with known links to the military, its intelligence agencies, and affiliated paramilitaries—such as, the ostensibly, banned Lashkar-e-Jhangvi—operate with widespread impunity across Pakistan.

In view of the above mentioned ethnic and sectarian clefts within the armed forces, the safety and security of Pakistan's nuclear weapons became the center of debates, in print and electronic media across the world. According to a US-based think tank report, Pakistan has the world's fastest growing nuclear program, capable of weaponizing up to 200 nuclear devices by the year 2020. In another report, Council on Foreign Relations noted. "Pakistan...is believed to have enough fissile material to produce between 110 and 120 nuclear warheads,"

In June 2014, after the terrorist attack on Karachi airport, there were concerns in Afghanistan, Russia, India, and Europe about the safety and security of Pakistan's nuclear weapons. In Pakistan and India, several commentators raised the issue of the safety of Pakistan nuclear weapons, and warned that the threat of nuclear proliferation in the region was matter of great concern. Pakistan has already expanded and upgraded its nuclear program with the help of China. The country's scientists are striving to enhance the range of deficiencies of its delivery systems. What is most frightening is that Jihadist organizations in Pakistan have easy access to nuclear weapons, through their colleagues in the armed forces.

During the last 16 years, Pakistan doubled the number of its nuclear warheads, making them the fastest-growing nuclear weapon state in the world. However, India deployed a nuclear triad of bombers, missiles, and a submarine capable of firing nuclear weapons. Pakistan also developed a network of nuclear weapons factories, plutonium reactors and nuclear missiles. India invested heavily in spy satellites, aircraft, drones and early warning radar, while Pakistan developed spy and modern-warning systems. At present, both the states hold considerable nuclear stockpiles, which have doubled since 1998. Both the states have developed cruise missiles, and are seeking nuclear submarines. More worrisome is that India and Pakistan have developed military doctrines that increase the prospects of nuclear use. Although India has pledged not to resort to nuclear weapons as a first strike, it has increased its readiness to launch "Cold Start" conventional military strikes against Pakistan calibrated to deter Pakistani military or terrorist incursions. Meanwhile, Pakistani military planners insist that Pakistan will use nuclear weapons immediately if India attacks.

Now, China's tacit support to Pakistan in boosting the country's nuclear weapons is considered to hold strategic implications for India. The nuclear power relationship between Pakistan and China is widely seen as a continuing effort to respond to the India–U.S. civilian nuclear deal, which, among other things, ended a decades-long moratorium on U.S. companies selling nuclear technology to India, despite India not being a signatory to the Nuclear Non-Proliferation Treaty. The China–Pakistan deal is in violation of China's NPT obligations, and transgresses, the Nuclear Suppliers Group guidelines, that forbid

NPT-signatory states from supplying nuclear technology, and fissile material to states not party to the NPT.

The threat of Islamic State (ISIS) using WMD might present threatening situation, since the threat lies at the nexus of two subjects—ISIS terrorism and weapons of mass destruction—that are both characterized by high level of dynamism. Terrorist groups in Pakistan are trying to access bio-weapons to use against civilian populations in India and Afghanistan, as these groups have established strong networks inside the army quarters.

International media recently carried out stories of the presence of Islamic State (ISIS) and its recruitment centers in Afghanistan and Pakistan--funded by the Taliban, sectarian groups, drug smugglers and radicalized business firms. This terrorist group also poses a bigger challenge for the Afghan and Pakistani security forces. In September 2014, more than 800 members of the ISIS terrorist group stormed the Ajristan district of Ghazni province, killing 100 people including the ANA soldiers. The Daish group is also in contact with Lashkar-e-Jhangavi (LeJ), and Lashkar-e-Toiba in Punjab. On 11 December 2014, former Interior Minister of Pakistan Mr. Rahman Malik told a local news channel that Daish or Islamic State (ISIS) had established recruitment centers in Gujranwala and Bahawalpur districts of Punjab province. The wall-chalking campaign and leaflets prompted fears about the terrorist group making inroads in the country. According to the leaked government circular in Baluchistan and Khyber Pakhtunkhwa provinces, the Islamic State recruited more than 10,000 to 12,000 fighters for next sectarian war in Pakistan. I am sure, as they have already retrieved nuclear explosive from Iraq, they will start their jihad in Pakistan with the use of nuclear explosive devices.

However, on 09 August, 2013, New York Times reported Pakistan's nuclear forces were abruptly ordered, to be on high alert for a possible Taliban attack, on the country's military installations. Taliban and their allies had a plan to sabotage the country nuclear facilities and use a dirty bomb. On 07 September, 2012, Pakistan army deployed commando force at one of the country's biggest nuclear site, in Dera Ghazi Khan District of Southern Punjab, after an intelligence report warned of a possible Taliban attack. Even a minor attack on Pakistan's nuclear facilities would change the face of the country. In November 1999, Pakistani authorities used the Baghalchur area of Dera Ghazi Khan District as a dumping ground for nuclear waste, produced elsewhere in the country. "Barrels containing nuclear waste brought from Dera Ghazi Khan, Mianwali and other parts of Punjab were initially dumped in Baghalchur," a local Baloch told Herald Magazine. In 2005, the Magazine reported people from Baghalchur resorted to district and sessions court in Dera Ghazi Khan against the dumping of the waste.

After testing a nuclear bomb in Baluchistan, in the 1998, at the time of the Taliban rule, Pakistan dumped its nuclear waste in Afghanistan's Helmand and Kandahar provinces. In 1998, after India announced its nuclear capability, Pakistan also tested its nuclear bomb in the Chaghi area of Baluchistan province, 30 km from the Afghan border. Afghan experts and officials in the office of environment protection department said, that radiation from the Pakistan atomic bomb remained in the region, where the atomic bomb was tested. Muhammad Kazem Humayon, the President of National Environment Planning for the Office of the National Environment Protection Department of Afghanistan said, Pakistan at the time of Taliban rule in Afghanistan had taken opportunity from the friendly relation with the Taliban, and dumped their nuclear waste in Helmand and Kandahar provinces.

The future relationship between the army and jihadist groups and the possible use of weapons of mass destruction by the Islamic State (ISIS) raises many questions about the safety of country's nuclear weapons. A recent report of The Washington Post also warned that extremist groups could seize components of the stockpile or trigger a war with India. There were also reports from the US intelligence agencies that during the Kargil war, Pakistan army readied its nuclear weapons without the knowledge of Prime Minister Nawaz Sharif. A prominent Pakistani scientist, Dr. Parvez Hoodbhoy, also warned that the country's nuclear weapons could be hijacked by extremists, as a result of increasing radicalization within the army barracks. "If Pakistan did not have nuclear weapons, Kargil would not have happened... It was the first instance that nuclear weapons actually caused a war."

In 2013, secretary of Welfare Department of the Punjab government and columnist Orya Maqbool Jan warned, in a TV debate, that jihad against India is mandatory on every Pakistani Muslim. Thus India's fear became genuine. On 16 May 2009, Israeli website, Debka reported that former Indian Prime Minister Mohan Singh had warned President Barack Obama that nuclear sites in Pakistan's Khyber Pakhtunkhwa province were "already partly" in the hands of Islamic extremists. Before this statement, in 2005, Mr. Singh told CNN that his government was worried about the security of Pakistan nuclear assets after President Musharraf. In his 2014 book, author Mark Fitzpatrick quoted former Army Chief of Pakistan General Kayani's speech in August 2012. In his speech, the Army Chief condemned extremism and said it could lead Pakistan to civil war.

In a Pakistan without the bomb, jihadist groups, who felt protected by the nuclear shield, would feel strongly constrained, and could not expect to freely attack India. There are speculations that Pakistan's nuclear weapons could be stolen or smuggled out of the country, during periods of great instability, notwithstanding Washington's $100 million assistance to Pakistan in securing its nuclear weapons.

Pakistan is also developing a new generation of tactical nuclear weapons (TNWs) that target not only Indian cities but Indian military formations on the battlefield. The purpose of these is "to counterbalance India's move to bring conventional military offensives to a tactical level." The threat implied by Pakistan is based on two assumptions: Pakistan believes that the use of TNW would bring about such a material and psychological shift in hostilities, as to stun India into a halt. The rise of tactical nuclear weapons has been well documented over the past two years. What has received less scrutiny, however, is the doctrine on which this rise has been based. Pakistan's advances in perfecting tactical nuclear weapons are quite dangerous.

In general understanding, Pakistan's nuclear doctrine means that, in case of an Indian military attack, the government in power would be left with no other option except to retaliate with nuclear weapons. By using nuclear weapons, Pakistan wants to prevent India from disintegrating the country. If Indian armed forces enter Pakistan in large numbers, and the Pakistani security forces are unable to intercept their advance towards Islamabad, there might be the only option of using nuclear weapons against India.

The fear of nuclear weapons and materials escaping the protective custody of Pakistan's army is well founded. On 05 May 2006, Baloch militants attacked the dumping site near Baghalchur uranium mine in Dera Ghazi Khan District. In 2007, terrorists attacked two air force facilities in Sargodha, associated with nuclear installations.

The threat of nuclear weapons theft and bioterrorism in South Asia once again came under discussion in International press that terrorist organizations in both Pakistan and India, are trying to retrieve biotechnology and nuclear weapons, and use it against the civilians and security forces. Border skirmishes between Pakistan and India, the cloud of civil war in Afghanistan, and the emergence of ISIS terrorist organization in Pakistan, further justified the possibilities of the complex threat of chemical and biological terrorism. As Pakistan and Afghanistan have been the victims of terrorism and Talibanization during the last three decades, the establishment of ISIS networks in South Asia may possibly change the traditional concept of terrorism and insurgency in the region.

There is a general perception that extremist organizations in South Asia could use some advanced technologies against civilian populations. If control over these weapons is weak, the possibility of theft increases. The problem of nuclear and biological terrorism deserves special attention from all South Asian states, including Afghanistan. As nuclear weapons, missile technologies, and bio-weapons proliferate, there is a grave danger that some of them might fall into the hands of ISIS group, Taliban, or Indian and Afghani extremist groups. In the Seoul Summit, Indian Prime Minister Manmohan Singh warned that South Asia is under threat. Two incidents in Karachi and another in Baluchistan proved that terrorists were trying to retrieve nuclear weapons, to use them against military or nuclear installations.

During the last 20 years, Islamabad made remarkable advances in nuclear weapons technology, and successfully countered all of India's offensive mechanisms, targeting its deployments. The military politics of retaliation between the two states, prompted a huge cost, when India set up the Air Defense Shield or Prithvi series of missiles, and Pakistan developed multiple independently targetable re-entry vehicles (MIRVs) for its ballistic missiles. As a bigger economy, India can afford these military confrontations but it is a huge burden on Pakistan's national budget. Islamabad is in trouble on the Cold Start Doctrine (CSD) of India that allows the country's military to strike 50 kilometers inside Pakistan's territory at short notice. To counter this threat, Islamabad developed tactical nuclear weapons and threatened that in case of India's attack, it would use them against the country. To exhibit its power, on 05 November 2013, Pakistan fired the Nasr missile capable of carrying a 200 kilogram plutonium warhead, and thus introduced tactical nuclear weapons on land.

On 21 August 2008, terrorists attacked ordinance factories in Wah. In July 2009, a suicide bomber struck a bus that may have been carrying A.Q Khan Research Laboratory scientists, injuring 30 people. Moreover, two attacks by Baloch militants on suspected Atomic Energy Commission facilities at Dera Ghazi Khan also drew international attention. On 10 October 2009, nine terrorists, dressed in army uniform—attacked GHQ. On June 2014, two suicide bombers killed high ranking military officers linked to Pakistan's nuclear program, in Fateh Jang,

Radicalization within the military ranks, as evident from the Mehran Naval base incident, and the Lashkar-e-Toiba terrorist activities, all point towards a tilt in balance from the military to the Jihadists. The recent killing Punjab Home Minister, poor governance, the overriding role of radical Salafi and Wahabi Sunni sects, acknowledge that worst may still lie ahead. Pakistani generals use nuclear weapons as a tool for achieving foreign policy objectives.

In 2009, Pakistani Taliban threatened to launch an attack against the country's nuclear and military installations. National Terror Alert reported that Al-Qaeda and the Taliban had developed some expertise in making bio-chemical weapons. In April 2009, Inspector General Police Khyber Pakhtunkhwa province, Mr. Malik Navid revealed before Pakistan National Assembly's standing committee, that Taliban retrieved about expertise in making chemical and biological weapons. Malik Navid warned that Pakistani government needed to urgently focus on containing militancy as it spreads from its bases.

In the end, I would like to thank my intellectual friends from India, the late journalist Mr. Rajinder Puri, and Mr. Rana Banerji, former Special Secretary of Cabinet Secretariat, India; my endearing friends Afghan businessman Muhammad Hafiz Skandari, Afghan thinker and lawyer, Mr. Miftahuddin Haroon, Pakistan's communist politician and lawyer, Mr. Anwer Dhoolan, and friends in the armed forces of Pakistan and Afghanistan. However, I am highly indebted to my publishers and editors, Martin DeMers and Andrea Sengstacken, for their encouragement and cooperation.

Musa Khan Jalalzai
London: September 2015.

SUMMARY

The construction of two nuclear power plants in Khushab (a Saraiki District of Southern Punjab, Pakistan), and Karachi raised serious questions about the intentions of Pakistan military establishment, that wants to further expand its nuclear weapons program. Notwithstanding international concerns on these nuclear power plants, On 20 June 2015, the Sindh Environmental Protection Agency (SEPA) approved the twin nuclear project, and allowed its construction. The 2008 Mumbai terrorist attacks and the Line of Control incidents prompted deep distrust between India and Pakistan.

In June 2015, Indian security forces carried out military operations against insurgents in Myanmar, warned that it could happen in Pakistan as well. Pakistani Prime Minister Nawaz Sharif and Defense Minister Khwaja Muhammad Asif responded with strong words. Mr. Asif warned India that Pakistan was a nuclear state, and the country does not maintain a nuclear bomb just to use it, as a firecracker. "If forced into war by India, Pakistan will respond in a befitting manner; our arms are not meant for decoration," he said. Former President General Pervez Musharraf also responded aggressively in turn, saying that Pakistan would adopt a tit-for-tat approach, and would react immediately: "Don't attack us, don't challenge our territorial integrity because we are not a small power, we are a major nuclear power."

In 1999, during the Kargil war, Indian military leaders had decided to enter a limited war against Pakistan, but as Indian secret services (RAW) failed to truly interpret Pakistan's motives, the planned war was procrastinated. In his book, former RAW's Chief, Major General V K

Singh regretted on the performance of his intelligence agency, during the Kargil war: "After the Kargil intrusion in 1999, the government constituted the Kargil Review Committee to go into the intelligence failure that contributed to the fiasco. When the report was placed before parliament, about 15 pages dealing with intelligence were removed, on grounds of security. Not one of the honorable members sitting in the house questioned the implied insult and aspersion on their integrity." Just two years after the Kargil war, an attack on the Indian parliament led to a six months standoff.

After the Kargil war, to effectively counter the Indian nuclear threat, Pakistan army attached importance to the development of short-range nuclear-capable systems, and tactical nuclear weapons. India also tried to develop nuclear missiles, to achieve a strategic deterrent against Pakistan and China. The recent modernization of China's land-based ballistic missile force, which the country has equipped with Multiple Independently Targetable Re-entry Vehicles (MIRVs), is a bigger challenge for India. The recent annual report of the US military command on Chinese missile technology development indicated, that the Chinese army has shown an interest in developing technology for MIRVs. Military experts in the US understand that a Chinese MIRV missile will be adorned with multiple warheads, allowing a single missile to hit a number of different targets at once.

In addition to China, Russia is also interested in a fair rapprochement with Pakistan. Military cooperation between the two states has become irksome for the Indian army. As a strong military power, the Russian Strategic Missile Force (RVSN) will have a modern Inventory of Silo-Based Intercontinental Ballistic Missiles (ICBMs) by 2020. At present, the RVSN possesses 400 Intercontinental Ballistic Missiles (ICBMs). The 100-tonne SARMAT-ICBM with a range of 5,500 km is expected to replace the current SATAN by 2018-20. According to Chief Engineer of Russia's Almaz-Antey Defense Corporation, Pavel Sozinov, the Russian military is working on its own Missile Defense System (MDS), similar to the Terminal High Altitude Area Defense (THAAD), and Ground Based Midcourse Defense (GMD) of the US. China and Pakistan have agreed to boost maritime security cooperation in the Indian Ocean.

China wants to sell eight Diesel Electric Air Independent Propulsion (DEAIP) equipped submarines capable of carrying nuclear weapons to Pakistan. Like the US signed a strategic partnership agreement with India, Pakistan decided to approach Russia for military ties. In November 2014, Russian Defense Minister

Sergie Shoigu visited Islamabad, and signed a military cooperation agreement with Pakistan. Russia too has lifted the arms embargo on Pakistan. For Pakistan, with consecutive instability, nuclear weapons are an umbrella against India. Broadly speaking, the two countries are operating in a strategically competitive environment, where their dangerous weapons have become a constant threat to peace and stability of the region.

The threat of chemical, biological and nuclear terrorism in South Asia also causes deep frustration and anxiety, as the region hosts many militant organizations. The addition of ISIS into the South Asian volatile politics, added to the concern of nuclear experts, that this fundamentalist group may possibly use nuclear or biological, and chemical weapons in the region. This group has already learnt the technique of making nuclear explosive devices, and the illegal transactions of poorly protected materials. The Subcontinent is the most volatile region because India and Pakistan are engaged in a dangerous nuclear arms race. India's National Security Advisor admitted in one of his recent speeches that a fourth generation war is being fought against Pakistan with different tactics and dimensions.

The jihadist organizations in South Asia, and even the Islamic State (ISIS), and Taliban, have already demonstrated their interest in retrieving chemical and nuclear weapons, but at present, there is no evidence of their attempts to get access to these weapons. The ISIS recently claimed that it is engaged with Pakistan for nuclear weapons delivery, but Pakistan remained tight-lipped. There are confirmed reports that ISIS retrieved chemical weapons from Iraq, and jihadist groups in South Asia also struggling to obtain chemical weapons capability.

By using nuclear weapons, Pakistan wants to prevent India from smashing the country to bits. If Indian armed forces enter Pakistan in large numbers, and Pakistani security forces are unable to intercept their advance towards Islamabad, they may have no option but to use nuclear weapons against India.

Pakistan's military establishment understands that, just as India dismembered Pakistan in 1971, and continues to challenge the country by various means, so a nuclear bomb is the only umbrella to protect the country from the military might of India. Today, the armies of both states are eyeball-to-eyeball in Punjab and Kashmir, and India continues to become the strongest military power in the region. Therefore, Pakistan has concerns about its national security, and wants to convince Indian leaders that the use of nuclear weapons can prompt disastrous consequence. The deployment of Pakistan's tactical weapons, according to nuclear experts, means to use them against India, if it attacks Pakistan's territory in an effort to disintegrate it.

Pakistan's tactical nuclear weapons, and the China's shifting strategy of a new nuclear doctrine, created confusion for the Indian, and called for a re-think of its nuclear position in the region. On 15 August 2014, Prime Minister Narendra Modi elucidated the position of his government on the national security of India. During the last 20 years, Islamabad has made remarkable advances in nuclear weapons technology, and has successfully countered all of India's offensive mechanisms, targeting its deployments. The military politics of retaliation between the two states prompted a huge cost, when India set up the Air Defense Shield, or Prithvi series of missiles, and Pakistan developed Multiple Independently Targetable Re-entry Vehicles (MIRVs) for its ballistic missiles.

Islamabad is in trouble on the Cold Start Doctrine (CSD) of India that allows the country's military to strike 50 kilometers inside Pakistan's territory, at a short notice. To counter this threat, Islamabad developed Tactical Nuclear Weapons (TNW), and threatened that in case of India's attack, the country would use them against India. To exhibit its power, on 05 November 2013, Pakistan fired the Nasr Missile capable of carrying a 200 kilogram plutonium warhead, and thus introduced Tactical Nuclear Weapons on land. India also invested a lot on Spy Satellites Aircraft Drones (SSAD), and Early Warning Radar (EWR), while Pakistan developed Spy and Modern Warning Systems (MWS). At present, both the states hold a massive nuclear stockpile, and the size of this stockpile has doubled since 1998. Both states have developed Cruise Missiles and are seeking nuclear submarines. China's tacit support to Pakistan for boosting the country's nuclear weapons is considered to have strategic implications for India. All these weapons and strategic developments in both the states mean that confidence-building measures remain only on paper, with no one wanting to extend the hand of cooperation.

CHAPTER-1: NUCLEAR JIHAD IN PAKISTAN: THE ISIS AND TALIBANIZATION OF THE ARMED FORCES

Policy makers and military experts have longstanding worries about the purported radicalization of Pakistan's armed forces, fearing that extremist elements within the army might facilitate the TTP or Islamic State (ISIS) to attack nuclear installations. Now, as the Islamic State (ISIS) has been added to the list of Pakistani extremist networks, the danger of nuclear terrorism further intensified.

Recent events in Pakistan and its war on Pashtuns, extrajudicial killings in Swat, and the killings of children in Waziristan and FATA regions, raised serious questions, that now trained terrorists and extremist elements like Lashkar-e-Toiba, TTP and Islamic State (ISIS), or their colleagues within the army, may well resort to nuclear, biological, radiological or chemical weapons. The Daish group or Islamic State (ISIS) has established close contacts with Lashkar-e-Jhangavi (LeJ), Punjabi Taliban, and Lashkar-e-Toiba in Punjab. On 11 December 2014, former Interior Minister of Pakistan, Mr. Rahman Malik told a local news channel that Daish (ISIS) established recruitment centers in Gujranwala, and Bahawalpur districts. The wall-chalking campaign and leaflets prompted fears about the terrorist group making inroads in the country. According to the leaked government circular in Baluchistan and Khyber Pakhtunkhwa provinces, the Islamic State recruited more than 10,000 to 12,000 fighters for the next sectarian war in Pakistan, and continues to expand its terror network, within the state institutions.

In November 2014, Pakistan's National Counter Terrorism Agency (NACTA) warned that Islamic State is spreading like a viral disease across the country, while the group leader, Mr. Abu Baker Al Baghdadi, appointed an Afghan writer, Abdul Rahim Muslim Dost as chief of its Khurasan chapter, and started gearing up to muster the support of former jihadist leaders. Mr. Abdul Rahim Muslim Dost (Afghan National) was arrested by Pakistani agencies in Peshawar after the 9/11 terrorist attack in the United States. After his release, he wrote a book (Pashto language) against the brutalities and torture tactics of Pakistani intelligence agencies against the detainees. No sooner as the book was released by a local publisher in Peshawar, then the ISI arrested him again, and forcefully disappeared for quite a long time. On 04, September 2013, one of Pakistan's leading newspapers, the News International reported a 178-page summary of the United States intelligence community, about the US intelligence surveillance of Pakistan's nuclear weapons. Pentagon and CIA focused on Pakistan's nuclear facilities that might come under attack by TTP or ISIS.[1]

The Washington Quarterly report diverted the attention of international community towards the problem of illicit nuclear trade. The trade appears to be growing worse as technologies and capabilities proliferate in South Asia. During the last 13 years, terrorists not only attacked civilians but also targeted military installations and nuclear bases in Pakistan. The greatest threat to Pakistan's nuclear infrastructure emanated from the rogue elements within the army, TTP, and the Islamic State (ISIS).[2]

In October 2014, Pakistani Taliban announced allegiance to the Islamic State (ISIS). The IS established its networks in Pakistan, and invented its previous contacts within the extremist groups, and the ranks of the armed forces. More than 60 out of 400 extremist groups operating in Pakistan (NCMC of Pakistan) joined the ISIS terrorist network and, send their fighter to Iraq and Afghanistan. In September 2014, Afghan military intelligence sources told me that there were so many ISIS fighters in the country, who appeared to be in Afghan dress with Pakol caps on their heads. Five Tehreek-i-Taliban Pakistan (TTP) commanders announced their oath of allegiance to Abu Baker al-Baghdadi, a self-proclaimed caliph of the Islamic State. In December

---

1 *The News International*, 04 September, 2013
2 *Detecting and Disrupting Illicit Nuclear Trade after A.Q. Khan*, David Albright, Paul Brannan, and Andrea Scheel Stricker, Published in the *Washington Quarterly*, Vol-33, 24 March, 2010. http://csis.org/files/attachments/130828_Detecting%20and%20Disrupting%20Nuclear%20Trade.pdf.

2014, Muttahida Qaumi Movement (MQM) Chief, Altaf Hussain warned that the Iraqi militant group, Islamic State, established its networks in Pakistan. Daily Dunya News reported MQM Chief saying that a large number of Taliban were seeking memberships in the ISIS. Analysts in Pakistan believe that if the country's army failed to undermine the threat of ISIS and Taliban network, the terrorist groups might inflict more fatalities on the country.

In September 2014, wall chalking in Waziristan, Khyber Pakhtunkhawa and parts of Afghanistan started, asking the people of both the states to join and support Islamic State. City transport, buses and cars also had ISIS stickers pasted on them. Daily Telegraph reported Tahrik-e-Khilafat, a previously unknown extremist group established its bases in Karachi, and swore allegiance to the ISIS terrorist group. This became a new challenge to the military establishment in Pakistan, which is deeply embroiled in the fights against the TTP in Waziristan, and FATA regions. In 09 June 2014, when terrorists attacked Karachi air port, and killed two military officers, government stepped up security around nuclear installation across the country. This was a fresh warning from terrorists, radicalized elements, and those, whose relatives had been ruthlessly killed during the military operations in Baluchistan, FATA and Waziristan. The attack raised serious doubts about the professionalism of the ISI and civilian intelligence agencies.

International media continues to report concerns about the growing threat of nuclear and biological terrorism in Pakistan, but the country continues to sign multilateral nuclear agreements with different states, in order to exhibit its challenging military might. Pakistan's nuclear relations with China and US indicate that the country wants to defend its nuclear status. The country's nuclear doctrine is, in fact, a military strategy that promotes retaliation to nuclear attack by India.[1]

In general understanding, Pakistan's nuclear doctrine means that, in case of any attack from the Indian side, the government in power would be left with no other option except to retaliate with nuclear weapons. By using nuclear weapons, Pakistan wants to prevent India from disintegrating the country. If the Indian armed forces entered Pakistan in large numbers, and Pakistani security forces were unable to intercept their advance towards Islamabad, the only option they might have is; to use nuclear weapons against India. Pakistan's military establishment understands that, as India once dismembered Pakistan in 1971, and continues to challenge the country by various

---

1 Indrani Bagchi, *Times of India*—07 August, 2014.

means, therefore, a nuclear bomb is the only umbrella to protect the country from its military might.[1]

The Nawaz Sharif government is committed to bring India and Pakistan to a close and ease the political and military tension between the two states. In his General Assembly speech (2014), Prime Minister Nawaz Sharif said:

> As a responsible nuclear weapon state, we will continue to pursue the goals of disarmament and non-proliferation and adhere to the policy of Credible Minimum Deterrence, without entering into an arms race. We would not, however, remain oblivious to the evolving security dynamics in South Asia, nor would we agree to arrangement that is detrimental to our security and strategic interests. Our position on the proposed Fissile Material Treaty is determined by our national security interests and the objective of strategic stability in South Asia. Safe, secure and peaceful use of nuclear energy, without discrimination, is essential for economic development. Pakistan qualifies for full access to civil nuclear technology for peaceful purposes, to meet its growing energy needs, for continued economic growth. By the same token, as a mainstream partner in the global non-proliferation regime, Pakistan has impeccable credentials to join the multilateral export control regime, including the Nuclear Suppliers Group. Pakistan will continue to participate constructively in the Nuclear Security Summit (NSS) process, which is a laudable initiative.

In 2003, India's cabinet committee for security affairs reviewed the operationalization of the nuclear doctrine. The balance of power in South Asia became deeply complicated as India started campaigning to retrieve more nuclear reactors by signing agreements with Australia, the US and European states, while Pakistan also dragged China into this game. India is larger than Pakistan, Bangladesh and other South Asian neighbors by a wide margin. There were speculations in Pakistan, that Prime Minister Narendra Modi might adopt a new nuclear strategy vis-à-vis Pakistan as China continues to help expanding the country's nuclear weapons program.

In the international press, there has been an unending stream of criticism against Pakistan's tactical nuclear weapons. Nuclear experts fear that as bigoted elements in the army have close relations with extremist groups, like Lashkar-e-Toiba, TTP and Islamic State (ISIS), the danger of nuclear terrorism cannot be ruled out in South Asia. The danger of acquiring nuclear explosive by terrorists is real

---

1 Jagdish Singh, *Jerusalem Post*-02 June, 2014.

and its consequences would be appalling. Islamic State or Taliban can try to kidnap officials working in nuclear facilities.

The possibility, that terrorists could kidnap or allure some official working in the nuclear establishment cannot be ruled out. India and Pakistan are nuclear states, each with over 100 nuclear weapons and building more, and have become the worst enemies in the region. When Pakistan decided to deploy tactical nuclear weapons along the Indian border, there was deep criticism of the country's stance on the use of nuclear weapons against India.

The deployment of Pakistan's tactical weapons, according to nuclear experts, meant to use them against India, if it attacks Pakistan's territory in an effort to disintegrate it. Pakistan's Nasr missile was a ballistic missile, launched from a Mobile Twin-Canister Launcher. The test of this missile on 05, November 2013, prompted concern in South Asia. Afghanistan was more anxious about the possible use of this missile against the country. However, India has also given itself the right to use nuclear weapons, if its territory is attacked by a nuclear state. According to India's nuclear doctrine, nuclear weapons will not be used against a non-nuclear state. Pakistan's tactical nuclear weapons and the Chinese shifting strategy created confusion for the Indian government, and called for a re-think of its nuclear position in the region. On 15 August, 2014, Prime Minister Narendra Modi elucidated the position of his government on the national security of India.[1]

During the last 30 years, Islamabad made remarkable advances in nuclear weapons technology and successfully countered all of India's offensive mechanisms, targeting its deployments. The military politics of retaliation between the two states prompted a huge cost when India set up the Air Defense Shield or Prithvi series of missiles, and Pakistan developed Multiple Independently Targetable Re-entry Vehicles (MIRVs) for its ballistic missiles.

As a bigger economy, India can afford these military confrontations, but it might be a huge burden on Pakistan's national budget. Islamabad was in trouble on the Cold Start Doctrine (CSD) of India, which allows the country's military to strike 50 kilometers inside Pakistan's territory, on short notice. To counter this threat, Islamabad developed tactical nuclear weapons and threatened that in case of India's attack, it would use them against the country. To exhibit its power, on 05, November 2013, Pakistan tested the Nasr missile, capable of carrying

1 China's military challenge, Ashley J. Tellis and Travis Tanner, *Strategic Asia*, 2012-13.

a 200 kilogram plutonium warhead, and thus, introduced tactical nuclear weapons on land.[1]

As in my previous research papers, I warned that terrorists and extremist groups, like the Taliban and Islamic State (ISIS) can use nuclear explosive devices (NED) in Pakistan. Material for such a bomb is easily available in the country. It became reality, when terrorists attacked the country's nuclear installations time and again. Terrorist groups attacked Karachi, and the Air Force aviation base in Quetta, which were similar to the ones that occurred in Wah, Mehran base, Sargodha and Kamra. This was confirmed by the Southern Command Commander General Nasir Khan Janjua in his statement to journalists. He admitted that 12 terrorists were killed and 14 soldiers also lost their lives.

The very next day, the Army Chief visited Quetta and said that Pakistani nation rejected terrorism and resolved to overcome it as soon as possible. General Raheel was deeply frustrated during his address to security personnel. His blood pressure was high and it was evident from his face, as Prime Minister, Nawaz Sharif showed reluctant response to the attack by not even condemning it open heartedly. General Raheel said, his forces would continue to respond promptly to defeat the nefarious designs of the terrorists.

The test of Pakistan's ballistic missile, Nasr, capable of carrying a nuclear warhead, and India's ballistic missile, Prahaar and others, complicated nuclear weapons race in South Asia. India's tactical nuclear weapons are more dangerous than Pakistan. Indian nuclear missiles like Agni-I, Agni-III, VI and V present a bigger threat to the national security of Pakistan. India also launched various military and surveillance satellites to enter into an anti-satellite weapons and ballistic missile Defense race with China.[2]

Pakistan has two major strategic assets: its nuclear weapons and the Afghan Taliban. Both are controlled by the army, and more specifically by its intelligence agencies. The army, which gives itself the right of the guardian of the country's "ideological frontiers," still sees India as its main enemy, and views Afghanistan as part of its fifth province. Pakistan continues to create threatening environment in South Asia by developing different types of tactical nuclear weapons. Author Arun Sahgal suggested that these military developments and

---

1 "India and Pakistan's Nuclear Doctrines: A Comparative Analysis." Mohammad Badrul Alam. The Society for the Study of Peace and Conflict (SSPC), 11 April, 2012.
2 Editorial Board, *New York Times*, 09 April, 2014.

the modernization of Chinese army and its military influence in South Asia raised serious questions:

> China's military modernization, and capacity-building, infrastructure development in Tibet, and moves into the Indian Ocean pose serious challenges to India's security. China's growing footprint in South Asia and attempts to bring peripheral states into its circle of influence only add to these concerns. There is a duality in approaches to dealing with these challenges: while broader political discourse underscores cooperation and downplays competition, there is nonetheless a growing realization that India needs to develop credible hard power as a dissuasive strategy against China. India's strategic dilemma thus lies in shaping its political response to external balancing. Although there is the understanding of a strategic convergence between India and the U.S., there is little consensus on how to shape this relationship to further India's strategic interests. New Delhi continues to face a policy dilemma on whether to be a regional balancer, a swing state, or a strategic hedge.[1]

Military confrontations between India and Pakistan and between China and India can also be judged from the Ashley J. Tellis and Travis Tanner analysis which also describes Chinese interests in South Asia:

> At the geopolitical level, the United States is confronted with a challenge that it never faced in its rivalry with the Soviet Union: the growing dependence of its own allies and key neutrals in Asia on China for markets, capital, goods, and in many cases even technology. China's enormous size and its huge economy have made it the center of a highly integrated Asian economic system, where the growth of every country on its periphery increasingly depends on the extent and density of the linkages enjoyed with China. Such intermeshing inevitably produces geopolitical effects insofar as it makes the littoral nations, even when formally allied with the United States, more sensitive to Chinese interests than they would otherwise be in the absence of regional integration. Even if this process does not lead eventually to the creation of a hermetic trading bloc that excludes the United States—an unlikely prospect for now—it creates an expanded Chinese sphere of influence that, enveloping the United States' allies and important neutrals, complicates their decision-making as they attempt to juggle competing demands pertaining to security and prosperity.[2]

---

1 China's Military Modernization: Responses from India, Arun Sahgal, *The National Bureau of Asian Research.*
2 China's military challenge, Ashley J. Tellis and Travis Tanner, *Strategic Asia*, 2012-13.

As a strong state, India has adopted a very practical approach to nuclear race in South Asia, and continues to create more opportunities for Pakistan and other neighbors, to re-think about their attitude towards the country. The 2008 Mumbai attacks and the Line of Control incidents prompted deep distrust between the two states. In June 2014, Indian Prime Minister Narendra Modi issued a stern warning to Pakistan: "I had told you on television that this is not Manmohan Singh's government, it is Narendra Modi's government. If you do something, we will also do but we cannot sit quiet."[1]

Indian Law Minister, Ravi Shankar Prasad criticized Pakistan and its support to extremist groups across the border. Mr. Ravi Shankar demanded the resignation of Prime Minister Nawaz Sharif. However, Pakistan-based terrorist groups used the same language against Mr. Modi's government. In its video message, an extremist group, *Ansar-ul-Tawheed fi Belad Hind* (Brotherhood for Monotheism in India) warned Mr. Modi of retaliation for the Gujarat massacre. Given the fast growth of militant organizations within Pakistan in collaboration with foreign terrorists, encouraged by the Pakistan army to achieve their foreign policy objectives, the real fear is that Pakistan's nuclear weapons may possibly fall into the wrong hands.[2]

Journalist Zahid Husain (2014) asked how Prime Minister Nawaz Sharif would deal with the problem of militancy and religious extremism in his home province. Mr. Zahid Hussain argued that counterterrorism efforts have been focused entirely on the tribal areas and Khyber Pakhtunkhawa, and the state has conveniently shut its eyes to militant activities in the country's most powerful province.

In September 2014, the suspension of talks between India and Pakistan, set off alarm bells in the US and China, the stakeholders in the relationship between both the states. When Pakistani High Commissioner to India, Mr. Abdul Basit met a Kashmiri separatist leader, without the consent of the Indian authorities, it further inflamed Mr. Modi's colleagues in parliament. During his Kashmir visit, Prime Minister Modi warned Pakistan with a strong statement, and in his Laddakh visit, Mr. Modi said the Indian armed forces were suffering more casualties from terrorism than from any war.

Prime Minister Modi said that Pakistan continued to support a proxy war against India. Moreover, various politicians in India issued different statements against Pakistan, creating a hostile environment

---

1 *Daily Times*, 24 August 2014.
2 India's Nuclear Doctrine: Stirrings of Change. P. R. Chari, 04 June 2014.

in the region. In military circles, India's Army Chief, Dalbir Singh Suhag, warned Pakistan, and said that the country is unable to intercept cross-border infiltration.[1]

The exponential terrorist networks of sectarian and extremist organization in Pakistan are a real threat to the country's national security. These groups desperately seek nuclear materials, to prepare nuclear explosive devices and use it against India and foreign forces in Afghanistan. Nuclear installations, research reactors and uranium enrichment plants, might, at any time, come under potential attack from these organizations, and their allies within the armed forces. There are speculations, that TTP or the Islamic State (ISIS) might steal fissile material from a military or civilian facility, to construct an improvised nuclear device, and use it in towns and cities. In June 2014, after the Karachi Attack, there were concerns in Afghanistan, Russia, India, and Europe, that the country's nuclear weapons are not in safe hands.[2]

Pakistani nuclear analysts warned that the safety of systems can fail catastrophically. An important lesson of Fukushima, they noted, is that nuclear establishments underestimated the likelihood, and severity of possible accidents. Another important lesson they noted is that Pakistani establishment also overestimates its ability to cope with a real nuclear disaster.[3]

The possibility of a nuclear attack in Pakistan might be of several types; a commando type attack that might cause widespread dispersal of radioactivity, aircraft crash into an atomic reactor, suicide attack, attacks by the army officers (whose relatives were forcefully disappeared and killed by the army, drones and so called military operations in Swat, Momand, FATA and Waziristan regions), and cyber attack, all are possible.

After several incidents of terror attacks on Pakistan, including the Karachi terror attack, nuclear facilities (Wah, Kamra, Mehran base, Dera Ghazi Khan, Sargodha), and the desertion of large number of Pakistani soldiers to Taliban from 2004 to 2014, it has become clear that the TTP, Punjabi Taliban, and Islamic State (ISIS) can gain access to nuclear facilities, with the help of their radicalized allies in the armed forces.

The availability of nuclear materials in Pakistani black market, specifically in tribal regions, has raised serious questions about the

---

1 *Dawn,* 13 August 2014.
2 *Daily Times,* 14 August 2014.
3 *Dawn,* 13 December 2014.

security of the country's nuclear weapons facilities. There is a danger that terrorist groups, or their allies within the army, may possibly attack Pakistan's nuclear facilities, by detonating a small and crude nuclear weapon.[1]

Now, nuclear and military experts in Europe and the United States understand that Pakistan is simply a state that cannot be trusted. The investment of some Arab states including Saudi Arabia in the country's nuclear weapons raised serious question about the credibility and sincerity of the civilian and military leadership. This investment further jeopardized the peaceful environment in South and West Asia.

Since General Muhammad Zia-ul-Haq was killed in 1988, the army managed to control the security of nuclear installations across the country. Army Chief, General Musharraf established National Security Council comprising of 13 military and civilian leaders, to consolidate Nuclear Command and Control in 2000. Pakistan's Space and Upper Atmosphere Research Commission (SUPARCO) came under NSC. The commission was established in 1980 to help the development of ballistic missiles.[2]

In May 1999, Prime Minister Muhammad Nawaz Sharif announced credible deterrence policy; which was part of Pakistan's nuclear policy after the 1998 nuclear test. After the test, the country planned to establish nuclear force to protect its nuclear installations. From 2001 to 2008, Gen Musharraf adopted various policies regarding his country's nuclear weapons.

Director General of Strategic Planning Division, Lt General Kidwai, once said that more than 70,000 experts were working in 15 atomic plants across the country, including 8,000 well trained scientists of which more than 2,000 scientists have sensitive knowledge. Pakistan continues to develop its nuclear weapons, and appears to have built a force of 25,000 strong and well-trained soldiers. In 2008, the International Panel of Fissile Materials (IPFM) estimated that Pakistan had developed more than 80 nuclear weapons, but some reports confirmed that the country developed 100 nuclear weapons.

In December 2011, an article in Atlantic Magazine labeled Pakistan as the "ally from hell." The article warned that Pakistan was transferring its nuclear weapons from one place to another in very low security vans, to hide them from CIA. The inability of Pakistani armed forces was evident from the fact that instead of transferring

1 *Daily Times*, 03 October 2013.
2 *Daily Times*, 09 June, 2014.

nuclear weapons in armored vehicles, they were shifting them in unsafe vans hired from local transporters.[1]

The involvement of Pakistani generals in nuclear smuggling put the country in ordeal. There is plenty material on Pakistan's involvement in the smuggling of nuclear weapons to Korea, Iran, Libya and other Arab states, which caused harassment and fear in South Asia, and the Middle East. Pakistani generals had established a strong network of nuclear smuggling in 1980s and 1990s, and smuggled weapons in large quantity. David E. Sanger has reproduced the main contents of a letter of Korean official to Dr. Abdul Qadeer Khan regarding the sale of nuclear weapons. In his New York Times article, Mr. David named some Pakistani generals who were paid millions dollars from the North Korean army:

> The letter is said to have been written to Abdul Qadeer Khan, the Pakistani who built the world's largest black market in nuclear weapons technology, by Jon Pyong Ho, a North Korean whom American intelligence has long put at the center of the North's trade in missile and nuclear technologies. It reports that the chief of the Pakistani Army at the time, Gen. Jahangir Karamat, had been paid $3 million and asked that "the agreed documents, components, etc." be placed on a North Korean plane that was returning to Pyongyang, the North's capital, after delivering missile parts to Pakistan. The publication of the letter comes at a particularly inopportune moment for the Pakistani military. Already discredited inside Pakistan for its failure to detect the American commando raid that killed Osama bin Laden in Abbottabad, the military has veered from crisis to crisis since then. If authentic, the letter seems certain to rekindle questions about whether Pakistan's most respected institution played a key role in the proliferation of nuclear weapons technology".[2]

On 20 November 2013, NDTV reported US official warned about the threat to the nuclear weapons of Pakistan. "Are we endangering our own safety and that of Israel by over-exaggerating the nuclear threat posed by Iran while drastically under-estimating the growing threat posed by Pakistan? Someone in authority had better answer that question before it's too late," said Douglas MacKinnon. Pakistan, which conducted its nuclear tests in 1998, is battling with the Taliban and Islamic State (ISIS), which threatens to paralyze the state. In

---

1 Nuclear Karachi, A.H. Nayyar, Pervez Hoodbhoy and Zia Mian, *Dawn*, 16 December 2013.
2 *Atlantic Magazine*, December 2011, *Daily Times*, 03 October 2013, and 14 November 2013, *Daily Telegraph*, 07 November 2013.

the past, Taliban not only attacked civilians but targeted military installations and nuclear bases as well.[1]

Pakistani officials assess that these risks are tractable despite Pakistan's difficult internal threat environment given concerted and professional efforts at nuclear stewardship by the country's military. Some international experts say that the Taliban and Islamic State (ISIS) have their eyes on Pakistan's nuclear warheads. Pakistan remains one of the most likely sources of nuclear risk globally through theft of its nuclear material.

On 16 August 2012, Daily Telegraph reported Pakistani government sought to allay American concerns that its nuclear facilities are under threat from Taliban and al-Qaeda terrorists. A Pakistani Defense Ministry insider told London-Telegraph that nuclear warheads are kept "decoupled" from their delivery systems under the country's strategic weapons security policy, and are not stored at Kamra or any other air force base. The newspaper reported.[2]

On 16 November 2009, in his New Yorker analysis, Seymour M. Hersh also warned that nuclear weapons in Pakistan are not in safe hands as terrorists had carried out attacks in Rawalpindi and other cities:

> In the most brazen strike, ten gunmen penetrated the Army's main headquarters in Rawalpindi, instigating a twenty-two-hour standoff that left twenty-three dead and the military thoroughly embarrassed. The terrorists had been dressed in Army uniforms. There were also attacks on police installations in Peshawar and Lahore, and, once the offensive began, an Army general was shot dead by gunmen on motorcycles on the streets of Islamabad, the capital. The assassins clearly had advance knowledge of the general's route, indicating that they had contacts and allies inside the security forces.[3]

Writer Evan Braden Montgomery (2010) shares these concerns and analyzes the proliferation of nuclear weapons and warns over the future threat of nuclear terrorism in South Asia:

> There are two major dimensions of the nuclear terrorist threat: the "supply" side of nuclear proliferation and the "demand" side of violent Islamist extremism. Over the past decade, longstanding concerns over proliferation have become increasingly acute in light of a number of worrisome developments, including the status of India and Pakistan as overt nuclear weapon states, North Korea's two nuclear weapons

---

1 *New York Times*, 07 July 2011.
2 *NDTV*, 20 November 2013.
3 *Daily Telegraph*, 16 August 2012.

tests, the international community's failure to restrain Iran's nuclear ambitions, and the fear that an Iranian nuclear weapons program could spark further proliferation throughout the Middle East.[1]

Author Samuel Kane (2012) noted the threat posed by Pakistan's nuclear weapons, and warned that terrorist groups can at any times attack nuclear plants:

> In Pakistan, the threat of nuclear materials falling into terrorist hands is a multi-faceted danger, composed of several different scenarios, such as (1) insiders within the Pakistani nuclear program proliferating nuclear assets and knowledge to terrorist groups; (2) a terrorist group stealing nuclear materials from a Pakistani facility; and (3) a radical Islamist group seizing control of the Pakistani government and nuclear arsenal, through a coup or democratic elections.... The threat of an individual inside the Pakistani nuclear program transferring nuclear materials or know-how to a terrorist organization is a serious one, and is indeed one that Pakistan has already been forced to confront in various forms.[2]

On 19 March 2015, an official of the Strategic Planning Division, Brigadier Tahir Raza Naqvi disclosed important facts about the inner pain of Pakistan's nuclear establishment. He abruptly revealed that "some people" working with the country's nuclear program were sacked to keep it safe. He was speaking at a seminar on 'Future Security Outlook of South Asia: Trends and Challenges.' The seminar was organized by an Islamabad-based think tank, Centre for International Strategic Studies, and a political foundation, the Konrad Adenauer Stiftung of Germany. The sacked nuclear workers could not clear the Personnel Reliability Program that was started in mid-2003/04 to screen the employees working on the sensitive program, Raza said. All employees of the nuclear program are periodically checked for family background, education, political affiliation and religious inclinations.

Brigadier Raza Naqvi did not say how many were sacked over the years or why they failed to clear the screening. "We filtered out people having negative tendencies that could have affected national security," Raza Naqvi told Dawn. Those sacked were the "incorrigible" ones, he said, and quickly added: "Our checks are very solid." At least 12 people linked to Dr Abdul Qadeer Khan were removed when the

---

1 *The New Yorker*, "Defending the Arsenal in an unstable Pakistan," Seymour M. Heresh 16 November 2014.
2"Understanding the threat of nuclear terrorism," Evan Braden Montgomery. SBA, the Centre for Strategic and Budgetary Assessments. 22 April 2009.

proliferation scandal surfaced in 2003. But those firings took place before Personnel Reliability Program was instituted.

On 21 January 2014, PTI news reported the head of Indian Mujahedeen leader, Ahmad Zarar Siddiq, who admitted that he had asked his Pakistan-based friend Riyaz Bhaktal in a phone conversation that if he could be given an atomic device to use it against India. With this attempt, the security of Pakistan's fissile materials became a leading security concern for the United States.[1]

Thirty-six years later, an international chorus still warns that Pakistan presently armed with 90 to 110 nuclear weapons is the epicenter of violent extremism, where terrorist groups actively seek nuclear weapons. Pakistan army and its intelligence arm, the Inter-Services Intelligence (ISI), gained considerable experience in aiding, abetting and fuelling insurgencies and terrorism in Afghanistan, and Kashmir. Terrorists seeking to unleash massive violence and destruction may climb the escalation ladder to the highest rungs: nuclear weapons. Writer Farooq Tariq criticized the government policies on extremism and militant groups, and warned that a large number of religious schools are causing sectarian violence and jihadism:

> In Pakistan the main tool for the growth of Islamic religious fundamentalism is the madressah. According to conservative estimates, there are approximately 20,000 madressahs (USCIRF 2011). There are five main types, which are divided along sectarian and political lines: Deobandi, Barelvi, Shia, Ale-Hadith/Salafi (a minority sect which is close to Wahabism) and Jamaat-e-Islami. Eighty-two percent of those belonging to Deobandi madressahs view the Taliban as their model (Ali, 2010). They have been an alternative to public schools in a country where less than two percent of the total government budget is spent on education. Almost all donations to religious charities end up in the coffers of these madressahs.[2]

According to the Indian newspaper, Pakistan is struggling to secure its nuclear weapons with the help of the United States. Pakistan wants to secure its nuclear weapons as it fears that its nuclear arsenal could be in jeopardy in the event of a conflict with India.[3]

Pakistan has been building more and more nuclear weapons when India started decreasing its stockpile. In their Newsweek analysis,

---

1 "Preventing Nuclear Terrorism: Nuclear Security, the Non-proliferation Regime, and the Threat of Terrorist Nukes" by: Samuel Kane. 2012.
2 *PTI News*, 21 January 2014.
3 Farooq Tariq, *PTI News*, 04 June 2014.

Dr. Pervez Hoodbhoy and Mr. Zia Mian noted a deep public concern about the safety and security of Pakistan's nuclear weapons:

> Nuclear supporters in Pakistan point to the International Atomic Energy Agency (IAEA) and highlight that it visits nuclear power plants and makes sure they are safe. But the fact is that after the Fukushima accident, while addressing his board of governors, and the world, on March 21, 2011, the director-general of the IAEA stated categorically that, "We are not a nuclear safety watchdog ... responsibility for nuclear safety lies with our member states." Unfortunately, there is evidence that nuclear evacuation plans have not been dealt with seriously in Pakistan. In its survey of the Karachi reactor site, the PAEC assumed that about 8 million people live within about 30 kilometers of the site as of 2011 and only 12 million people live within about 50 kilometers of the site. But it is obvious even to the casual observer that all of Karachi falls within this distance of the reactor site and Karachi has a lot more than 12 million people living in it. The real population of Karachi may be closer to 20 million.[1]

Sanskar Shrivastava has also raised the same question of the safety and security of Pakistan's nuclear weapons. He also noted that Israel and some other Western states want Pakistan to eliminate nuclear weapons:

> There are elements within the government of Pakistan who don't run on any order or ideology but on the feeling of revenge and religion. At this it becomes very necessary to help the civilian government which formed in the country after many years of military rule, in protecting the nuclear arsenals. It is believed that U.S, Israel and some western nations have been planning to dismantle Pakistani nuclear program but nothing has been confirmed till now and Pakistan enjoys no discrimination in continuing its nuclear program unlike Iran. It is true that Pakistan didn't receive nuclear deals from US and other countries other than China unlike India which has bagged nuclear deals with more than 12 countries.[2]

On 25 December 2013, DW TV quoted Farooq Sulehria about the safety of nuclear weapons. Mr. Sulehria said that Pakistan's nuclear program is not safe:

> Nuclear programs are never safe. On the one hand there is perhaps too much hype about the Pakistani nuclear program in Western media, on the other there is genuine concern," The London-based Pakistani journalist and researcher Farooq Sulehria told DW. "The

---

1 *Chandigarh Tribune*, India, 11 June 2014.
2 *Newsweek*, Pervez Hoodbhoy, Zia Mian, 17 May 2014.

Talibanization of the Pakistan military is something we can't overlook. What if there is an internal Taliban takeover of the nuclear assets?" Mr. Sulehria said.[1]

In the quarterly journal of International Security (2013), Keir A. Lieber, Daryl Press defined the foundation of US Foreign policy regarding the proliferation of nuclear weapons in South Asia. The United States wants the solution of the crisis emanated from the threat of Pakistan's nuclear weapons:

> The concern that a nuclear-armed state might transfer weapons to terrorists is part of the foundation of U.S. no-non-proliferation policy. Non-proliferation is pursued for a variety of reasons, including the fear that new nuclear states will use their weapons directly against adversaries, even in the face of a clear risk of retaliation loss control of their nuclear weapons, or material through regime incompetence, corruption or instability, trigger regional proliferation cascade among nervous neighbors, or be emboldened to use nuclear weapons as a "shield" for undertaking aggressive diplomatic and military action confident that other states could thus be deterred from responding forcefully.[2]

In Pakistan and India, several commentators raised the issue of the safety of Pakistan nuclear weapons during the 2013, and warned that the threat of nuclear proliferation in Pakistan is matter of great concern. Pakistan has already expanded and upgraded its nuclear program with the help of China, and the country's scientists are striving to enhance the range of deficiencies of its delivery systems. The most frightening prospect of nuclear terrorism in South Asia is that Jihadist organizations in the country have an easy access to nuclear weapons through their colleagues in the armed forces. There are scary scenarios of Taliban return, dismemberment of Afghanistan and the access of Pakistani extremists to nuclear weapons.

---

1 *The World Reporter*, May 26, 2011. "Are Pakistan's Nuclear Weapons in Safe Hands"? Sanskar Shrivastava http://www.theworldreporter. com/2011/05/are-pakistans-nuclear-weapons-in-safe.html
2 On 25 December 2013, *DW TV* quoted Farooq Sulehria about the safety of nuclear weapons.

CHAPTER 2. BLACK MARKET AND THE DANGER OF NUCLEAR JIHADISM IN PAKISTAN

The abrupt jump of Islamic State (ISIS) into the war zones of Afghanistan and Pakistan can prolong war against terrorism in the region. The Islamic State (ISIS) is struggling to retrieve the support of the local population. Pakistani newspapers reported the Islamic State (ISIS) presence in Karachi, and its campaign of wall chalking in Manghopir, Sohrab Goth, and Gulshan-e-Maymar. The Tehreek-e-Taliban's regional commanders of Khyber, Peshawar, Kurram, Orakzai, Mardan, Kohat and Hangu, announced allegiance to the Islamic State. According to the Hindustan Times report, the appearance of ISIS in Pakistan is a cause of worry for the Army. Pakistan Army will now have one more powerful entity to contend with. Pakistan's overt and covert support to the Taliban against the Afghan army, and the arrest of Pakistan trained terrorists in Helmand and Kunar provinces, raised serious questions about the country's sincerity and cooperation with the Afghan national army.

Afghan and India focused militants continue to operate from Pakistani territory to the detriment of Afghanistan and regional stability. Pakistan uses these proxy forces to hedge against the loss of influence in Afghanistan, and to counter India's superior military, the Pentagon told Congress in its report on the current situation in Afghanistan. In a letter sent to Secretary of State John Kerry, Chairman of the House Foreign Affairs Committee and US Representative, Eliot Engel sternly demanded to consider implementing travel restrictions, suspending portions of assistance and sanctioning Pakistani officials who maintain relationships with designated terrorist groups.

The ISIS has a plan to join the TTP fight against Pakistan army in North Waziristan, and FATA region; therefore, it started distributing jihadist literature, titled "victory," in Pashtu and Persian languages, which can easily be read by Afghan and Pakistani citizens. The organization introduced itself as Daulat-e-Islamia (Islamic State) in the pamphlet, made an appeal to the local population for supporting its struggle for the establishment of an Islamic caliphate in South Asia. In Afghanistan, the ISIS established its network in some provinces bordering Pakistan. C. Christine Fair suggests that the ISIS quickly captured the imagination of Muslims in South Asia. By many accounts, which cannot be independently verified, hundreds of Pakistani fighters—if not more—have already made their way to Syria and Iraq.

The Ahrarul Islam militant groups is also working on the line of Islamic State, and receiving country-wide support, both in case of money and weapons from local business communities. The group doesn't believe on boundaries between Muslim states, and even says borders must be undermined between Afghanistan, Pakistan and India. In India, another development making headlines in print and electronic media is an Al Qaeda network in Kashmir. Al Qaeda leader Ayman al Zawahri in his recent video message said that his network will support Muslims in Kashmir, Burma, Bangladesh and Assam.

It is Sunni extremism, which has been nurtured by the Pakistan Army to serve as its jihadist proxy in India, and Afghanistan. The jihadist amoeba has since given birth to a number of radical groups, like the Sipah-e-Sahaba Pakistan (SSP) and its offshoot Lashkar-e-Jhangvi (LJ). Many of them are based in South Punjab and act as life-line to the Afghan Taliban and Pakistan. They are a part of the campaign to usher in the Khalifat. Now, both the Islamic State (ISIS) and al-Qaeda are making a play for pre-eminence in the world, and Pakistan.

Saudi Arabia has deployed thousands of troops from Egypt and Pakistan along its border with Iraq, amid fears of invasion by the Islamic State (ISIS). India Today reported Pakistani fighters including retired army personnel and civilians from militant groups, Lashkar-e-Toiba (LeT), and the Lashkar-e-Jhangvi (LeJ), fighting in Iraq and Syria. "Hundreds of our mujahedeen have moved to Syria. Others are preparing to join them soon," Abu Wahab, commander of a pro-Pakistan militant group claimed. The groups in Iraq are believed to be from the 'pro-government' groups like LeT and LeJ, not the Tehreek-e-Taliban Pakistan (TTP) that attacked Karachi airport on 08 June 2014, against which the Pakistan army launched an offensive in North Waziristan.

Major (Retired) Agha Amin, according to the India Today report, a Lahore-based Defense analyst, believes that Pakistani fighters went to Syria and Iraq with the tacit knowledge of the government. He mentioned the late General Hamid Gul, former Chief of Pakistan's spy agency ISI, between 1987 and 1989, as a key facilitator in the movement. The army supported General Hamid Gul's efforts to take former Pakistani soldiers to Iraq and Syria. "There is a strong possibility that the Mosul attack was supported by the Pakistani state, both civilian and military," Major Amin said.

Saudi Arabia was in hurry to strengthen its borders Defenses during the Islamic State advance towards Riyadh. The country took drastic step of calling in military assistance from its close allies to shore up the long 500-mile border. Saudi Arabia spent an estimated 35 billion pounds on Defense in 2013, beating Britain as the world's fourth largest military spender. All this throws up the possibility of the IS, Afghan Taliban and al-Qaeda closing ranks for common cause namely Pan-Islamism. It should be reason enough for Pakistan to worry since Pakistan projects itself as "an ideological state".

Saudi Arabia quietly signed an agreement of nuclear-cooperation with South Korea, and seeking Pakistan's nuclear weapons as well. Some experts warned that Saudi could seek Pakistan's aid in developing nuclear technologies—or even buy an atomic bomb—if it sees an agreement with Iran as too weak. Saudi officials have told successive U.S. administrations they expect to have Pakistan's support in the nuclear field, if called upon, because of the kingdom's massive financial support for the South Asian country. In March 2015, Prime Minister Nawaz Sharif visited Saudi Arabia and discussed military cooperation with the King. Current and former U.S. officials have often said they remained skeptical that Pakistan would directly sell or transfer atomic weapons to Saudi Arabia in response to the perceived threat of Iran. But they said they couldn't discount Islamabad deploying some of its weapons in the kingdom, or establishing a nuclear-defense umbrella.

Already, the TTP members in Karachi and Punjab are looking for nuclear materials to prepare explosive devices. Mr. Charles D. Ferguson and William C Potter noted the use of fissile material and other explosive devices: Two types of fissile material could be used for this purpose, highly enriched uranium (HEU) or plutonium, but the former would be far easier to make into a successful IND, as explained in detail, below.[1] According to the conservative figures used by the International Atomic Energy Agency, only 25 kilograms of HEU or 8 kilograms of plutonium would be needed to manufacture a weapon. These materials have been produced in great quantity in nuclear weapon and civilian nuclear energy programs around the world.[2]

There were speculations that on 10 June 2014, terrorists were facilitated by their colleagues within the army to enter the Karachi airport. Once again, the law-enforcement and intelligence apparatus were shown to be inadequate. And even the most secure sites were penetrated. Pakistanis reminded of just how vulnerable everyone is. And yet again, the government was nowhere in sight. Former Taliban spokesman Shahidullah Shahid claimed that the attack was a revenge for the killings of Hakeemullah Mehsud and others in airstrikes.

In 1980s, Pakistani state encouraged the Mujahedeen to fight a proxy war against the Soviet forces in Afghanistan. Most of the Mujahedeen were never disarmed after the war ended in Afghanistan, and some of these groups were later activated at the behest of Pakistan, in the form of Lashkar-e-Toiba, Harkat-ul-Mujahedeen, and others, like the Tehrik-i-Taliban Pakistan (TTP). Rajesh M. Basrur and Prof. Friedrich Steinhäusler suggest that once terrorists obtained radioactive material, and classified, they will need more knowledge about the use of such a weapon:

> Once terrorists have obtained radioactive material, they still have to fulfill several logistical requirements before they actually carry out an act of radiological terrorism, such as: knowledge about the targeted facility; provision of adequate manpower and vehicles to transport the source; access to tools for dismantling the source. These kinds of attacks would result in a wide range of radiation doses to the victims and First Responders (police, paramedics, and fire-fighters), though in most cases unlikely to be life-threatening. However, it is questionable whether initially Indian authorities would even be aware of the fact that a terror act involving radioactive materials has occurred, since most first responders are neither trained, nor technically equipped to detect the presence of radiation at the site of a terror attack. It is safe to presume that terrorists in India would have to inform the media

---

1 Charles D, Ferguson and William C Potter.
2 *Ibid*

first about the deployment of radioactive material in order to achieve the desired level of panic among the general public.[1]

The authors also mentioned security risk and warned that several types of attacks can be carried out by extremist and terrorist organizations in India. India is no doubt, the most vulnerable country where several insurgencies are in operation across the country. These groups would also try to retrieve weapons of mass destruction (WMD) or nuclear weapon. In these circumstances, India's nuclear weapons are also under threat from several terrorist and extremist groups. A small team of trained terrorists can gains access to an NPP, possibly with an insider's assistance, and detonates explosives at sensitive points to cause a release of radioactivity. The authors are of the opinion that the truck bomb attack is possible, acknowledging that in case of the detonation of a biggest conventional bomb, it might cause huge damage.[2]

Nuclear weapons constitute the strategic asset of Pakistan army. Islamabad continues to expand nuclear technology and delivery systems. The country wants to placate more states for investing money in its controversial program. James E. Doyle also raised the issue of nuclear terrorism and possibility of nuclear war in the future:

> A chain of events leading to nuclear war can emerge even when no political leader believes it is in the interest of the state to initiate war, and both sides act in a manner intended to avoid it. This long list of nuclear accidents, malfunction, mishap, false alarms and close calls, often initiated by mechanical and human error, continues to grow. Such incidents include crashes of nuclear armed aircraft and submarines, warning system mistaking flocks of geese or reflection of sunlight for enemy missiles launches, maintenance crews dropping tools and blowing up missile silos, and the temporary loss or misplacement of nuclear weapons.[3]

The future relationship between Pakistan army and jihadist groups, and the use of weapons of mass destruction (WMD), may cause huge destruction. Pakistan's contribution in the military buildup of ISIS raised serious question about the mercenary nature

---

1 "Why States Won't Give Nuclear Weapons to Terrorists" , *International Security*, Keir A. Lieber, Daryl Press volume 38, issue 1, Summer 2013, Belfer Center Programs or Projects: *Quarterly Journal: International Security*.
2 "Nuclear and Radiological Terrorism, Threat for India": Risk Potential and Countermeasures, Rajesh M. Basrur and Prof. Friedrich Steinhausler. http://jps.anl.gov/vol1_iss1/3-Threats_for_India.pdf.
3 *Ibid*

of the country's army. Authors Gary Ackerman and Jeremy Tamsett warn that terrorists may use WMD in future:

> The future nexus of jihadists and WMD is a topic of some controversy. On the one side, are those who view the use by al Qaeda and other jihadist of WMD as all but "inevitable"? These observers generally point to jihadist's demonstrated capacity for mass casualties' attacks, their evolving capabilities, eroding technical constraints, and the increased availability of the raw materials with which to produce WMD. On the other side are those who take a more skeptical approach, highlighting persisting technical obstacles to the efficient weaponization of CBRN agents, as well as the lack of sufficient incentives (based on both "pragmatic and jurisprudential reasons"), for jihadists to expand serious efforts on attaining WMD relative to more conventional weapons.[1]

The issue of Pakistan's nuclear danger has received considerable attention from international community as the TTP, and ISIS seek nuclear weapons, to use it either in Afghanistan or India. Some Kashmiri militant groups are trying to retrieve these weapons, and use it against the Indian army. Over the last ten years, there have emerged renewed concerns over the future direction of the country's nuclear program. Some see it as a worrisome possibility; some believe it is an exaggerated danger. Sadia Tasleem supports Pakistan's stance on the safety of its nuclear weapons:

> Islamabad appears confident in its ability to prevent any such eventuality. This, combined with the confidence that Pakistan draws from its close cooperation with the United States, prevents Pakistanis from perceiving US nuclear deterrence policy as a threat. Pakistan's threat perceptions continue to focus elsewhere. Nonetheless, disenchantment with the United States is heavily reflected in Pakistan's popular discourse. The disenchantment mainly centers on drone attacks and the implications of the Indo-US strategic partnership.[2]

India and Pakistan, with little experience and less contact, have virtually nothing to guide them in a crisis but mistrust and paranoia. If weapons proliferate in the Middle East, as Iran and then Saudi Arabia, and possibly Egypt join Israel in the ranks of nuclear powers, each will have to manage a bewildering four-dimensional stand-off. Foes such as India and Pakistan can foster stability simply by talking.

1 *Survival*, 2013, Vol, 55, Number-1.
2 *Jihadists and Weapons of Mass Destruction*, edited by Gary Ackerman, Jeremy Tamset, CRC Press, 2008

According to the National Security Policy of Pakistan, the urban areas in four provinces of the country have been the focus of terrorists for the last three decades. Analysis of the Ministry of Interior and its National Crisis Management Cell (NCMC) indicates that:

From 2010 to 2013, terrorists largely targeted seven agencies of FATA, Karachi, Peshawar, Kohat, Bannu, Hangu and Swabi districts of Khyber Pakhtunkhwa, and Quetta, Dera Bugti, Turbat and Kech districts of Baluchistan. There are sufficient grounds for such concerns even though there has been so far no direct evidence of international terrorist organizations conducting work to build improvised nuclear devices.[1]

Amulya Ganguli argues that Pakistan's army collusion with terrorists has created alarming situation in South Asia. The country uses terrorist against both India and Afghanistan:

> The threat is apparently greater than any other in recent history. For a start, it is for the first time ever that the army of a country is openly in collusion with the terrorists with the rest of the world not only unable to break this sinister alliance but even to condemn Pakistan in unequivocal terms. The danger is worsened by Pakistan's stockpiling of nuclear weapons, including - the most chilling of all - tactical battlefield nuclear armaments evidently for use in the event of an India-Pakistan war. This eager compiling of the so-called doomsday weapons is probably the result of India formulating the so-called Cold Start doctrine, which is said to envisage a swift military response to another Mumbai-type outrage. The belief in Pakistan apparently is that the possibility of such an operation leading to a nuclear conflict will scuttle the Cold Start project.[2]

Besides its primary responsibility of ensuring the territorial integrity of Pakistan, the army considers itself the protector of Islam and the guarantor of the idea of Pakistan. In this capacity, it has intervened several times to take direct charge of the day-to-day affairs of the country, by overthrowing lawfully elected civilian governments. As the CIA already highlighted al Qaeda's general interest in weapons of mass destruction, including nuclear weapons, the Islamic State (ISIS) has already retrieved these weapons from Iraq. Nuclear terrorism remains a discrete possibility, hence it should be designated a low probability high consequence event. Writer Vladimir Dvorkin (2012) warns about the fatalities of nuclear terrorism:

---

1 "Deterring nuclear terrorism: Reflections from Islamabad," *Bulletin of the Atomic Scientists*, Sadia Tasleem, 06 May 2013.
2 *Pakistan - a rogue state with a rogue army*, Amulya Ganguli, IANS, Dec 04, 2010,

Severe consequences can be caused by sabotaging nuclear power plants, research reactors, and radioactive materials storage facilities. Large cities are especially vulnerable to such attacks. A large city may host dozens of research reactors with a nuclear power plant or a couple of spent nuclear fuel storage facilities and dozens of large radioactive materials storage facilities located nearby. The past few years have seen significant efforts made to enhance organizational and physical aspects of security at facilities, especially at nuclear power plants. Efforts have also been made to improve security culture. But these efforts do not preclude the possibility that well-trained terrorists may be able to penetrate nuclear facilities.[1]

Pakistan often engaged in discussion with the United States on its controversial nuclear weapon program, at various levels, and in different circumstances, for more than 30 years, but, according to some research reports, U.S and international community is not satisfied with Pakistan's nuclear safety measures. Pakistan's supply of nuclear materials to some Arab states including Saudi Arabia, created more suspicion about its Islamic Nuclear Bomb. Pakistan's envoy to UN, Mr. Munir Akram expressed deep concern about the increasing US-Pakistan distances and emerging differences regarding it supply of nuclear weapons to Saudi Arabia:

> Clearly, Pakistan and the US need to address their nuclear differences urgently and constructively, The US in concert in other major powers, are also well placed to promote a more stable nuclear security environment between Pakistan and India. Absent some measures of mutual assurance, accommodation and cooperation on the nuclear issue, the continuing US military presence in Afghanistan is likely to further intensify Islamabad's concerns and Pakistan-US tensions and affect their positions on other issues, such as counterterrorism and Afghanistan's stability, where their objectives appear to be increasingly convergent.[2]

The threat of terrorist networks acquiring chemical, biological and nuclear weapons (CBRN) to develop and use it is real. In the intellectual circles, there is a general perception that as the Islamic State (ISIS) already used some dangerous gases in Iraq; it could use biological weapons against civilian populations in Pakistan. If control over these weapons is weak, or if it is available in open market, there would be a huge destruction in the region. In July 2014, the government of Iraq notified that nuclear material was seized

---

1 Vladimir Dvorkin, 2012.
2 "It's mostly about N-Pakistan," *Dawn*, Munir Akram, 02 February 02, 2014.

by the ISIS army from Mosul University. The laptop retrieved from university contained a 19-pages document in Arabic which explains how to develop biological weapons. In the laptop, there was a 26 pages religious FATWA, which allows the use of weapons of mass destruction. "If Muslims cannot defeat the kafir [unbelievers] in a different way, it is permissible to use weapons of mass destruction," warns the FATWA.

The effects of chemical weapons are worse as it cause death or incapacitation, while biological weapons cause death or disease in humans, animals or plants. We have two international treaties, which interdict the use of such weapons. Notwithstanding of all these preventive measures, the threat of chemical or biological warfare persists. In 2011 and 2013, there have been complaints, and allegations, that some states target Pakistan with biological weapons. The country has been trying to counter biological attacks but failed due to the limited funds and medical advancement.

The fatalities of Dengue and Ebola viruses in Pakistan, and West Africa are the worse forms of bioterrorism. In 2011, Pakistan medical Association called on intelligence agencies to investigate fears of deliberate spread of the deadly disease in the Punjab. There are speculations that in future, TTP or Islamic State (ISIS) might possibly use Measles, Dengue, Polio and the Ebola viruses in Pakistan. Some states might use drones for the purposes of bio-war against their rival states. The University of Birmingham Policy Commission Report warned that terrorists could also turn the remotely-piloted aircraft into flying bombs by hooking them up to improvised explosive devices. Writer Mushfiq Murshed urged that religiously motivated groups in Pakistan can retrieve nuclear weapons:

This is accomplished by obtaining clerical sanctions through religious edicts (FATWAs) that are primarily based on de-contextualized quotations from the sacred text. The edicts that al Qaeda has pursued and propagated clearly are an indication of what strategy they intend to pursue.[1]

As the country is a failing state and the infrastructure of terrorist organization is well established, there are possibilities that these groups can gain access to nuclear materials. Research scholars, Rajesh M. Basrur and Friedrich Steinhäusler also noted some atomic sites of Pakistan and their vulnerabilities:

---

1 "The Possibility of WMD Terrorism," Mushfiq Murshed, Vol, 8 No 4, WMD, *Criterion Quarterly*, Oct 31, 2013.

Though its overall nuclear infrastructure is relatively small, the possibility of leakage is widely feared because of the general sense of the country as a failing state. Pakistan's main uranium enrichment facility is at Kahuta (Khan Research Laboratories). Smaller uranium enrichment facilities exist at Sihala and Golra, and possibly at Gadwal. Plutonium extraction work is done at the New Lab, Nilhore, and at Khushab in central Punjab. Pakistan has two nuclear power plants. One is located at Karachi, the other at Chasma. Its nuclear weapons are believed to be in an unassembled state, with the fissile core kept separate from the bomb assembly. The bomb components and the wider infrastructure are under military control. In February 2000, a National Command Authority was established. In January 2001, the Pakistan Nuclear Regulatory Authority (PNRA) was created to regulate the civilian infrastructure.[1]

In his research article, Indian scholar, B. Raman (2004) noted Russian President, Vladimir Putin's concern about the safety of Pakistan's nuclear weapons during his India visit:

> When President Vladimir Putin of Russia visited India a year ago, he stated in an interview that Musharraf had repeatedly assured him that Pakistan's nuclear and missile assets were in the safe hands of the Army and that there was no question of their leakage to Al Qaeda or other jihadist terrorists. Putin added that while he had no reasons to distrust Musharraf, he continued to be concerned over the dangers of individual members of the Pakistani scientific community helping the jihadist terrorists to develop a WMD capability.[2]

In his article, journalist Ansar Abbasi also analyzed the terror incidents in Pakistan: "From 2001 to 2013 there were 13,897 incidents in Pakistan, which is marginally less than Iraq. During the year 2013, there have been 1,361 incidents of terrorism. A trajectory of terrorist incidents in Pakistan shows that after the Marriott bombing in Islamabad and Lal Mosque incidents, the number of suicide attacks in Pakistan increased alarmingly".

The threat of Pakistani jihadists using WMD might present threatening situation, since the threat lies at the nexus of two subjects—jihadist terrorism and weapons of mass destruction—that are both characterized by high level of dynamism. Terrorist groups in

---

1 "Nuclear and Radiological Terrorism, Threat for India: Risk Potential and Countermeasures," Rajesh M. Basrur and Prof. Friedrich Steinhäusler. http://jps.anl.gov/vol1_iss1/3-Threats_for_India.pdf.
2 "Pakistan and Danger of Nuclear Jihad," B. Raman, Paper No. 904, 27 January 2004, http://www.southasiaanalysis.org/paper904.

Pakistan are trying to retrieve bio-weapons and use it against civilian population in Afghanistan.

In his detailed article (2014), Dr. Agha Inamullah Khan argued that bioterrorism has already killed numerous poor women and children in Pakistan: "We had Dengue, Measles and now again alarming figures of Polio. The first incidence of dengue fever was reported in 2003 in Lahore with an earlier outbreak in Karachi almost a decade ago". The disease reappeared in 2006, hitting on alternate years until 2010 and returning with even greater fury following year. Also many Pakistanis, especially in rural areas, view vaccination campaigns with suspicion as a western plot to sterilize Muslims.

In 2013, Global Policy, a journal produced by the London School of Economics, warned about the prospect of Ebola being used as a terrorist weapon. Amanda M. Teckman also warned that the Islamic State might possibly use Ebola as a weapon against civilian population: "It remains to be seen if a terrorist group like ISIS—which has demonstrated a willingness to engage in large scale mass murder, including the uninhibited murder of civilians—has the capability to produce a weaponized version of Ebola." Author of *Bioterrorism*, Mr. Daniel M. Gerstein noted that terrorist might not carry out large scale attacks which negatively influence their support:

> Terrorists will act in ways they consider rational, even if this rationality is not obvious to outsiders. They will maintain a core raison d'être that will propel their actions and modulate their behavior to positively influence their constituencies. This will be very important as in the case of moderating behavior. Terrorists generally will be disinclined to engage in large-scale attacks with large number of civilian casualties (i.e., death, disease and morbidity greater than one thousand people) because this would tend to negatively influence their support base.[1]

---

1 "Nuclear and Radiological Terrorism, Threat for India: Risk Potential and Countermeasures," Rajesh M. Basrur and Prof. Friedrich Steinhäusler. http://jps.anl.gov/vol1_iss1/3-Threats_for_India.pdf. *Dawn*, 09 June 2014, *Daily Times*, and the *Express Tribune*, Pakistan. *Deccan Chronicle*, 17 June 2014, "Terrorist Tactics in Pakistan Threaten Nuclear Weapons Safety," Shaun Gregory, "*CTC Sentinel*," Volume-4 Issue-6, and 01 June 2011, "Afghanistan-Pakistan-Iran Radical Islam, Nuclear Weapons and Regional Security," Rana Banerji, *IPCS Issue Brief, Paper No. 191*, May 2012. Centre for Internal and Regional Security, IPCS http://www.ipcs.org/pdf_file/issue/IB191-RanaBanerjee-BGS.pdf. *The Crisis State: Pakistan's Security Dilemma*, D. Suba Chandran, Center for Internal and Regional Security, IPCS, No. 192, May 2012. http://www.ipcs.org/pdf_file/issue/IB192-Suba-BGS.pdf.

Terrorism experts understand that unless the tacit support of Pakistan army to the terrorists is undermined, the possibilities of nuclear terrorism cannot be ruled out. Writer Ramtanu Maitra argues that the links between Pakistan army and Kashmir based terrorist groups as a dangerous development. These groups, Mr. Ramtanu suggests are flourishing and harboring by US and Pakistan:

> What are disturbing are the direct ties between the Pakistani military and the terrorists, particularly the anti-India terrorist such as a Kashmiri fighter, who was a commando in Pakistan's Special Services Group (SSG), and was once rewarded by Gen. Pervez Musharraf as a hero for a terror attack in Indian Kashmir. Moreover, a slew of terrorists, who were recruited from the Mideast, North Africa, and Asia, and funded, trained, and harbored by the Americans, British, Saudis, and Pakistanis, continue to flourish inside the vast, virtually ungoverned areas of Pakistan.[1]

Writing on possible nuclear attack and the availability of radiological materials in India and Pakistan, Kishore Kuchibhtla and Mathew McKinzie argued that terrorists can disperse radioactive materials in major cities, where the psychological and economic impacts would undoubtedly be far worse:

> The threat of nuclear, or radiological, terrorism is not limited to the confines of the United States. South Asia continues to be a volatile region that hosts many militant groups and sources of radioactive material. Because of these and other factors, nuclear and radiological terrorism remains a frightening possibility in India and Pakistan. If terrorists dispersed radioactive materials in a major city, the psychological and economic impacts would undoubtedly be far worse. Widespread availability of radioactive materials worldwide makes the threat of radiological terrorism plausible. The use of radioactive materials in medicine and industry has been globalized. Radioactive materials are stored and used throughout India and Pakistan for cancer therapy, food irradiation, and medical product sterilization.[2]

Political instability in Pakistan and the fear of nuclear arsenals falling into wrong hands has attracted international attention. In

1 "Central Asia, Kashmir Face New Jihadi Threat; Concerns in Russia." http://www.larouchepub.com/eiw/public/2013/eirv40n41-20131018/40-43_4041.pdf. Also, *Nuclear and Radiological Terrorism threat from India: Risk Potential and Countermeasures*. Rajesh M. Basrur and Freidrich. *Bioterror in the 21st Century: Emerging Threats in a New Global Environment*, by Daniel M. Gerstein, Naval Institute Press, and 01 September, 2009.
2 *Nuclear Terrorism and Nuclear Accidents in South Asia*, Kishore Kuchibhtla and Mathew McKinzie. Stimson Centre.

analyzing the likelihood of nuclear and bioterrorism in Pakistan, we have a lot of material indicating the possible collaboration of jihadists and military officers in carrying out attacks against civilian population in Afghanistan and Pakistan. Nuclear experts understand that bioterrorism in the country is a disastrous threat. Michael Krepon has raised the same questions about the vulnerability of Pakistan nuclear weapons. As Pakistan has been poorly governed for a long time, therefore, according to Michael Krepon argument, Islamic extremists turned against the organs of the state:

> Pakistan has been poorly governed for so long—both by military rulers and by civilians—that its demise has been repeatedly predicted. The nation's cadre of civil servants, its public education system, and its social services has progressively degraded. Political leadership in Pakistan has become a life time appointment, few business opportunities offer as much prospect of success as being as elected official...Islamic extremism once a favored tool of the Pakistan military to dislodge the Soviet Union from Afghanistan and to punish India across the Kashmir divide, has turned against the organs of the state. Acts of violence are on the rise in Pakistan and have been directed against former paymasters in the Pakistan military.[1]

On 22 June, 2011, Brigadier Ali Khan was arrested on the charges that he consorted with extremist organizations. His wife confirmed to journalists that Mr. Khan was against the killing of Osama bin Laden and drone attacks in Waziristan. Former Director General Inter Services Press Relations (ISPR) Major General Athar Abbas once warned in an interview that the trend of jihadism in army and its links with terrorist groups could be harmful for armed forces. The investigation report of the Abbottabad Commission criticized the ISI for its inconsideration policy and regretted that after 2005, it had closed the file of bin Laden and was no longer actively pursuing him. Former ISI Chief Ahmad Shuja Pasha, while recording his statement before the commission vowed that Pakistan was a failing state.

In his policy analysis paper, Mr. Subhodh Atal noted that Mr. Musharaf investigated some of the country's nuclear scientists for their links with al Qaeda. He also noted that Pakistan shared its nuclear technology with North Korea, and possibly with Myanmar and Saudi Arabia:

> Even worse, Pakistani nuclear experts are under investigation for links with al-Qaeda...Pakistan is reported to have shared its nuclear technology with North Korea, and possibly with Myanmar and Saudi

---

1 *Pakistan's Red-Carpet Treatment*. Michael Krepon, 27 October 2013.

Arabia, thus contributing to the problem of nuclear proliferation. A nation that is penetrated by Islamic radicals and that possesses dozens of nuclear weapons and proliferate them to other dictatorial countries poses a tangible and immediate problem. But U.S. policy toward Pakistan does not reflect that reality. In the absence of pressure from the United States, Pakistan has not found it necessary to take serious action against Islamic extremists or to end its proliferation activities.[1]

During the Taliban regime in Afghanistan, al Qaeda sought nuclear weapons assistance from Pakistan military warlords. Pakistani scientists who helped Taliban and al Qaeda groups were Sultan Bashiruddin Mahmood, a retired officer of Atomic Energy Commission, and Choudhry Abdul Majeed. They met Osama bin Laden in August 2001, and discussed with him a nuclear weapons infrastructure in Afghanistan. The threat of nuclear terrorism is a challenging problem for Pakistan. In 2001, according to Graham Allison's analysis, Sultan Bashiruddin Mahmood and Choudhery Abdul Majeed visited Osama bin Laden in Kabul. Over the course of three days of intense conversation, they finally reached a conclusion that Pakistan will help Osama in developing weapons of mass destruction in Afghanistan. Sultan Bashiruddin Mahmood had spent 30 year as a uranium expert in Pakistan's Atomic Energy Commission, and had been a key figure in Kahuta Atomic Plant.

Writer, Mr. Paul K. Kerr's suggests that the two men were seeking an approval of developing nuclear weapons:

> Mahmood and Majeed met with Osama bin Laden and Ayman al-Zawahiri in August 2001 in Afghanistan to discuss, among other topics, what would be needed to develop a nuclear weapons infrastructure, details of nuclear bomb design, and how to construct radiological dispersal devices. Mr. Mahmood was a public figure well-known for his eccentric and extreme views about science and Islam and he was demoted in 1999 to a lower rank in part because of his radicalism. Mr. Mahmood then sought early retirement and started the UTN organization.[2]

---

1 *Extremist, Nuclear Pakistan: An Emerging Threat?* By Subodh Atal, CATO Institute, 05 March, 2003, Policy Analysis No-472. http://www.cato.org/publications/policy-analysis/extremist-nuclear-pakistan-emerging-threat, and also, "Nuclear terrorism: How Big a Threat? Is al Qaeda Trying to Get a Bomb"? US Documents, 7 September 2012. *Daily Times*, 14 November 2013.
2 "Pakistan's Nuclear Weapons: Proliferation and Security Issues," Paul K. Kerr, Mary Beth Nikitin, 19 March 2013.

In 1999, General (Retd) Pervez Musharraf turned to extremist forces to undermine Prime Minister Nawaz Sharif's government. Mr. Musharaf also used these forces in the Kargil war. The army's close links with extremists and Taliban is evident from the fact that in the Kargil war; more than 200 Afghan Taliban fighters sacrificed their lives for Pakistani armed forces.

On 26 March 2014, Daily Times in its editorial page published a long but interesting story about the Prime Minister Nawaz Sharif use of the platform of Nuclear Security Summit in Hague. In his address, Prime Minister Nawaz Sharif outlined Pakistan's nuclear security architecture, including an effective command and control system, safety and security of nuclear materials, and preventive measures to prevent any leakage of such materials. Having operated civilian nuclear power facilities safely for 40 years, Mr. Nawaz Sharif plugged Pakistan as qualifying to be part of the international nuclear energy regime, including membership of the Nuclear Suppliers Group.[1]

On the issue of nuclear confidence measures and peace in South Asia, writer Sitara Noor argued that the relatively poor record of radiation safety and security in India raised serious concern that nuclear and other radioactive material might enter into the country. She also suggested that India and Pakistan face serious threat from the non-State actors who may try to use nuclear or radioactive material for an improvised nuclear device or a radiological dispersal device.[2]

Pakistan understands that nuclear weapons are the only guarantors for its national security, while writer Mr. Adil Sultan defends his country and supports the idea that Pakistan needs nuclear weapons for its protection:

The growing conventional asymmetry and the salience of nuclear deterrence during various crises reinforced Pakistani conviction that nuclear weapons are the only guarantors for its national security. Several factors contribute to a state's nuclear choices, but in Pakistan's case, the concern about national security has been the chief catalyst. The salience of nuclear weapons in Pakistan's security policy and the fact that it has played vital role during various crises

---

1 Congressional Research Service Report. http://fpc.state.gov/documents/organization/171369.
2 "Nuclear confidence-building measures and peace making in South Asia," Sitara Noor, http://www.issi.org.pk/publication-files/1361514703_89851329.pdf.

with India, has provided successive leaders an opportunity to claim credit for successful nuclear stewardship.[1]

Non state actors in South Asia are causing challenges and problems. Nuclear terrorism is yet another challenging problem. Though Pakistan's overall nuclear infrastructure is relatively small, the possibility of leakage is widely feared because of the general sense of the country as a failing state. The insiders in Pakistan's armed forces can help terrorists in obtaining nuclear weapons.

The main source of a nuclear-terrorist threat, therefore, stems from the Islamic State (ISIS) and TTP that have taken up arms in Waziristan, FATA and Baluchistan, because Pakistan's links to terrorism and Islamic radicalism are well known. Research scholars, Rajesh M. Basrur and Friedrich Steinhausler, in their research report underlined the theft of nuclear materials from India, where several incidents of natural uranium stolen occurred in the past:

> In India, numerous cases of theft have occurred in recent years. For instance, in July 1998, the Central Bureau of Investigation seized over eight kilograms of natural uranium stolen from the Indira Gandhi Center for Atomic Research (IGCAR) in Chennai ("Uranium Racket Unearthed," 2002). Besides, it is difficult to ensure security over materials that are outside the direct control of the state, such as radiological sources in the possession of hospitals and industries. In July 2002, a gamma radiography camera containing Ir-192 with an activity of 729-GBq was stolen during transportation in the north-eastern state of Assam. A disturbing aspect of the incident was that the camera, a highly radioactive device, was left unlocked in the trunk of a public bus in a region plagued by terrorist activity ("Radiation Scare in Assam," 2002). Although Atomic Energy Commission (AEC) Chairman Anil Kakodkar claimed there was no need to panic, the fact remains that the camera was a powerful potential source for a dirty bomb ("No Chance of N-Material Falling into Wrong Hands," 2002). Again, in August 2003, a large quantity of Co 60 was stolen from a steel plant in Jamshedpur.[2]

The threat of nuclear terrorism existed in both India and Pakistan as their nuclear weapons are under threat from extremist groups.

---

1 "Pakistan's emerging nuclear posture: impact of drivers and technology on nuclear doctrine," Adil Sultan, *Strategic Journal of the Institute of Strategic Studies Islamabad*, http://www.issi.org.pk/publication-files/1340000409_86108059.pdf.
2 "Nuclear and Radiological Terrorism, Threat for India: Risk Potential and Countermeasures," Rajesh M. Basrur and Prof. Friedrich Steinhäusler. http://jps.anl.gov/vol1_iss1/3-Threats_for_India.pdf.

Having realized the sensitivity of the threat, on 09 August, 2013, The New York Times reported Pakistan's armed forces were abruptly ordered to be on high alert for a possible Taliban attack on the country's military installations. Taliban and their allies had a plan to sabotage the country nuclear facilities and use a dirty bomb. On September 7, 2012, Pakistan army deployed commando force at one of the country's biggest nuclear site in Dera Ghazi Khan District of Southern Punjab after an intelligence report warned of a possible Taliban attack. Even a minor attack on Pakistan's nuclear facilities would change the face of the country.[1]

South Asian Monitor also noted the efforts of terrorists getting a ready-made nuclear device and having the expertise and wherewithal to detonate it remains a far-fetched proposition. They may obtain minor quantities of fissile material and use these to produce a 'dirty bomb.' Pakistan, so far has not changed its position on the last resort proclamation, which thus appears to be at odds with its unwritten nuclear doctrine. Prof. Muhammad Sadiq of Qaid Azam University Islamabad, Pakistan argues that terrorist group might drag India and Pakistan into war:

Islamic militants may drag Pakistan and India into a war through their malicious acts such as replicating Mumbai (2008) like carnage. Everyone knows 'war is a slippery road,' it may escalate to a doomsday scenario where both states could use nuclear weapons against each other. The strategic dynamics between both the countries could drift into increasingly dangerous proportions if the militants go for a major attack on Indian interests anywhere in the world.[2]

A study (2010) of the Belfer Center for Science and International affairs concerned that Pakistan's stockpile face a greater threat from Islamic extremists groups. In 2011, for example, terrorist groups attacked Minhas air base some 25 miles away from Islamabad, where several nuclear warheads were stored. In that battle, one soldier and eight militants killed.[3]

---

1 *The New York Times*, 9 August, 2013.
2 *Ibid*, 9 August 2013.
3 "Report of Belfer Centre for Science and International affairs",2010

Chapter 3. Pakistan's Nuclear Weapons, ISIS, Taliban, and Global Concern

On 29 December 2014, Abhishek Singh, a first Indian secretary to the UN Mission, told the UN General Assembly that the threat of nuclear terrorism is one of the pressing challenges, facing the international community. There are more than 100 incidents of theft or misuse of nuclear material each year. At present, there are 25 states possessing nuclear weapons and nuclear facilities, and continue to expand into dangerous neighborhoods around the globe. Now, the most challenging problem for the Islamic State (ISIS) in Pakistan would be, to obtain fissile material necessary to construct a nuclear explosive device. Terrorists of the Islamic State and TTP could attempt to exploit many acquisition routes.

Pakistan faces a greater threat from Islamic extremists seeking nuclear weapons than any other nuclear stockpile on earth. As the potential spread of nuclear weapons in South Asia is a major threat to regional and global peace, the Islamic State (ISIS), and other extremist groups in the country are struggling to retrieve nuclear material, and use it against military and nuclear installations. Washington Post in one of its reports warned that Pakistani extremist groups could seize components of the stockpile or trigger a war with India.

There are reports from the US intelligence agencies that during the Kargil war, Pakistan readied its nuclear weapons without the knowledge of Prime Minister Nawaz Sharif. Known Pakistani scientist, Dr Parvez Hoodbhoy also warned that his country's nuclear weapons could be hijacked by extremists, as a result of increasing radicalization within the army barracks. "If Pakistan did not have nuclear weapons, Kargil would not have happened. My intention is that it was the first instance that nuclear weapons actually caused a war," Hoodbhoy said.[1]

The threat of nuclear weapons theft, and bioterrorism in South Asia has become centre of discussion in International press, that terrorist organizations in Pakistan and India are trying to retrieve biotechnology and nuclear weapons, and want to use it against civilian's population and security forces. The recent border skirmishes between Pakistan and India, the cloud of civil war in Afghanistan, and the emergence of Islamic State (ISIS) in Pakistan and Afghanistan, further justified the possibilities of the complex threat of chemical and biological terrorism in the region. As Pakistan and Afghanistan have been the victims of terrorism and Talibanization during the last three decades, the establishment of Islamic State (ISIS) in South Asia may possibly change the traditional concept of terrorism and insurgency in the region.

There is a general perception that forces of the Islamic State (ISIS) can use biotechnologies against the security forces in South Asia. If the control on those weapons is weak, the possibilities increased. The nucleation is that the problem of nuclear and biological terrorism deserves special attention from all South Asian states, including Afghanistan. As nuclear weapons and missile technologies, and bio-weapons proliferation, there is a grave danger that some of them might fall into the hands of TTP, or Islamic State (ISIS), Indian and Afghani extremist groups, which might cause destruction and disease.

On 26 September 2014, Dawn reported the outgoing Peshawar corps commander Gen Khalid Rabbani expressed deep concern about the militancy problem in Pakistan. Squarely indicating that regions outside his operational command of FATA, and Khyber Pakhtunkhwa had a potent and varied mix of militancy, that needed to be tackled urgently, the newspaper reported. By citing militant hotbeds in other provinces, the commander of the ongoing operation Zarb-i-Azb in North Waziristan Agency should not be seen as trying to deflect responsibility, but should be applauded for attempting to put the fight against militancy in its proper context—which means regarding Zarb-i-Azb as an important, but by no means final, step in the right direction. Dawn reported.

---

1 *Anniversary: What if Pakistan did not have the bomb?* Pervez Hoodbhoy, 28 May, 2011, http://tribune.com.pk/story/177622/anniversary-what-if-pakistan-did-not-have-the-bomb/, *Daily Times*, 03 October 2013. "The-Prospect-of-Nuclear-Jihad-in-South-Asia"-Musa-Khan-Jalalzai. Daily Times, 03 October 2013.

Some Pakistani clerics, army generals and politicians suggest that jihad against India is mandatory on every Pakistani Muslim. Thus, the fear of India became genuine. On 16 May, 2009, an Israeli website, Debka reported former Indian Prime Minister Manmohan Singh warned President Barak Obama, that nuclear sites in Pakistan's Khyber Pakhtunkhwa province are "already partly" in the hands of Islamic extremists. Before this statement, in 2005, Mr. Singh told CNN that his government was worried about the security of Pakistan nuclear assets after General Musharaf.[1]

In July 2012, EU Non-Proliferation Consortium published a Non-Proliferation Paper No: 19, in which author Bruno Tertrais painted a balanced picture of Pakistan nuclear weapons. Mr. Bruno analyzed the mixed consequences of India and Pakistan nuclear weapons and established the fact that a single incident can lead to a full-scale war in the region:

> The induction of nuclear weapons in South Asia has had mixed consequences. Since 1998 there has been no major conventional war in the region, but the propensity for risk taking remains high: Pakistan risked war in 1999 by sending armed militants across the Line of Control, wrongly believing that India would be deterred from reacting; both countries went to the brink of war in the winter of 2001–2002; and India was close to retaliating against Pakistan after the 2008 Mumbai terrorist attacks. India has attempted to checkmate Pakistan and block the avenues that it thinks Pakistan might open with its nuclear capability. The 1999 incident led to India stating that it would not hesitate to wage a limited war. The 2001–2002 crises led to India's adoption in 2004 of the Cold Start doctrine: a fast campaign with limited objectives, capturing territory up to 50–80 km inside Pakistan, but without months of mobilization—leaving no time for Pakistan or the international community to react.[2]

Nuclear weapon materials could fall into the hands of terrorists during a period of political turmoil. Research scholar, Reshmi Kazi argued that Pakistani extremist groups can acquire nuclear weapons

1 "The prospect of nuclear jihad in South Asia," Musa Khan Jalalzai. *Daily Times*, 03 October 2013. On May 16, 2009, an Israeli website, *Debka*, Indian Prime Minister Singh warned President Barck Obama that nuclear sites in Pakistan's Khyber Pakhtunkhwa province are "already partly" in the hands of Islamic extremists.
2 In July 2012, EU non-proliferation consortium published a non proliferation paper No-19, in which author Bruno Tertrais painted a balanced picture of Pakistan nuclear weapons. *Pakistan's nuclear programme: a net assessment*, Bruno tertrais, Foundation for Research, June 13, 2012, http://www.frstrategie.org/barreFRS/publications/rd/2012/RD_201204.pdf.

by stealing or purchasing assembled nuclear weapons from their friends within the armed forces:

> The situation in Pakistan has further taken a turn for the worse which increasing political instability prevailing in the country giving rise to international concerns on the potential threat of Islamabad's nuclear weapon falling into the hands of terrorists. It is feared that Pakistan might lose control over it national 'crown jewels' to radical elements like Tehrik-i-Taliban Pakistan (TTP) and Lashkar-e-Taiba (LeT) many of who keep close ties with al Qaeda.[1]

In May 2014, Prime Minister Nawaz Sharif visited National Command and Control Center, which oversees Pakistan's nuclear facilities. After his visit, he said that his country wanted peace in the region, and would not be part of an arms race.[2]

Times of India also reported that Pakistan established a 25,000-strong Nuclear Special Force (NSF), and put in place extensive measures to protect and manage its strategic assets, including its nuclear arsenal. But, notwithstanding the presence of this strong nuclear force, Taliban carried out successful attacks on Pakistan's nuclear installations. Research reports have documented the UN, US, and Indian government who notified 35 Terrorist Organizations under the unlawful activities (Prevention) Act.[3]

The international community continues to express deep concern about the safety of Pakistan's nuclear weapons, and demand additional measures. Pakistan's strategic objective has been expanded to the acquisition of a "full spectrum capability" comprising a land, air and sea-based triad of nuclear forces, to put it on a par with India. Thus the recent shifts in Pakistan's nuclear strategy cannot be ascribed solely to the traditional construct of India-Pakistan hostility.[4]

After the 1965 Indo-Pakistan war, Zulfikar Ali Bhutto aggressively began advocating the option of "nuclear weapons programs" but such attempts were dismissed by Finance Minister Muhammad Shoaib and Chairman I.H. Usmani. The India and Pakistani War of 1971

---

1 *Nuclear terrorism, the New Terror of the 21st Century*, Reshmi Kazi, IDSA Monograph Series, No. 27 October 2013, Institute for Defense Studies and Analyses, New Delhi. http://idsa.in/system/files/Monograph27.pdf.
2 Not in arms race but will not neglect defense needs: Nawaz Sharif, *PTI News*, 20 March 2014, and *Economic Times*, http://articles.economictimes.indiatimes.com/2014-03-20/news/48401935_1_arms-race-prime-minister-sharif-pakistan.
3 *Times of India*, 22 June, 2013.
4 "Dealing with Pakistan's brinkmanship," *Daily the Hindu*, 07 December 2012.

was a crushing defeat for Pakistan. On 20 January 1972, in a Multan (Oldest City of Pakistan) meeting, Bhutto stated: "What Raziuddin Siddiqui, a Pakistani, contributed for the United States during the Manhattan Project, could also be done by scientists in Pakistan, for their own people"?

In 1975, Dr. Abdul Qadeer Khan considerably advanced these efforts. As a nuclear state, Pakistan jeopardized its weapons and installations by directly supporting jihadist militias in Syria, Iraq and Bahrain. The Saudi-Pakistan partnership is certain to boost the jihadist organizations and the Pakistani intelligence agencies, which are nurturing them, thereby transforming Pakistan into a complete jihadist military state in near future.[1]

At the behest of Saudi Arabia, Pakistan made a strategic shift on Syria's civil war—to one that portends to back the Syrian rebels and even provide them with arms through Riyadh.[2] Pakistan's military establishment sold its soldier to Saudi Arabia, and allowed the country to use them against the Syrian regime and Iraq.[3]

It also sold its soldiers to the US to use them in Afghanistan and Bahrain, and tomorrow its soldiers might be used against communist China. Pakistani media reported Saudi Arabia requested for Pakistani soldiers following Pakistani Prime Minister Nawaz Sharif's visit to Riyadh in March 2015. Pakistan has good relations with Iran than Saudi Arabia does, but ultimately it is more dependent on Saudi Arabia. China publicly links recent attacks in Xinjiang province to Pakistan.

China has repeatedly addressed the issue in talks with Pakistan, arguing that Uighur terrorists received training from Pakistani security forces. In 2003, ETIM's leader Hasan Mahsum was killed in a raid by the Pakistani army at the border between Afghanistan and Pakistan. However, it is just as possible that China will itself be alienated from Pakistan due to Pakistan's role in incubating Uyghur radicals. China sees Pakistan's involvement in the bloodiest violence in Xinjiang between ethnic Uyghurs and Han Chinese—both civilians and government forces. Over 100 individuals died in the latest bout of violence, which began when Uyghurs attacked police stations in Kashgar.

---

1 *Saudi Arabia's Nuclear Thinking and the Pakistani Connection*, Reshmi Kazi, 7 January 2014, Institute for defense studies and Analysis. India. *The Guardian* reported, Saudi Arabia playing nuclear games. Pravda newspaper-11.11.2013
2 *Daily Times*, 02 May 2014.
3 "ISI and Media Infighting," Shaukat Kadir, *The Nation*, 09 May 2014.

Pakistan's opposition parties slammed the government for what its leaders called "a policy about turn." It was Saudi Arabia that hosted Nawaz Sharif during his decade long exile after a coup in 1999. Saudi Arabia is also more threatened by Iran and its nuclear program than the United States. Iran has increased its influence in Iraq and through Hezbollah in Lebanon, and if Assad stays in power, Iran wins in Syria too.[1]

Mr. C Raja Mohan in his article (March 2015) in the Indian Express reported that Saudi Kingdom is seeking Pakistan's military support to shore up its internal and external defense amidst mounting regional tensions. Saudi Arabia's regional security environment has gotten worse since then. Riyadh has been deeply concerned about the gains made by the Shia Houthi rebels in Yemen, with which Saudi Arabia shares a restive frontier. On 02 May 2014, in his Daily the News International article, Zubair Torwali' reported the confusion of Pakistan army and its inability to defeat the Taliban:

A straight answer of the failure against the terrorists is the confusion that is experienced on a national level. This confusion does not seem self-inflicted or the fault of the peoples. Neither does this confusion seem to be the outcome of any communication strategy of the militants. Where there is confusion there exist some trust deficit; and certain acts, covert or overt, produce this lack of trust. In Swat the people surrendered to terrorists because they—the people—did not know exactly who their real enemies were. On the contrary they regarded the entire insurgency a covert arrangement of the intelligence agencies. In Fata the tribesmen do not fight the militants because they see them as extensions of the army.[2]

Pakistan continues to establish more nuclear plants in Karachi with the help of China, but the procrastination of Chinese President scheduled trip to Pakistan in 2015, created misunderstanding between the two states. Amid growing violence across the country, and terror threat, the country is steadily expanding its nuclear weapons stockpile. In her research paper, Reshmi Kazi noted Pakistani extremist groups and their possible access to nuclear weapons:

The volatile situation in Pakistan has become further unstable with the existence of terrorist groups like Jaish-e-Muhammad and Harakatul Jehad al Islami who is being influence by the al Qaeda led pan-global jihadist ideology and is intensely active in the Indian sub-continent.

1 *Dawn*, 02 May 2014.
2 "The confusion of Pakistan army and its inability to defeat the Taliban," *Daily the News International*, 02 May 2014, in his, Zubair Torwali. And also, *Daily Naya Akhbar*, 8 February 2014.

The degree of the crisis merits solemn deliberation since the al Qaeda has articulated its aspiration to attain nuclear/radiological material and weapons, and have touched base with diverse individuals and militant groups to obtain these sensitive technology and material for purpose of weaponization. Investigations into the recent Mumbai blasts of November 26 2008 have provided credible information of the involvement of the LeT operating from Pakistan soil. It is alleged that the LeT had the backing of the ISI which shared intelligence with the Lashkar and provided it protection in the Mumbai terror attacks.[1]

On 11 December 2013, Daily Times reported the Nawaz Sharif government discourse on the prohibition and elimination of nuclear weapons. Pakistani government reiterated that in case of major offensive from India, they will be left with no option but to use nuclear weapons first. In the context of South Asia, the danger of nuclear war is very high because India and Pakistan have already fought three wars from 1948 to 1971 and a limited war in 1999. On August 2013, Pakistan started work on two large nuclear power plants designed by China, in Karachi.[2]

The story of Pakistan nuclear weapons and its smuggling received considerable attention from international community. The network of Pakistan and China and Pakistan and Saudi nuclear has become a challenging problem in South Asia and the Middle East. On 7 July 2011, the Guardian newspaper reported:

The story of the world worst case of nuclear smuggling took on new twist when documents surfaced appearing to implicate two former Pakistani generals in the sale of Uranium enrichment technology to North Korea in return for millions of dollars in cash and jewels handed over in a canvas bag and cardboard boxes of fruit. The source of the document is AQ Khan, who confessed in 2004 to selling parts and instructions for the use of high-speed centrifuges in enriching uranium to Libya, Iran and North Korea. Extracts were published in the Washington Post, including a letter in English purportedly from a senior North Korean official to Khan 1998 detailing payment of $3m to Pakistan former army chief, General Jahangir Karamat and another half million to lieutenant General Zulfiqar Khan who was involved in Pakistan's nuclear bomb test.[3]

---

1 "Nuclear terrorism, the New Terror of the 21st Century," Reshmi Kazi, IDSA Monograph Series, 27 October 2013, Institute for Defense Studies and Analyses, New Delhi.
2 Daily Times, 11 December 2013.
3 The Guardian, 7 July 2011.

On 29 July 2013, Institute for Science and International Security, published a research paper of authors David Albright, Andrea Stricker, and Houston Wood, in which they raised important questions about the nuclear material smuggling in future. The report identified states that smuggle nuclear weapons across the world. The authors also indentified methods used in the preparation of nuclear weapons:

> Gas centrifuges are expected to remain a preferred pathway to making HEU. As a result, gas centrifuges warrant particular consideration. They are relatively widespread and are currently favored by proliferating states as the pathway to obtain fissile materials for nuclear weapons. Gas centrifuge procurements dominate illicit nuclear trade cases. This trend is not expected to change over the next decade. Nuclear reactor coupled with a plutonium separation plant. Over the next five to ten years, the main source of plutonium for nuclear weapons is expected to remain nuclear reactors and associated plutonium separation plants. Although there are other ways to produce plutonium, such as by particle accelerators, these methods are judged as less likely to be significant sources of plutonium in this time period.[1]

In the United States, Pakistani merchants of menace were desperately looking for nuclear material to smuggle it to their country in 2011. Police and intelligence agencies were in hurry to monitor the activities of Pakistani smugglers. On 05 April 2011, The Hindu reported a top Washington think tank argued that nuclear smuggling from the United States to Pakistan needed to be monitored. David Albright, President and founder of the Institute for science and International Security (ISIS) said the "U.S government and the nuclear industry need to be working closer together" if such smuggling rings were to be detected.[2]

In April, 2011, in his interview with Arms Control Today, National Security coordinator Mr. Gary Samore suggested that Pakistan is very serious about the security of nuclear materials:

> What I worry about is that, in the context of broader tensions and problems within Pakistani society and polity—and that's obviously taking place as we look at the sectarian violence and tensions between the government and the military and so forth—I worry that, in that broader context, even the best nuclear security measures might break down. You're dealing with a country that is under tremendous stress

---

1 *Future World of Illicit Nuclear Trade: Mitigating the Threat*, David Albright, Andrea Stricker, Houston Wood Institute for Science and International Security, Houston, 29 July 2013.
2 *The Hindu*, 05 April 2011.

internally and externally, and that's what makes me worry. They have good programs in place; the question is whether those good programs work in the context where these broader tensions and conflicts are present.[1]

Nuclear weapons in a country where terrorists or their proxies are at the door step if not already in the bedroom, is too grim to contemplate. On 14 May 2009, in Japan Times, Brahma Chellaney argued that both jihadists and Pakistan army generals are a threat to international peace:

> The choice in Pakistan is not between Islamists and US sponsored generals, who actually reared the forces of jihad and still nurture many jihadists. Both are a threat to international peace and security... Pakistan's descent into a jihadist dungeon tellingly occurred not under civilian rule but under military rule.... Pakistan's descent into a jihadist dungeon tellingly occurred not under civilian rule but under military rule. While one military dictator, General Zia ul-Haq, let loose the jihadists he reared, another dictator, Musharraf, pushed Pakistan to the very edge of the precipice.[2]

Extremist infrastructure and widespread terror networks of militant groups, along with poor governance, created a climate of fear across the country. Militant networks in Southern Punjab have established training centers for extremist forces. Punjab is home to 80 million people, and a web of Punjabi Taliban activities. Punjab's Chief Minister, Shahbaz Sharif supports Punjabi Taliban. Militant and extremist tendencies have spread everywhere, and militancy has gained a foothold in all major cities. Seventy percent of Sunni Muslims in Pakistan follow the Barelvi sect, which have their own networks of extremism. Deobandi sects support jihadism.

In 13 November 2012, James Martin Center for Non-proliferation studies published an article of Phil Lai on its website, which mainly focused on the threat of nuclear terrorism in South Asia:

Nuclear terrorism is traditionally understood to take one of four forms: direct acquisition and deployment of a nuclear device, independent fabrication of a device using stolen materials, release of radiation by attacking nuclear facilities, or release of radiation through other means of dispersal. But the particular circumstances of the South Asian security situation raise the troubling possibility of a

---

1 *Arms Control Today, National Security coordinator*, Mr., Gary Samore's interview. Pursuing the Prague Agenda: An Interview with White House Coordinator Gary Samore. April 2011.
2 *Japan Times*, 14, May 2009.

fifth scenario: a nuclear exchange intentionally provoked by terrorist activity that is not itself inherently nuclear.[1]

In a Pakistan without the bomb, jihadist groups, who felt protected by the nuclear shield, would feel strongly constrained and could not expect to freely attack India. Experts warned about a danger that Pakistan's nuclear weapons could be stolen or smuggled out of the country, during periods of great instability. Washington has spent up to $100 million to assist Pakistan in securing its nuclear weapons. Nevertheless, terrorists planning a nuclear attack would face considerable difficulties in acquiring a nuclear weapon or stealing fissile material for the production of a weapon.

On 03, March, 2014, Daily Dawn reported a London based scholar's remarks about Pakistan's nuclear danger. The author voiced alarm about Pakistan's nuclear arsenal, the world's fastest growing, which he said would likely expand until at least 2020. Fitzpatrick said no solution was ideal, but he called for Western nations to offer Pakistan a deal along the lines of a 2005 accord with India, which allowed normal access to commercial nuclear markets despite its refusal to sign the Non-Proliferation Treaty.[2]

"The time has come to offer Pakistan a nuclear cooperation deal akin to India's," Fitzpatrick said as he launched a new book, "Overcoming Pakistan's Nuclear Dangers," in Washington. "Providing a formula for nuclear normalization is the most powerful tool that Western countries can wield in positively shaping Pakistan's nuclear posture," Fitzpatrick said. In his book, Mr. Fitzpatrick expressed concern over an arms race, and said Pakistan was constrained by its lack of uranium ore. Fitzpatrick said Pakistan's production may end in 2020, by which time it would have some 200 nuclear weapons, about double the current estimate.[3]

South Asian states are facing the threat of terrorism and violent extremism. The unending civil war in Afghanistan and Pakistan has destabilized the whole region. Terrorism in Afghanistan affects Pakistan and its heat touches Iranian border, while the flames are clearly seen in China and Russia.

The debate about bioterrorism is not entirely new in the region as both Pakistan and India have developed these weapons to use them

1 *A New Path to Accidental Nuclear War in South Asia? Diversion isn't the only danger confronting Pakistan's nuclear arsenal.* Phil Lai, 13 November, 2013. James Martin Center for Nonproliferation Studies.
2 *Dawn,* 03 March 2014.
3 *Overcoming Pakistan's Nuclear Dangers,* Mark Fitzpatrick, The International Institute for Strategic Studies (IISS), 11 Mar 2014.

in a future war. On 03 December 1984, the worse chemical disaster occurred in the city of Bhopal in India, which caused the death of thousands people. If a nuclear war were to break in South Asia, experts believe that it is most likely to happen in India and Pakistan. This kind of war would have dire consequences. In the Seoul Summit, Indian Prime Minister Manmohan Singh warned that South Asia is under threat. Two incidents in Karachi and another in Baluchistan proved that terrorists were trying to retrieve nuclear weapons, to use it against military or nuclear installations.

The Indian government recognized the threat from bioweapons as real and imminent. Both the Ministry of Defense and Ministry of Home Affairs placed high priority on this issue. India understands that Pakistan based terrorist groups may possibly use these weapons in Kashmir in near future. Pakistan too has expressed deep concern about the use of these weapons against its security forces either by Taliban or Baloch insurgents. The emergence of recent polio and bird flu cases in Pakistan, which killed dozens people in Khyber Pakhtunkhwa province and Baluchistan is the primary warning of danger. In order to fashion a nuclear explosive, a terrorist group would need additional technology, equipment, and materials. One concern is that terrorists could buy detailed nuclear weapon designs from black marketers or rogue suppliers, easing their task of building improvised explosive devices.

Once TTP or other terrorist group stolen biological and nuclear weapons, they will use it against military and nuclear installations. National security experts in the UK and US believe that the most likely way terrorists will obtain a nuclear bomb will not be to steal or purchase a fully operational device, but to buy fissile material and construct their own. Today, illicit nuclear trade efforts aim to procure nuclear direct use and dual use goods, many of which are controlled by national and international trade control regimes. The problem of illicit nuclear trade appears to be growing worse as technologies and capabilities proliferate. The world could in fact become far more dangerous. With the global spread of technology and rapid growth in international trade, traffickers could find it easier to ply their dangerous trade. However, the example of Pakistan highlights that developing states can run into significant additional problems, even with the advantage of critical foreign assistance.

The precarious domestic and economic situation in Pakistan could be exploited by radical groups to foment unrest and subversion. The creeping fundamentalism throughout Pakistani society sparks an additional concern about insider collusion that might enable terrorists to evade security measures. According to a research report on the possibility of nuclear terrorism:

> The Global Initiative to Combat Nuclear Terrorism is a first step, which has been valuable in focusing countries' attention on the issue of nuclear terrorism and building legal infrastructure, capacity for emergency response, law enforcement capabilities, and more.... Hostile states are highly unlikely to consciously choose to provide nuclear weapons or the materials needed to make them to terrorist groups, for such a step would risk retaliation that would end their power forever. Nevertheless, the risk of such transfers is not zero and more states with nuclear weapons would mean more sources from which a nuclear bomb might be stolen.[1]

The IISS Strategic Dossier on Nuclear Black Markets provides a comprehensive assessment of the Pakistani nuclear program from which the Abdul Qadeer Khan network emerged, the network's proliferation activities, and the illicit trade in fissile materials. General Musharraf allowed the training camps of extremist organizations fighting in Central Asia, Chechnya, and Kashmir. In a serious dialogue with Taliban, the US repeatedly made it clear that it would be held responsible for any terrorist attacks undertaken by Osama Bin Laden while he was in Afghanistan.

General Musharraf's war against terrorism and sectarianism vigorously targeted sectarian terrorist groups in Pakistan. The basic characteristics of Pakistan's extremist and terror infrastructure are critical to its democratic transition. We are not going into the details of ethnic distribution of the country. In my opinion, military governments limited the evolution of institutionalized mechanisms to solve the contradictions between ethnic and religious identities. The threat of the Punjabi Taliban movement in Punjab has often been mentioned in government circles and the media as well, but was never discussed in detail and was limited to exaggerated statements most of the time.

Jaish-e-Mohammed was banned in Pakistan in 2002, and designated as "foreign terrorist organization" by the US. Most of the JeM's cadre and material resources have been drawn from the militant groups, Harakat ul-Jihad al-Islami (HUJI) and the HUM. The JeM had close ties to Afghan Arabs and the Taliban. Jaish has

---

1 *Preventing Nuclear terrorism: An Agenda for the Next President*, Matthew Bunn and Andrew Newman, Belfer Centre, http://www.fmwg.org/sitefiles/bunn_preventing_nuclear_terrorism-an_agenda_nov08.pdf.

good contacts in the UK and receives a lot of financial support from various Pakistani sources. Members of the group are working in and outside the UK and support it financially. The JeM also collects funds through donation requests in magazines and pamphlets.

Lashkar-e-Toiba is one of Pakistan's most extremist religious groups, whose growth dates back to the 1980s and Pakistan's role in the Afghan-Soviet war, which was won in large part by a Pakistan backed Mujahedeen. The militant sectarian group has restored contacts with al-Qaeda terror networks in both Pakistan and Afghanistan. Admiral Mike Mullen warned that Lashkar-e-Toiba had become a very dangerous organization and a significant regional and global threat. Pakistan itself is no stranger to sectarian violence, which has intensified in recent years. If the Bahraini regime falls as the Saudis and American's fear, it would be seen as and portrayed by Iran as a victory of her interests.

The Punjabi Taliban has been the main fighting force in Indian Kashmir since the 1990s. They went underground or migrated to the tribal areas when Musharraf clamped down on them under pressure from the US. In the tribal belts of Pakistan and Afghan, these militant groups established ties with the Afghan Taliban. Intelligence reports in Pakistan say that up to 15% of militants in Pakistani tribal areas are Punjabis. Having quoted a US intelligence report said: "Pashtun Taliban and Arab militants, who are part of the al-Qaeda organization, have money, shelter, training sites and suicide bombers".

Experts believe that there are possibilities of nuclear war between Pakistan and India in near future, as Pakistan tried to use these weapons in the Kargil war, in 1999. In India, the threat from nuclear Pakistan is two-fold; Pakistan is like a monkey can any time explode the bomb without assessing the fatalities and cost of human life in Afghanistan and India. On 30 April 2014, India and Afghanistan signed an agreement, under which the country would pay Russia to transfer light and sophisticated weapons to the Afghan National Army before the withdrawal of NATO, US and their allies from Afghanistan in the end of 2014.[1]

When President Ghani came to power in 2015, he refused to accept Indian weapons. India's interest in Afghanistan is evident from its strategic partnership with the country, under which it has guaranteed military assistance. After the fall of the Taliban regime in 2001, and the US military intervention, Afghanistan became India's largest foreign aid recipient, as the country has invested $2 billion

---

1 *Daily Outlook Afghanistan*, 30 April 2014.

in various reconstruction projects. On 02 January, the Wall Street Journal reported, 'India which has long dropped any pretension to an independent foreign policy, has been more than amenable to serving as America's surrogate in the region—a role that, much to its irritation, had for long been assigned to Pakistan.' As per my personal intellectual approach, India's deepening influence in Afghanistan is not new, but it is evident from the fact that the country showed more avidity to strengthen its political and military influence in the country, and warn Pakistan that it has no more concern about the country's use of Taliban insurgent in Indian Kashmir.[1]

Indian military experts understand that after the NATO withdrawal from Afghanistan, India will stay in the country with its full military might to further improve the fighting capabilities of Afghan National Army (ANA). This decision of Indian military establishment exacerbated Pakistan's concern as the country has already complained about the Afghan land, being used against the country, and time and again, Pakistan provided proofs of Indian involvement in FATA and Baluchistan. Pakistan's military establishment has reservations that India is exploiting the present volatile situation in Pakistan. In the end of 2014, President Ashraf Ghani and General Raheel Sharif started working on the improvement of relations between the two countries but, unfortunately, the recent interview of the former president, General Musharraf, with a UK newspaper once again caused misunderstanding and distrust.

India's neighbor and rival Pakistan is likely to be angered by any move to help arm Afghan forces, even if indirectly. Pakistan shares a long border with Afghanistan and has traditionally exerted considerable influence on Kabul. But under President Karzai, and since the ouster of the Taliban movement in 2001, relations between the two states deteriorated amidst accusations that Pakistan has failed to stop militants crossing into Afghanistan and launching frequent, deadly attacks.

Russia's Federal Service for Military Technical Cooperation, the state agency responsible for arms and military cooperation deals, declined comment on the agreement. Mr. Karzai's "shopping list" was submitted to New Delhi in 2013, comprised 66 items ranging from tanks to spares for Afghanistan's small fleet of helicopters. India´s difficult relationship with Pakistan has so far impeded a stronger strategic and

---

1 "New Year resolution for India: Stay out of Afghanistan mess, India should avoid military involvement in Afghanistan, no matter what the temptation or compulsion or provocation," *Wall Street Journal*, 02 January 2014, G. Sampath.

political role for India in Afghanistan. Islamabad's pursuit of a policy of 'strategic depth' that is, control over Afghanistan's government to hedge against India's interests.

Today's Pakistani Taliban is no longer confined to the tribal areas straddling the Pakistan and Afghan border. Until now, secret Saudi funds for the improvement of Pakistan's nuclear arsenal didn't include the transfer of nuclear weapons and their missile delivery system to the kingdom. The next phase of the secret compact may well include the transfer of nukes to the kingdom. Pakistan's nuclear insecurity is intensified by its nuclear strategies. The country is rapidly expanding its stockpile; it now boasts one of the world's fastest growing arsenals. There is no doubt that recent attacks on military targets in Pakistan have increased in number and boldness. So far, however, the targets of the attacks have not been military installations that contain nuclear weapons or components.

The most extreme form of risk would be takeover of the state by radical Islamists, a scenario that Bruce Riedel has documented at some length. While the Islamist Pakistan that Riedel describes is disturbing, neither Riedel nor other analysts have a convincing narrative of how the Pakistan of today gets there. In response to my article published in daily Times in 2013 on nuclear jihad in South Asia, Pakistan army published three articles in the same newspaper, denouncing my assessment of Pakistan's nuclear safety and security and, the threat of Taliban insurgents. Writer, Mr. Usman Ali Khan defended Pakistan's nuclear safety and security in his article.

This article is a response to the recent column published titled as: "The prospect of nuclear jihad in South Asia" (Daily Times, October 3, 2013) by Musa Khan Jalalzai. In this article the writer made several pronouncements about the nuclear safety, security and the current status of nuclear position, showing concern that nuclear arsenal may be used by non state actors. The article states:

> The availability of nuclear materials in black market, specifically in Pakistan's tribal regions, has put the country's nuclear weapons facilities under threat. There is concern that TTP, Punjabi Taliban or its allies may possibly attack Pakistan's nuclear facilities by detonating a small, crude nuclear weapon. Pakistan has been active in improving the safety of its nuclear weapons in recent years. Facing international pressure over safety of its nuclear weapons, Pakistan has said it has taken steps to augment their security as it shares the concern that non-state actors or terrorists may acquire and use them. Pakistan shares concern that non state actors or terrorists may acquire and

potentially use nuclear materials and cause serious economic, political and psychological consequences.[1]

Usman Ali Khan contradicted my views and defended his country's nuclear weapons:

We have demonstrated through our political commitment and actions the importance that we attached to nuclear security. We have engaged constructively inter alia with the global initiative to combat nuclear terrorism and the Nuclear Security Summit processes. A positive development following the Washington Post report was the statement of the state department spokesperson, Jen Psaki, who said: "The US is confident that the government of Pakistan is well aware of its responsibilities and has secured its nuclear arsenal accordingly.[2]

Pakistan has been a nuclear power for three decades. Its nuclear weapons are estimated to 100 warheads. A senior Pakistani official who has close ties to former President Zardari revealed in an interview that after the 9/11 attacks, there had been an understanding between the Bush Administration and General Pervez Musharaf's regime over what Pakistan had and did not have. Today, he said, you'd like control of our day-to-day deployment. But why should we give it to you? A former State Department official who worked on nuclear issue with Pakistan after September 11th said, that he had come to understand that the Pakistanis believe that any information we get from them would be shared with others—perhaps even the Indians.

The future world of illicit trade may include a pariah country, unauthorized entities in a country, or criminal elements selling nuclear facilities or capabilities to other states—actors which are termed "rogue suppliers." North Korea is a rogue supplier and has demonstrated the capability and inclination to provide nuclear goods and capabilities to customers abroad outside normal commerce, and despite international norms and rules. Other states could emerge as rogue suppliers, particularly Iran. There is also growing concern that Iran and North Korea are undertaking nuclear cooperation. After my article on Pakistan nuclear jihadist strategy, Prime Minister Nawaz Sharif replaced General Khalid Ahmad Kidwai with General Zubair Mahmood Hayat.

---

1 *Daily Times*, 08 October 2013
2 *Ibid*, 08 Oct 2013.

CHAPTER 4. THE THREAT OF NUCLEAR TERRORISM FROM KARACHI TO PESHAWAR

The lack of effective security system for weapons useable nuclear materials in Pakistan is a major challenge. Notwithstanding several improvements in security systems in 2012, there is still no effective global system for how nuclear materials should be secured. In 2012, seven states; Austria, Czech Republic, Hungary, Mexico, Sweden, Ukraine, and Vietnam removed all or most of their weapons usable nuclear materials, and 13 other countries promised to decrease their quantity of materials. Despite all these efforts, 5 states increased their stocks of nuclear materials (Pakistan, Japan, The United Kingdom, India and North Korea). The future of illicit trade of nuclear materials in South Asia by non state actors, and terrorists may further jeopardize the security of the region. The problem of this trade appears to be growing worse as technologies proliferate. With the global spread of technologies and rapid illegal sale of uranium and plutonium, traffickers could find it easier to flourish their dangerous trade.

Pakistan's nuclear security faces the critical challenge from its own radicalized armed forces. The fear of nuclear weapons and materials escaping the protective custody of Pakistan's army is well founded. Former ambassador of the United States to Pakistan, Anne W Patterson expressed concerned that someone working in Pakistan's nuclear facilities, might smuggle enough nuclear materials out to make a weapon. The main threat to Pakistan's nuclear installation might also come from the virus or worm activated within the computer.

The issue is very complicated but Pakistani generals don't care about it. They want to expand the business of fear, terrorism and harassment across the world. They want to send terrorists to India and Afghanistan consecutively. They support ISIS and fight against Iraq and Syria. Though the United States assisted Pakistan in improving nuclear security, but there are speculations, that the Strategic Plan Division might be subjected to pressure by the ruling party to appoint its favorite individuals within the SPD security infrastructure, as the tussle between civilian and military leaders on the control of nuclear weapons has intensified.[1]

During the last five decades, Pakistan and India doubled the number of their nuclear warheads, making them the fastest nuclear weapon states in the world. However, India deployed a nuclear triad of bombers, missiles, and a submarine capable of firing nuclear weapons.[2]

At present, both the states hold a lot of nuclear stockpile which have doubled since 1998. Both the states have developed cruise missiles, and are seeking nuclear submarines. More worrisome is that India and Pakistan have developed military doctrines that increase the prospects of nuclear use. Although India has pledged not to use nuclear weapons first, it has increased its readiness to launch shallow "Cold Start" conventional military strikes against Pakistan, calibrated to deter Pakistani military or terrorist incursions. Meanwhile, Pakistani military planners insist that Pakistan will use nuclear weapons immediately if India attacks.[3]

On 29 September 2014, Dawn reported the 69th session of General Assembly of the United Nations observed the first ever annual day for the total elimination of nuclear weapons. In a message released by his office, UN Secretary General Ban Ki Moon urged member states: "the time has come for the total elimination of nuclear weapons stockpiles." While most active members of one group lobbied for a complete, ban on all nuclear arms, others quietly tried to put the spotlight on Pakistan.

As Prime Minister Modi said that the time has changed, and the killing of innocent men and women cannot be tolerated in Kashmir, it means, perhaps, the people of India and Pakistan need peace, prosperity and stability not military confrontation. Pakistani Prime Minister called for a resolution of the Kashmir dispute, by saying

---

1 *South Asian Monitor*, 21 Jul 2014.
2 *Daily Times*, 22 July 2014.
3 *Pakistan's Nuclear Future: Reining in the Risk*. Henry D. Sokolski, Strategic Studies Institute, 2009.

the UN was not the appropriate forum to raise the issue, and that his country was prepared for a bilateral engagement "in a peaceful atmosphere, without the shadow of terrorism," a reference to the unresolved investigation of the 2008 Mumbai attacks.

He was correct, of course; the General Assembly is no longer a platform for serious discussion, and it is a way for heads of state to build an image for their country, and themselves. In this regard, Prime Minister Modi's speech, with its references to Indian spiritual traditions, was written for the US public to consume, while Mr. Sharif's bland, narrow focus was everything that western publics feel is wrong with Pakistan—an obsession with India, desire for territory, and a total lack of charisma and likeability.

India and Pakistan need to puncture the tires of their unaffordable and sarcastic armies, which consumed the two nations for a long time. Pakistan's army adventurism in Afghanistan and Kashmir, through extremists and non-state actors, jeopardized the geographical existence of the country. India's diplomatic presence in Afghanistan also enraged Pakistan that India has encircled the country from all sides. Now Pakistan army considers this adventurism as the war of survival and strategic interests.

The consecutive firing from both sides shows that relationship remained tense, but Mr. Nawaz Sharif is still optimistic in his efforts. Mr. Sharif assured India that his country wants peace with India. The cauldron is still there. Some newspapers in both the states reported more than 63 violations of the ceasefire in October 2014 alone, and during the last 10 months, there have been as many as 209 violations. Now Mr. Modi understood that Mr. Nawaz Sharif is not sincere with India, he warned Pakistan that the time has changed.

The Indian Express said the remarks were in response to political opponents who charged the Prime Minister with not speaking directly about the fresh clashes—the worst in a decade. Mr. Modi took a different view: "When there is a challenge at the border, it is soldiers who answer with fingers on the trigger; it is not for politicians to respond."

India's Defense Minister also warned Pakistan to stop shelling in Kashmir, after the worst cross-border violence, to hit the disputed region in years. "If Pakistan persists with this adventurism, our forces will make cost of this adventurism unaffordable for it," Arun Jaitley told journalists in New Delhi. "Pakistan should stop this unprovoked firing and shelling if it wants peace on the border. "The nuclear-armed neighbors have traded blame for the cross-border violence that has killed at least 12 civilians. In October 2014, Pakistan responded to India's warning against any "adventurism" on the borders in Jammu and Kashmir by saying it is capable of responding to Indian aggression. Pakistan has the ability to reply to Indian aggression. We do not want the situation on the borders of two nuclear neighbors to escalate into confrontation; Pakistan Defence Minister Khawaja Asif was quoted as saying by the media. "India must demonstrate caution and behave with responsibility," Asif said soon after his Indian counterpart Arun Jaitley warned that the cost of any adventurism by Pakistan on the borders of J&K would be "unaffordable".

Meanwhile, under fire from the opposition over escalating ceasefire violations by Pakistan, Prime Minister Narendra Modi said India responded to the aggression with courage and lamented public debate on the issue for political gains. "Today, when bullets are being fired on the border, it is the enemy that is screaming. Our jawans have responded to the aggression with courage," Modi said. China's tacit nuclear support to Pakistan for boosting the country's nuclear weapons prompted strategic implications for India. The nuclear power relationship between Pakistan and China is widely seen as a continuing effort to respond to the India-U.S. civilian nuclear deal, which, among other things, ended a decades-long moratorium on U.S. companies, selling nuclear technology to India, despite India not being a signatory to the Nuclear Non-Proliferation Treaty.[1]

Prime Minister Nawaz Sharif said that Pakistan plans to build six more nuclear energy plants in coming decades. These nuclear plants would be built in partnership with China. Islamabad's turn toward more nuclear power also raises questions over the safety of the nation's nuclear reactors. India also needs nuclear weapons to establish strategic parity with China, and secondly, to deter Pakistan's intransigence. China, however, has been willing to provide Pakistan with assistance for nuclear power projects. The two countries have a historically close relationship. China's tactics to violate their international obligations were evident during the immediate period after the end of the cold war, with Chinese cold war, firms acting as fronts for transferring European technology to Pakistan.[2]

In fact, China's relations with the military establishment in Pakistan have never been strained during the last sex decades. China still helps Pakistan in many ways. Rivalry between India and China

1 *The Geopolitics of Energy in South Asia*, Marie Lall, Institute of Southeast Asian Studies, 01 January 2009.
2 "How Pakistan and China Are Strengthening Nuclear Ties," By Krista Mahr, *Time Magazine*, December, 02, 2013

intensified, while India sees itself as a rival to China as well for regional leadership and international influence. Beijing has measured itself alongside superpowers; similarly, Pakistan's rivalry with India is noticed in Delhi only for its use of asymmetric warfare from behind a nuclear shield. China has been bolstering Pakistan's nuclear capabilities for the past five decades in an attempt, to maintain parity between India and Pakistan. Not only has China played a crucial role in the North Korean and Iranian nuclear programs, its nuclear engagement with Pakistan potentially remains the most destabilizing factor in the global Management of nuclear technology.[1]

The nature of the China-Pakistan military and nuclear alliance makes it beneficial for China to extend its nuclear proliferation tentacles worldwide. In his article, published in Japan Times, Prof. Harsh V. Pant argued that military and nuclear relationship between Pakistan and China is in the interest of both the states by presenting India as a common rival:

> The China–Pakistan partnership serves the interests of both by presenting India with a potential two-front theatre in the event of war with either country. Not surprisingly, one of the central pillars of Pakistan's strategic policies for more than four decades has been its steady and ever-growing military relationship with China. And preventing India's dominance of South Asia by strengthening Pakistan has been a strategic priority for China. But with India's ascent in global hierarchy and American attempts to carve out a strong partnership with India; China's need for Pakistan is only likely to grow. A rising India makes Pakistan all the more important for Chinese strategy for the subcontinent.[2]

In an Asia Program paper, Rosheen Kabraji viewed Pak–China relations as a Chinese military influence in South Asia, to counter US–Indian influence in the region: As Pakistan and China strengthen their relations, questions have arisen around the changing nature of this alliance, the rhetoric that sustains it and the implications of greater Chinese influence in Pakistan for the region....China's strategic relationship with Pakistan and its approach to Indo-Pakistani disputes in the first decade after the Cold War reflected its desire for

---

1 "China-Pakistan nuclear axis defies non-proliferation aims," Harsh V. Pant, *The Japan Times*. 19 April 2013,http://www.japantimes. co.jp/opinion/2013/04/19/commentary/world-commentary/china-pakistan-nuclear-axis-defies-nonproliferation-aim.
2 *Ibid*, in his article, published in *Japan Times*, Prof. Harsh V. Pant (04 19, 2013) argued that: "military and nuclear relationship between Pakistan and China is in the interest of both the states by presenting India as a common rival."

better relations with India to advance its economic agenda. Analyst Syed Fazl-e-Haider also argued that when the US denied Pakistan civilian nuclear deal, then Pakistan turned to China:

> China has deepened co-operation largely in response to the civil nuclear energy deal signed between the US and India in 2008. That deal opened up a US$150 billion market for US nuclear trade with India, which was controversially granted an exemption from the Nuclear Suppliers Group. Neither India nor Pakistan, arch-rivals in many aspects, has joined the nuclear Non-Proliferation Treaty, yet both possess nuclear arsenals. The US denied Pakistan a civilian nuclear deal, saying that it first had to improve its nuclear proliferation record. Pakistan's nuclear arsenal has been a sensitive topic for the US as it tries to improve relations with its frontline ally in the campaign against Islamist extremists. The US has restricted nuclear-related exports to Pakistan since it conducted its nuclear tests in 2008.[1]

Pakistan's nuclear program, however, is essentially intended to counter its conventional forces inferiority vis-à-vis India. After the Pokhran-II in 1998, and the Kargil episode, the real nature of nuclear weapons was emphasized and the imperative of military involvement dawned on the establishment. The role of nuclear weapons in the India-Pakistan rivalry is disturbing and illuminating. The two sides haven't used their weapons, but their arsenals have changed their military and political strategies in ways that make the region more explosive and crisis prone.

What has caused this situation is the fixation with achieving military parity with India, and the precarious cocktail that the establishment has brewed in nurturing fundamentalist and terrorist organizations as instruments of their policies in Afghanistan and Kashmir. All these weapons and strategic developments in both the states means that confidence building measure remained only on paper, and no one desires to extend the hand of cooperation. Following the deal between the US and India, Pakistan ramped up its production of uranium and plutonium, and it seems, its nuclear weapons arsenal. Given that both nations have already come close to nuclear blows– the two countries nearly engaged in a war over Kashmir, which has been described as one of the tensest nuclear standoffs between India and Pakistan since independence in 1947. According to some reports, Pakistan currently has the world's fastest-growing nuclear arsenal, with enough fissile material to build 120 bombs and the potential

1 China's deepening role in Pakistan's nuclear development," Syed Fazl-e-Haider, *Insight & Opinion*, 01 September, 2014

to build at least 80 more by 2020. India has the ability to build 110 nuclear devices, but is also reported to have ramped up its production capacity.

After US President Barack Obama and Prime Minister Narendra Modi met in New Delhi on 25 January 2015, four key deliverables from the summit meeting were identified to be in the areas of nuclear energy, defense, climate change and the economy. Nonetheless, Obama and Indian PM Narendra Modi announced a break of the nuclear deal deadlock. "I am pleased those six years after we signed our bilateral agreement, we are moving towards commercial cooperation, consistent with our laws [and] international legal obligations," Modi said. Obama, in turn, spoke of a "breakthrough understanding on two issues that were holding up our ability to advance our civil nuclear cooperation." "Noting that the contact group set up in September 2014 to advance implementation of bilateral civil nuclear cooperation has met three times in December and January, the leaders welcomed the understandings reached on the issues of civil nuclear liability and administrative arrangements for civil nuclear cooperation, and looked forward to U.S.-built nuclear reactors contributing to India's energy security at the earliest," the two countries said in a joint statement.

This exacerbating militarization of conflict mechanism, the withdrawal of NATO and US forces from Afghanistan, and civil wars in the Middle East, intensified the war of interests between the two states. In the presence of all these weapons, the danger of nuclear terrorism, the potential spread of nuclear materials in black market, and the recent control of nuclear materials by Sunni terrorist groups, Islamic State (ISIS), raised serious questions about the safety and security of nuclear weapons in South Asia. Pakistan faces a series of threats to its national security. These threats come from ISIS and the likely potential use of chemical, biological, radiological, and nuclear (CBRN) devices by domestic terrorist groups.[1]

International Task Force on the Prevention of Nuclear Terrorism once warned that the "possibility of nuclear terrorism is increasing" because of a number of factors including "the conventional forms of terrorism," and the vulnerability of nuclear power and research reactors to sabotage and of weapons usable nuclear materials to theft. Recently the Islamic State uncovered a complex with stockpiles of WMD in Iraq. "We do not believe that the complex contains CW

---

1 *The Nation,* (Urdu Weekly) 07 August 2014, London, and also *Daily Times,* 22 July 2014

materials of military value," the U.S. State Department said on the IS matter of WMD discovery.[1]

The danger is that either states might support or back terrorist groups, in case of materials and funds, to prepare improvise nuclear device and use it against each other. Another development that has also worried nuclear scientists is the cyber attacks during the nuclear crisis management. Cyber warfare has the potential to attack or to disrupt a successful nuclear crisis management. India and Pakistan have developed strong networks of cyber armies, and often attacked each other's sensitive computers in the past.[2]

Cyber attack can make muddy signals being sent from one side to the other side during the nuclear crisis. Cyber warriors can disrupt and destroy communication channels for successful crisis management. Pakistan's nuclear weapons are under threat from violent cyber terrorists, operating across the border. Pakistan set death penalty for cyber terrorism in 2008. This was an unprecedented step of making cyber terrorism a crime punishable by death, according to a decree issued by former President Asif Ali Zardari. Cyber terrorism is described as the accessing of a computer network or electronic system by someone who then "knowingly engages in or attempts to engage in a terroristic act." "Whoever commits the offence of cyber terrorism and causes death of any person shall be punishable with death or imprisonment for life," according to the ordinance, which was published by the state-run APP news agency.[3]

The Prevention of Electronic Crimes law will be applicable to anyone who commits a crime detrimental to national security through the use of a computer or any other electronic device, the government said in the ordinance. The ordinance also set out punishments for other offences, including electronic fraud, electronic forgery, system damage, unauthorized access to codes and misuse of encryption. Punishments for those crimes ranged from three to 10 years in prison.[4]

Pakistan is a troubled country with deep divisions in its government. In this context, it is unclear how effective a Pakistani solution would

---

1 *The New Terrorism: Islamist International*, D.P. Sharma, APH Publishing, 01 January, 2005.
2 "Nuclear Crisis Management and "Cyber war," Phishing for Trouble"? Stephen J. Cimbala, *The Nation* (Urdu Weekly) 07 August 2014, London, and also *Daily Times*, 22 July 2014.
3 *Daily Times*, 22 July 2014.
4 "The ordinance also set out punishments for other offences, including electronic fraud, electronic forgery, system damage, unauthorized access to codes and misuse of encryption." *The Telegraph*, 6 Nov 2008.

be. Perhaps Islamabad could be persuaded to exercise its influence on the Taliban to bring them in conformity with international norms by closing down the terrorist camps and delivering Taliban leaders to justice authorities.[1]

The terrorist attack on Karachi airport showed that Pakistan's intelligence had badly failed to provide true information about the terrorist's networks in Karachi. This attack also highlighted the military capability of the Taliban and exposed the gap in the country's security apparatus. After this attack, and the killing of Shia Muslims in Taftan, every Pakistani citizen was referring to the previous daring attacks against the country's nuclear installations.[2]

The terrorists yet again exposed the failure of the intelligence agencies, which are already embroiled in protracted conflicts, and internal power games. The attackers on the airport were trained men who had planned to hijack one or two planes, loaded with bombs, and then use it against nuclear installations. This was a clear challenge for Strategic Plans Division of the armed forces, which has deployed 25,000 nuclear forces around nuclear facilities.[3]

On 05 May 2006, Baloch militants attacked the dumping site near Baghalchur Uranium mine in Dera Ghazi Khan District. In 2007, terrorists attacked two air force facilities in Sargodha, associated with nuclear installations. There are two F-16 squadrons in Sargodha. On 21 August 2008, terrorists attacked Ordinance Factories in Wah. In July 2009, a suicide bomber struck a bus that may have been carrying A.Q Khan Research Laboratory scientists, injuring 30 people.[4]

According to the Herald magazine report (11 March 2014): "In November of 1999, the PAEC closed down the Baghalchur mines because they had run out of uranium deposits, media reports said. Since then, nuclear authorities have used the site as a dumping ground for nuclear waste produced elsewhere in the country, complain local residents. "Barrels containing nuclear waste brought from Dera Ghazi Khan, Mianwali and other parts of Punjab were initially dumped in the open," the Herald reported.

Moreover, two attacks by Baloch militants on suspected Atomic Energy Commission facilities at Dera Ghazi Khan have also drawn

---

1 "The Taliban and Terrorism: Report from Afghanistan," Michael Rubin and Daniel BenjaminThe Washington Institute, 06 April, 2000.
2 "Mayhem in Taftan," *The Express Tribune*, 10 Jun 2014, http://tribune.com.pk/story/719525/mayhem-in-taftan/
3 *CNN*, 10 Jun 2014.
4 *Daily Times*, 22 July 2014

international attention. On 10 October 2009, nine terrorists, dressed in army uniform—attacked GHQ. On June 2014, two suicide bombers killed high ranking military officers linked to Pakistan's nuclear program, in Fateh Jang.[1]

Pakistan has established a nuclear force of 25,000 soldiers to safeguard its nuclear installations, but the successful attacks of terrorist show that the nuclear force has failed to protect the country's nuclear sites. India and Pakistan are geographically intertwined even as structural asymmetries between the two continue to widen. Pakistan's strategic planning began in the same year that its first nuclear tests were conducted.[2]

The way in which Pakistan has developed its nuclear policies and strategic forces is directly related to the nature of the security threat, and the structural power imbalance and widening conventional force asymmetry with India. Pakistan believes that the use of TNW would bring about such a material and psychological shift in hostilities as to stun India into a halt. Therefore, in Pakistani perception, the TNW is a deterrent at best, and a war termination weapon at worst. [3]

Writer Michael Krepon has also highlighted the situation in India-Pakistan context and argues that after testing nuclear devices in 1998, Indian and Pakistani spokespersons downplayed the value of short-range weapons. Instead, Pakistani military officers stressed that any use of a nuclear weapon would have strategic consequences. Mr. Michael Krepon argued that Pakistan was moving very slowly to gain the capabilities needed for successful, limited war options against well-defended territory. While India's Army continues to face many shortfalls, its Air Force is being qualitatively upgraded.[4]

In Amit Gupta warned that, an Indian attack on Lahore, Islamabad, and Karachi would essentially leave Pakistan with an economy and society that was in the 19th century. A similar Pakistani attack on Mumbai or New Delhi, according to Gupta, would put back India's developmental efforts by a couple of decades as not only would the nation struggle to recover but foreign investors would flee the country. One may argue, therefore, that nuclear deterrence has been achieved by both sides and neither has to worry about feeling vulnerable in this

1 *Ibid.*22 July, 2014.
2 Sipri Year Book Online, VII. *Pakistani nuclear forces,* http://www.sipriyearbook.org/view/9780199678433/sipri-9780199678433-div1-41.xml
3 IPCS Debate: Responding to Pakistan's Tactical Nuclear Weapons: A Strategy for India." Manpreet Sethi, 18 January 2014.
4 *Pakistan's Tactical Nuclear Weapons,* Michael Krepon, Stimson Centre, 24 April 2012.

spectrum of conflict. So what do TNW give either side? The answer is a higher level of instability and a much lower level of deterrence.[1]

Missiles tests in India and Pakistan prompted deep reaction in both the states. Mr. Gurmeet Kanwal and Monika also highlighted the missile race in their recent paper:

Pakistan believes that the successful testing of the 60-km nuclear-capable short-range missile Hatf-9 (Nasr) "adds deterrence value to Pakistan's strategic weapons development program at shorter ranges." In paradox, the fact remains that this step has further lowered Pakistan's nuclear threshold through the likely use of TNWs. The introduction of TNWs into the tactical battle area further exacerbates credibility of their control. Pakistan has not formally declared a nuclear doctrine, but it is well known that nuclear weapons are its first line of Defense.[2]

When India and Pakistan conducted their nuclear weapon tests in 1998, foreign experts repeatedly told them that, as the poor countries with weak institutions, they could not be entrusted with such awesome weaponry. Over a decade on, and multiple crises later— Kargil in 1999, a military standoff in 2001–2, and the Mumbai attacks of 2008—India and Pakistan experienced nothing quite as perilous as the Cuban scare. Pakistan is developing a new generation of tactical nuclear weapons (TNWs) that target not Indian cities, but Indian military formations on the battlefield.[3]

Mr. Hans M. Kristensen and Robert S. Norris suggest that Pakistan continues to develop more weapons, while concerns about Pakistan's nuclear weapons have deepened:

Despite its political instability, Pakistan continues to steadily expand its nuclear capabilities and competencies; in fact, it has the world's fastest-growing nuclear stockpile. In the aftermath of the US raid that killed Osama bin Laden, who had made his hideout in an Islamabad suburb, concerns about the security of Pakistan's nuclear weapons are likely to keep pace with the growth of Pakistan's arsenal.

1 "India, Pakistan and Tactical Nuclear Weapons: Irrelevance for South Asia." Amit Gupta. IPCS Debate
2 *Pakistan's Tactical Nuclear Weapons: Conflict Redux.* Gurmeet Kanwal (Editor), Monika Chansoria. K W Publishers Pvt Ltd, 15 Oct 2013.
3 *The Diplomat*, "New Year, New Problem? Pakistan's Tactical Nukes, Pakistan is developing a new generation of smaller "tactical" nuclear weapons. The dangers and challenges such arms present are very real." By Shashank Joshi, 02 January 2013, http://thediplomat.com/2013/01/pakistans-new-nuclear-problem/109 *Nuclear Notebook: Pakistan's nuclear forces*, Hans M. Kristensen Robert S. Norris, 07, 04, 2011. Bulletin of the Atomic Scientists, http://thebulletin.org/nuclear-notebook-pakistans-nuclear-forces-2011

Pakistan is building two new plutonium production reactors and a new reprocessing facility with which it will be able to fabricate more nuclear weapons fuel. It is also developing new delivery systems. Enhancements to Pakistan's nuclear forces include a new nuclear-capable medium-range ballistic missile (MRBM), the development of two new nuclear-capable short-range ballistic missiles, and the development of two new nuclear-capable cruise missiles.[1]

On 12 September, 2013, Reuter reported the analysis of the think tank of the International Institute for Strategic Studies, in which the panel expressed deep concern on the safety and security of nuclear weapons in South Asia: "An arms race in South Asia and Pakistan's development of tactical "battlefield" nuclear weapons are increasing the risk of any conflict there becoming a nuclear war, the International Institute for Strategic Studies (IISS) warned."

The think tank cited Pakistan's development of Short-Range Tactical Nuclear Weapons—which in theory could be used to stop any conventional Indian armored advance into Pakistani territory as a particular cause of concern. "The continuing expansion of Pakistan and India nuclear capabilities created ever greater concern about an intensifying nuclear arms race in South Asia," the IISS warned in its annual strategic survey.[2]

Mr. Alex P. Schmid and Ms. Charlotte Spencer-Smith (2012) shared the same concern about the security of nuclear weapons in South Asia. The issue of nuclear theft needs a considerable attention from International community:

> On March 26-27, 2012, leaders of 53 countries met for a summit in Seoul, Korea, in the framework of the American initiative to reduce and secure scattered nuclear materials which could offer terrorists an opportunity to acquire uranium or plutonium for exploding a nuclear weapon. It takes less than 25 kilograms of highly enriched uranium (HEU) and less than eight kilograms of plutonium (Pu) for constructing a viable atomic bomb. There are still between 1.300 and nearly 1.600 tons of highly enriched uranium and nearly 500 tons of plutonium stored in Russia and the United States and, to a lesser extent, in some 30 more countries. While the more than 100

---

1 *Nuclear Notebook: Pakistan's nuclear forces,* Hans M. Kristensen Robert S. Norris, 07, 04, 2011. Bulletin of the Atomic Scientists, http://thebulletin.org/nuclear-notebook-pakistans-nuclear-forces-2011
2 On 12 September, 2013, *Reuters,* "the analysis of the think tank of the International Institute for Strategic Studies, in which the panel express deep concern on safety and security of nuclear weapons in South Asia. Pakistan's "battlefield" nukes risk nuclear war," and also, *IISS think tank. Reuters,* 12 September, 2013.

military storage sites which contain some 19,000 assembled nuclear weapons (all but about 1.000 in the USA and Russia) are generally well-protected, some of the ca. 500 civilian nuclear power stations and some of the ca. 120 academic HEU-powered research reactors are in a number of cases much less well protected. Some of the latter are badly in need of better security than a chain-lock at the gates and a single night watchman on duty. There have been some twenty known cases of theft of plutonium and highly enriched uranium since 1990 and many more of other radioactive materials.[1]

On April 2014, Bloomberg TV reported a former Pennsylvania resident and two Pakistani nationals were indicted by a federal grand jury for smuggling technology to Pakistan, highlighting the U.S. Justice Department's focus on illegal exports that might be used for weapons of mass destruction. The men, the report said, used two corporations, Optima plus International, and Afro Asian International to export "dual-use" items, with both commercial and military or nuclear applications, for resale to the Pakistan Atomic Energy Commission, an arm of the Pakistani army, prosecutors said. Those indicted were Pakistanis; Shafqat Rana, formerly of Lancaster, Pennsylvania, and Abdul Qadeer Rana and Shahzad Rana, both of Lahore, Pakistan.[2]

The collusion of these factors raises the specter of a destabilized political State apparatus wherein the foolproof security of Pakistan's nuclear assets cannot be ensured. The failure of intelligence is also evident from the fact, that sectarian and ethnic affiliations in intelligence infrastructure of the country are becoming a challenging problem. Sectarian terrorists and those belonging to different school of thought receive strong support from their colleagues within the armed forces. The involvement of the army and air force in tackling insurgency in the tribal areas and Waziristan caused distrust between the state and the citizens.

On 22 June 2014, The Frontiers Post reported the Narendra Modi government's announcement that the International Atomic Energy Agency (IAEA) Additional Protocol had been ratified. According

---

1 Illicit Radiological and Nuclear Trafficking, Smuggling and Security Incidents in the Black Sea Region since the fall of the Iron Curtain— an Open Source Inventory, Alex P. Schmid & Charlotte Spencer-Smith, "Perspective on Terrorism, Vol 6, No 2, 2012.
2 On April 2014, Bloomberg TV; a former Pennsylvania resident and two Pakistani nationals were indicted by a federal grand jury for smuggling technology to Pakistan, highlighting the U.S. Justice Department's focus on illegal exports that might be used for weapons of mass destruction.

to the newspaper report, India had signed the IAEA Additional Protocol on 15 March, 2009, which was ratified after more than four years. However, by itself, it will not pave the way to the successful conclusion of negotiations with Westinghouse or GE or, for that matter, even AREVA. But dialogue with the U.S. lost momentum as did the quest for India's membership of the Nuclear Suppliers Group over the Nuclear Liability Law. The newspaper reported.[1]

The security of Pakistan's nuclear program has always received attention from international media due to domestic political instability and growing internal militant threats. In contrast, the security of the Bhabha Atomic Research Center (BARC) has been breached many times but there is little public discussion about threats to the security of India's huge civilian and military nuclear infrastructure. Instead, an overriding assumption exists that relevant agencies in India provide enough security to nuclear infrastructure.

The issue of making nuclear devices by terrorist organizations has become very complicated. Terrorist have the skills to prepare improvised nuclear device. In a comprehensive report (Future World of Illicit Nuclear Trade) for the Institute of Science and International Security (2013), David Albright, Andrea Stricker and Houston Wood have warned that the theft of nuclear materials and, cyber-theft and espionage pose new threats of leakage of sensitive information important to the development of nuclear weapons and the means to make them:

> In the future, there could be a greater availability of classified, proprietary, and other sensitive information about the technologies used to make HEU and plutonium and build nuclear weapons. For almost all proliferating states during the last several decades, their progress benefited from access to another country's classified information about nuclear weapons or the means to make HEU and plutonium. More recently, cyber-theft and espionage pose new threats of leakage of sensitive information important to the development of nuclear weapons and the means to make them. In addition, there are many dual-use technologies used in modern industries that are sensitive or proprietary and sought by other states. Some of these are critical to the development of a capability to make nuclear weapons, plutonium, or HEU. Preventing the unauthorized spread of classified, proprietary or other sensitive information will remain a difficult

---

1 On 22 June 2014, *The Frontiers Post*, the Narendra Modi government's announcement that the International Atomic Energy Agency (IAEA) Additional Protocol had been ratified

challenge. States and terrorists will likely continue to try to gain access to such information in their quest for nuclear capabilities.[1]

Five Eyes continue to focus on Pakistan as a potential source of nuclear bomb material. Yet unsecured highly enriched uranium elsewhere has been a worry for many years. Of particular concern have been the vast amounts of Weapons-Grade Uranium that were left relatively unguarded in Russia, Ukraine, Belarus and Kazakhstan, after the break-up of the Soviet Union. There are speculations that after the 9/11, the United States ordered General Musharaf to hand over all nuclear weapon to the US Special Forces as the threat of nuclear terrorism intensified. Some experts believe that the US safely controlled Pakistan nuclear weapons. Quoting the US Security Journal (Stratfor), Times of India reported that US delivered a very clear ultimatum to Pakistan:

> In a stunning disclosure certain to stir up things in Washington's (and in Islamabad and New Delhi's) strategic community, the journal Stratfor reported on Monday that the "United States delivered a very clear ultimatum to Musharraf in the wake of 9/11: Unless Pakistan allowed US forces to take control of Pakistani nuclear facilities, the United States would be left with no choice but to destroy those facilities, possibly with India's help." "This was a fait accompli that Musharraf, for credibility reasons, had every reason to cover up and pretend never happened, and Washington was fully willing to keep things quiet," the journal, which is widely read among the intelligence community, said. The Stratfor commentary came in response to an earlier New York Times story that reported that the Bush administration had spent around $100 million to help Pakistan safeguard its nuclear weapons, but left it unclear if Washington has a handle on the arsenal.[2]

"As the government of Pakistan totters, we must face a fact that the United States simply could not stand by as a nuclear-armed Pakistan descended into the abyss," proposed Frederick Kagan and Michael O'Hanlon, analysts at two Washington DC think-tanks. One possible plan would be a Special Forces operation with the limited goal of

1 *Future World of Illicit Nuclear Trade Mitigating the Threat*, David Albright Andrea StrickerHouston Wood, Science and International Security, 29 July 2013. http://www.nps.edu/Academics/Centers/CCC/PASCC/Publications/2013/Albright_Future_World_of_Illicit_Nuclear_Trade_PASCC.pdf
2 The US safely controlled Pakistan nuclear weapons. Having quoted the US Security Journal *(Stratfor)*, and, *Times of India* reported (20 November, 2007) that US delivered a very clear ultimatum to Pakistan.

preventing Pakistan's nuclear materials and warheads from getting into the wrong hands." In his research paper, published in World Affairs Journal (2011), Neil Padukone noted Lashkar Toiba's violent threat to peace and stability in South Asia:

> Global scrutiny after the 11/26 Mumbai attacks pressured the ISI to make Lashkar put its violent activities on temporary hold. But JuD (which after 2009 went by the name Tehreek-e-Tahaffuz Qibla Awal) has used the intervening time to build up a vast social services infrastructure that has solidified a broader Islamist movement throughout much of Pakistan. This movement recruits not only impoverished youth but highly skilled professionals. According to the Strategic Foresight Group, as early as 2005 LeT's assets included a 190-acre campus in Muridke, outside of Lahore, complete with 500 offices, 2200 training camps, 150 schools, 2 science colleges, 3 hospitals, 34 dispensaries, 11 ambulance services, a publishing empire, garment factory, iron foundry, and woodworks factories. It had more than 300,000 cadres at its disposal and paid salaries to their top bracket functionaries that were 12-15 times greater than similar jobs in the civilian sector.[1]

Pakistan's controversial nuclear scientist Abdul Qadeer Khan, who allegedly transferred nuclear technology to several states including North Korea, still resonate with ordinary Pakistanis and Islamists alike. Abdul Qadeer Khan was removed from his post as head of the country's nuclear program by former military dictator and President Pervez Musharraf in 2001. In Pakistan, not only militant groups, moderate religious parties invariably use nuclear rhetoric against India and Western nations. Terrorist groups, such as Islamic State (IS), are seeking to acquire the ability to build "improvised nuclear explosive devices," or crude atomic bombs.

Research scholar, Samuel Kane suggested that Pakistani extremist groups have the capabilities to attack the country's nuclear installations. He also warned that several factors are involved in extremist's attacks on Pakistan nuclear installations:

In Pakistan, the threat of nuclear materials falling into terrorist hands is a multi-faceted danger, composed of several different scenarios; such as (1) insiders within the Pakistani nuclear program proliferating nuclear assets and knowledge to terrorist groups; (2)

---

1 *World Affairs Journal*, 2011, "The Next al-Qaeda? Lashkar-e-Taiba and the Future of Terrorism in South Asia, Neil Padukone, noted Lashkar Toiba's violent threat to peace and stability in South Asia," http://www.worldaffairsjournal.org/article/next-al-qaeda-lashkar-e-taiba-and-future-terrorism-south-asia

a terrorist group stealing nuclear materials from a Pakistani facility; and (3) a radical Islamist group seizing control of the Pakistani government and nuclear arsenal, through a coup or democratic elections.[1]

International media continues to highlight the threat of nuclear terrorism emanating from the consecutively expanding network of Pakistan's nuclear weapons. Pakistan journalists and writers are not willing to criticize the network of Pakistan's nuclear weapons due to the fear of ISI violent action against their families. Moreover, the biggest threat to Pakistan's nuclear weapons emanates from jihadists organization in and outside Pakistan, and in South and Central Asia. Federation of American Scientists published numerous articles and research papers on the prospect of nuclear terrorism in South Asia, in which experts raised important questions about the safety and security of Pakistan's nuclear weapons.

Charles P. Blair warns the looming threat of the country's nuclear jihad and its fatalities. The Chatham House writers have also raised the same questions in their research paper (Too Close for Comfort Cases of near Nuclear Use and Options for Policy, April 2014). The authors highlighted Pakistan's nuclear command and its gradual development:

> Pakistan's nuclear command-and-control structure is officially divided between three authorities. The first is the National Command Authority, which is chaired by the prime minister. The second is the Strategic Plans Division (SPD), a body comprising government and military representatives set up as the result of command-and-control reforms between 1999 and 2001. The third is Strategic Forces Command, comprised of the military. The storage status of Pakistan's nuclear weapons during peacetime has not been explicitly clarified, but it is widely believed that the SPD exercises heightened vigilance against the possibility that they could go missing. Reports indicate that Pakistan does separate its warheads from its delivery systems, and that the warheads themselves are separated by 'isolating the fissile "core" or trigger from the weapon and storing it elsewhere.' While Pakistan's nuclear weapons are therefore not susceptible to being used while on a hair-trigger alert, the warhead's components

---

1 *Preventing Nuclear Terrorism: Nuclear Security, the Non-proliferation Regime, and the Threat of Terrorist Nukes,* Samuel Kane, was drafted by Samuel Kane as a project conducted in the summer of 2012 while serving as a Research Associate at Global Solutions.org https://globalsolutions.org/files/public/documents/Sam-Kane-Preventing-Nuclear-Terrorism.pdf.

are nevertheless stored at military bases and can be put together at short notice.[1]

In 1999, during the Kargil war, and in 2008, after the Mumbai attacks, Pakistan and India were on the verge of a military confrontation. Pakistan refused to restrain Lashkar-e-Toiba, and those involved in the Mumbai attacks, while India was adamant not to extend the hand of cooperation to Pakistan. In his research paper on Pakistan's nuclear Blackmailing, Dr. Rajesh Kumar Mishra (2002) argues that the threat of Jihadist groups to Pakistan's nuclear installations is intensifying:

> Jihadist zealots inside Pakistan as the epicenter of global terrorist network defy any international suggestion for peaceful resolution of disputes. They wield double-edged sword of terror—jihadist terrorist strikes and nuclear attacks, not only for India but also for the whole world. While speculations are still rife of possible use of nuclear weapons by Pakistan, the international apprehension of terrorists developing or using "dirty" bombs has also to do a lot with the so-called Jihadist sympathizers in Pakistan. Indo-Pak nuclear war remains only one aspect of nuclear terror. The potential nuclear terror if unleashed by Jihadist elements in Pakistan would be equally devastating for both India and the world community. Domestic and international illegal connection that prompts Pakistan to perpetuate nuclear terror may hardly ensure long lasting security and, so, requires timely international attention.[2]

David Albright, Andrea Stricker and Houston Wood have also warned about the rogue suppliers of nuclear materials. They also argued that greater availability of classified, proprietary and other sensitive information about the technologies used to make HEU and plutonium and build nuclear weapons is matter of great concern. They argued that there is also growing concern that Iran and North Korea are undertaking nuclear cooperation:

> The future world of illicit trade may include a pariah country, unauthorized entities in a country, or criminal elements selling nuclear facilities or capabilities to other states—actors which are termed "rogue suppliers." North Korea is a rogue supplier and has demonstrated the capability and inclination to provide nuclear goods

---

1 *Too Close for Comfort Cases of Near Nuclear Use and Options for Policy.* Patricia Lewis, Heather Williams, Benoît Pelopidas and Sasan Aghlani, Chatham House Report, April, 2014.
2 "Pakistan's Nuclear Blackmailing: Spreading fear of nuclear terror." Dr. Rajesh Kumar Mishra, Paper no. 482, 26. 06. 2002, *South Asia Analysis Group.* http://www.southasiaanalysis.org/paper482.

and capabilities to customers abroad outside normal commerce and despite international norms and rules. Other states could emerge as rogue suppliers, particularly Iran. There is also growing concern that Iran and North Korea are undertaking nuclear cooperation. In the longer term, there is reason to worry that Syria under the victorious, old, or a new, radical regime could restart a secret nuclear program and emerge as a rogue nuclear supplier, or that Pakistan's government, along with its nuclear arsenal, could fall into the hands of radical fundamentalists.[1]

Former member of the Pakistan Foreign Service, Asif Ezdi's recent article in the News International (July 07, 2014) narrates an interesting story of India's agreement with International Atomic Energy Agency that gives nuclear weapons inspectors the right of access to its civil nuclear sites. This is an important development, and is an ordeal for Pakistan:

> The agreement, called the Additional Protocol in IAEA terminology, was concluded as part of the India–US nuclear deal of 2008 under which India received a waiver from the Nuclear Suppliers Group's restrictions on the export of nuclear material and technology to countries that do not accept full-scope safeguards on their nuclear program. Far from being aimed at providing transparency of India's nuclear program, the main purpose of the additional protocol was to provide the US with another excuse, however threadbare, for its claim that exempting India from the NSG's restrictions on nuclear trade would "bring the country into the international non-proliferation mainstream.[2]

Nuclear terrorism in Pakistan is based on the assumption that the three major levels of Pakistan's nuclear complex, nuclear doctrine and command and control; the security of the nuclear arsenal, delivery systems, and fissile material production facilities; and the security of civilian nuclear facilities present opportunities for the theft or diversion of nuclear materials. According to Mr. Michael Rubin, if Islamist powers or groups did have the atomic bomb, they would gladly use that against Israel, India, or the United States. However, the NATO Review for 2014 also elucidated the nuclear dimensions of Jihadist terrorism:

> Suicide bombings are bad enough. But suicide nuclear bombs would spell catastrophe. Michael Ruhle looks at how jihadists' attempts

---

1 *Future World of Illicit Nuclear Trade Mitigating the Threat*, David Albright, Andrea Stricker, Houston Wood, 29 July 2013.
2 *The News International*, 07 July 2014.

to join the nuclear club have been thwarted—and what's needed to stave off this threat. The ideological appeal of jihadist terrorism is as weak as ever, and even in most parts of the Muslim world, radical Islam remains deeply unpopular. Jihadist terrorism can instill fear and cause serious disruptions within. Since "9/11," radical clerics have extended this logic even further. In his 2003 work, 'A Treatise on the Law of the Weapons of Mass Destruction Against the Unbelievers,' one Saudi radical scholar argued that since roughly ten million Muslims had been killed by Americans, killing that same number of Americans was permissible, including through the use of weapons of mass destruction. Such a fatwa (an Islamic scholar's or clergyman's analysis on interpreting Islamic law) effectively provides a religious blank cheque for mass murder. Against this backdrop, statements by some Islamists, including religiously fervent physicists who maintain that Pakistan's nuclear weapons 'belong to all Muslims' acquire a new, worrying significance.[1]

Bruce Riedel's paper about the future of Global Jihad (2011), suggests that Pakistani armed forces would, of course, use their nuclear weapons to defend themselves. A jihadist, nuclear-armed Pakistan is a scenario that must be avoided at all costs. In Edward A. Friedman (2014) research paper, he revealed the fact that in 1998, Osama bin Laden declared that it was his Islamic duty to acquire weapons of mass destruction. Because Islam deplores killing of women and children, religious justification was sought for such weapons. In 2003, three Saudi clerics associated with Al Qaeda provided justification in a fatwa that stated: "One kills in a good manner only when one can."[2]

---

1 *NATO Review for 2014*, "The nuclear dimensions of jihadist terrorism Suicide bombings are bad enough. But suicide nuclear bombs would spell catastrophe."
2 "A Scenario for Jihadist Nuclear Revenge, the Greatest Threat," Edward A. Friedman, spring 2014- Volume 67...Federation of American Scientists. Paul Bracken, "The Second Nuclear Age: Strategy, Danger, and the New Power Politics," Times Books, 2012, Published on June 23, 2014, "The Jihadi Menace Gets Real, Walter Russell Mead, the American Interests." *The new jihadists*, Anthony Bubalo, 12 April 2014

Chapter 5. Nuclear Smuggling and Saudi Investment in Pakistani Weapons

Nuclear black marketing and the investment of Saudi Arabia and other Arab States in Pakistan Nuclear Weapons, and its Weapons of Mass Destruction, raised serious questions that these weapons might fall into the hands of TTP, Islamic State (ISIS), or Punjabi Taliban. Huge investment of Saudi government and other Arab States in Pakistan's nuclear weapons is not a new thing; Libya, United Arab Emirate, China and wealthy individuals from Pakistan, and several other states contributed their share. Saudi Arabia has in the past been the subject of speculation regarding nuclear weapons ambitions. Among the charges leveled against it is the possession of undeclared nuclear facilities.[1]

Saudi Arabia denied manufacturing nuclear weapons, but the country allegedly allocated financial funds for its nuclear program, and received scientific assistance from Pakistan. Pakistani scientists and army experts are working with the country's army on various projects. A report of the BBC news exposed the race of nuclear weapons in the Middle East, pitting the Shia Iran against its Sunni-ruled rival, Saudi Arabia, which is allegedly aspiring to become a nuclear power. The BBC News reported that Saudi Arabia invested huge money in Pakistan's Atomic Program. According to a former Pakistani spy agent, he believed the Pakistanis

---

1 *Nuclear Black Markets: Pakistan, A.Q. Khan and the rise of Proliferation Networks.* Dossier of International Institute for Strategic Studies, 2007

certainly maintain a certain number of warheads on the basis, that if the Saudis were to ask for them at any given time, they would be immediately transferred.[1]

The facilities for nuclear installations, Saudi Arabia has, is sufficient for its nuclear program. Saudi Arabia desperately seeks nuclear weapons as the emergence of Iran as a nuclear state, created fear and deep dismal, among the Arab states. Therefore, Saudi generals and Wahabi establishment decided to invest in Pakistan nuclear weapons. In 1994, Muhammad Khilewe, the first secretary of Saudi mission to the United Nations claimed asylum in the United States, and revealed that his country wanted to obtain nuclear weapons.[2]

In 1988, Saudi Arabia also received CSS-2 DF-3 intermediate-range missiles from China. As the security of nuclear installation on its soil was very complicated, the country decided to invest huge money in Pakistan nuclear program. Pakistan received billions of dollars from Saudi Arabia, to prepare nuclear weapons for the country that faced a constant threat from Iran.[3]

In March 2015, Prime Minister Nawaz Sharif visited Saudi Arabia. Saudi Arabia's campaign to build a broad Sunni alliance to contain Iran has apparently suffered at least a setback from Pakistan. Pakistani Prime Minister Nawaz Sharif rejected, at least for now, Saudi Arabia's entreaties for Pakistani troops to help guard the Saudi border with northern Yemen, controlled by Iranian-backed Houthi Shiite forces. After the Iranian Revolution, Pakistani dictator Zia ul-Haq deployed an elite Pakistani armored brigade to the kingdom at King Fahd's request to deter any threats to the country. In all, some 40,000 Pakistanis served in the brigade over most of a decade. Today only some Pakistani advisers and experts serve in the kingdom. However, the ISIS is projecting itself as a champion of the 'Sunni' cause, putting up a fight against an expansionist, Shia Iran. Moreover, if the Sunni states remain ambiguous about their anti-ISIS policy, Islamists the world over will gravitate towards the extremist group as it continues

1"Saudi nuclear weapons 'on order' from Pakistan," *BBC*, 06 November 2013, http://www.bbc.co.uk/news/world-middle-east-24823846.

2 *Melbourne Daily Star*, 28 March 2014.

3 *Deadly Arsenals: Nuclear, Biological, and Chemical Threats*, Joseph Cirincione, Jon B. Wolfsthal, Miriam Rajkumar, Carnegie Endowment, 01 Dec 2011.*Middle East Turmoil and the Disintegration of a Nation State*, Prof. William R. Stanley—Transcend Media Service, Syria in Depth, 3 February 2014. https://www.transcend.org/tms/2014/02/middle-east-turmoil-and-the-disintegration-of-a-nation-state/, and also, *What the Future Holds for Syria and the Region*, Najmuddin A. Shaikh, 25.09.2012.

to play up its anti-Iran and anti-Shia credentials. Saudi Arabia link with Pakistan's nuclear and missile program has long been the source of speculation, which Pakistan might either station its nuclear forces on Saudi soil, or provide a nuclear umbrella to the Wahabi state, in return for oil supply; or that Saudi would purchase nuclear weapons from Pakistan.

The Saudi regime always counted on Pakistan to provide the Praetorian Guards of the regime if a need arose. The Iranian reports suggest that there could be Pakistani personnel numbering 100,000 already serving in the security-related spheres in Saudi Arabia. Saudi Arabia has stationed some brigades of Pakistan military on its soil, and continues to support Islamic State (ISIS), to prevent Iranian invasion. However, more than 30,000 thousand soldiers of Pakistan's Blackwater (Fuji Foundation) are fighting in Bahrain, and Yemen, against the Shia population. Pakistan also provided military unites to protect the kingdom. In Bahrain, Pakistani Blackwater militias are fighting Saudi war against the majority Shia population.[1]

As India Today Magazine reported hundreds of Pakistani militants and army soldiers supporting the ranks of Islamic State, these fighters are believed to be retired army personnel and civilians from militant groups like Lashkar-e-Toiba (LeT) and the Lashkar-e-Jhangvi (LeJ). "Hundreds of our mujahedeen have moved to Syria, and others are preparing to join them soon, "Abu Wahab," commander of a pro-Pakistan militant group claimed. The groups in Iraq are believed to be from the 'pro-government' groups like LeT and LeJ, and not the Tehreek-e-Taliban Pakistan (TTP) that attacked Karachi airport on June 8, 2014, against which the Pakistan army is fighting in North Waziristan.

In this chapter, I want to highlight nuclear relation between Pakistan and Saudi Arabia, and the Saudi demand of its share in Pakistan's Islamic bomb. After some of my articles published in newspapers, a considerable amount of debate started in international press regarding Pakistan's controversial nuclear program. I received serious death threats from Pakistan's military establishment and intelligence agencies. In my argument, I raised the question that how

---

1 *Saudi Arabia's Nuclear Aspirations: Challenges, Opportunities and Options*, Reshmi Kazi, http://www.pugwashindia.org/pdf/saudi. pdf. And also, *Issue brief, Saudi Arabia's Nuclear Thinking and the Pakistani Connection*, Reshmi Kazi, 07 January, 2014, Institute for Defense Studies and Analysis, http://idsa.in/issuebrief/ SaudiArabiasNuclearThinkingandPakistan_rkazi_070114. Nuclear Terrorism. And also Kazi, *The New Terror of the 21st Century*, Reshmi Kazi, IDSA, 27 October 2013.

many Muslim and non-Muslim states invested in Pakistan Islamic bomb, and how much money the country received so for. Research scholar Reshmi Kazi's analysis of Saudi Arabia's nuclear thinking and Pakistani connection provides my readers with good information in the context of Iranian nuclear threat in the region:

> Saudi Arabia worries that the West will turn its focus away from Iran once the problem over the Iranian nuclear programme is diffused. Riyadh anticipates that in the long run a nuclear Iran will be emboldened in Saudi Arabia's proxy conflict with Iran in states like Palestine, Bahrain, Yemen and most recently Syria. Amidst such concerns, Riyadh's rejection of a coveted seat at the United Nation Security Council in October 2013 followed by the revelation of the BBC news about possible nuclear weapons cooperation between Saudi Arabia and Pakistan in November 2013 has raised questions whether Riyadh aspires to acquire nuclear weapons capability? What has been the level of nuclear cooperation between the two Islamic nations...President Hassan Rouhani has already emphasized in an interview to the financial Times that Iran will not fully dismantle its nuclear programme as part of a comprehensive agreement.[1]

Pakistan's military contribution in the Islamic State (ISIS) can be judged from the revelations of a former officer of Pakistan army. Major (Retd) Agha Amin, a Lahore-based defense analyst told India Today that Pakistani fighters went into Syria and Iraq with the tacit knowledge of the government. He mentioned Lt-General Hamid Gul, former chief of the ISI, as a key facilitator in the movement. The army, however, supported Lt-General Hamid Gul's efforts to take former Pakistani soldiers to Iraq and Syria. "There is a strong possibility that the Mosul attack was supported by the Pakistani state, both civilian and military, Major Amin said.

Saudi Arabia invested in Pakistan's nuclear bomb and now wants to obtain the bomb. While the Saudis quest for these weapons has also been set in the context of countering Shia Iran and it is now possible for the Wahabi Sheikhs to deploy these weapons quickly than Iran. As a nuclear state, Iran wants to establish hegemony in the region, and Saudi Arabia views Iran's influence in Middle East and Persian Gulf, as a bigger threat. The Saudi investment in Pakistan nuclear bomb raised many questions.[2]

Facilities and capabilities that Saudi Arabia is known to possess would be insufficient for any military nuclear program. Allegations

1 Saudi Arabia's Nuclear Thinking and the Pakistani Connection, IDSA, 07 January 2014
2 *BBC*, 06 November 2013,

that Saudi sought an indigenous nuclear weapons capability from Pakistan have now become reality. Pakistani scientists helped Saudi Arabia's National Nuclear Program (NNP). The rise of nuclear Iran in the Persian Gulf and Middle East regions, ISIS and the torment of the Arab world, and their desperately seeking nuclear weapons, have been two interesting issues of debates in international press. In the end of 2013, Iran settled its controversial issue and extended hands of friendship to the West. Author Reshmi Kazi highlights the anxiety of Saudi rulers and their encirclement of Iran:

> Riyadh's goal is to encircle Iran in the region, weaken its allies and cap its regional aspirations. However, the nuclear deal concluded between the global powers led by Washington and Iran seemingly appears to scuttle Riyadh's goal in countering Tehran influence in the region. What bother Riyadh more is the belief that the diffusion of the Iranian nuclear problem, Washington would eventually turn its attention away from the Middle East leading to a deterioration of US protective umbrella in the region? The Obama administration's abandonment of its long-standing regional ally in Egypt's Hosni Mubarak and its recent diplomatic initiatives in Syria and Iran bears testimony to Iran's apprehensions.[1]

On February 2014 we saw the first visit of Pakistan's Army Chief to Saudi Arabia since he replaced General Kayani in November 2013, after the controversial news reports about the Saudis' investment in the country's Islamic bomb, and this confirmed international news reports that Pakistan was planning to deliver nuclear bomb to the country. Pakistani newspapers scrupulously reported his mission, but newspapers in the United Kingdom termed his visit of great importance, as both the states faces the threat of ISIS terrorism. In Pakistan, a new Islamic terrorist threat of ISIS is on the rise as Saudi Arabia wants to strengthen its military relations with the country on one hand, and support Taliban insurgents against the ISIS on the other.[2]

---

1 *Saudi Arabia's Nuclear Thinking and the Pakistani Connection*, Reshmi Kazi, 07 January, 2014, Institute for Defense Studies and Analysis.
2 "Pakistan's Top General in Saudi Arabia to Discuss Defense Cooperation, Pakistan's chief of army staff is in Riyadh to expand their strategic partnership." By Ankit Panda, *The Diplomat*, 06 February, 2014, http://thediplomat.com/2014/02/pakistans-top-general-in-saudi-arabia-to-discuss-defense-cooperation/. And also, "Pakistan" trump card in the deck Saudis," Igor Nikolayev, *Russian Information Agency*, 11 April 2014, http://eng.iran.ru/news/analytics/102/Pakistan_trump_card_in_the_deck_Saudis.

On 08 February 2014, Daily Naya Akhbar reported Saudi authorities asking Pakistan army Chief, Raheel Sharif, to dispatch two more divisions' forces (30,000) to the kingdom as part of bilateral agreement between the two states. Another Pakistani newspaper, Daily Ummat (Urdu) stated that Pakistani troops will train Saudi troops, but military observer fear that these troops might be used in sectarian conflicts in the Middle East. On 20 January 2014, Saudi Deputy Defense Minister, Prince Salman visited Pakistan to discuss the emergence of nuclear Iran and the emergence of ISIS in the Middle East.[1]

Dawn reported on 7 March 2014 that the Pakistani government was pursuing plans for a "new era in strategic partnership" with Saudi Arabia, which it desired to be anchored in time-tested Defense relationship. Plans were also afoot for expanded Defense cooperation with China. Foreign Office spokesperson Tasneem Aslam said at the weekly media briefing that the possibility of collaboration in Defense production was discussed during the visit of Saudi Crown Prince Salman bin Abdul-Aziz. "Nothing has yet been finalized... these discussions are continuing," she said.[2]

Dawn reported about the impending Pak-Saudi Defense and friendly relations with China. Chinese, Defense Minister visited Pakistan and discussed bilateral cooperation between the two states. "While we do not want to indulge in an arms race and spend our meager resources on buying arms, at the same time, we cannot be completely oblivious to what is happening in the region. We have to keep a level of conventional stability," Foreign Office Spokeswoman said. It is a fact that Saudi Arabia is integrating Pakistan as a key player in its regional strategies. The mystery of the $1.5 billion 'gift' deposited by Saudi Arabia in the State Bank of Pakistan, according to Mr. Bhadrakumar's argument, is falling in place. What emerges is that Saudi Arabia needs Pakistani weapons for equipping the forces, which serve as Riyadh's proxies in various regional theatres.[3]

In his Friday Times editorial, journalist Najam Sethi also confirmed the grant of $1.5 billion Saudi help to Pakistani Prime Minister, Nawaz Sharif: The Saudi Kingdom has granted $1.5b to the Nawaz Sharif government... A quick fix of $3b is a lot of free money for Pakistan's forex-strapped economy that is struggling to cope with significant international debt payments and a rising trade gap that

---

1 *Daily Naya Akhbar*, (Urdu Newspaper), 08 February 2014,
2 *Dawn*, 7 March 2014
3 *Ibid*, 7 *March 2014*.

is putting pressure on the rupee and fuelling inflation. Indeed, the Saudi injection has reversed the rapid fall of the rupee, proving that the finance minister, Ishaq Dar, was not bluffing when he warned exporters six weeks ago not to hoard their dollars.[1]

Mr. Najam Sethi also hinted towards the threat of Shiaism arising from Iraq and Syria, which Saudi Arabia wants to counter it effectively. Saudi knows that nuclear Iran is threat to its security and stability, therefore, the country wants to engage Pakistan in the region:

> The Saudis and the Emirates-Gulfdoms are feeling insecure because of the Shia revival in their heartlands. This is because the restless Shias are sitting on their oil reserves. Iran, too, is unremitting in opposing Saudi influence. Iraq and Qatar, two competitive energy suppliers, are not playing ball either. Egypt and Libya haven't bought into the Saudi Islamist line. Worse, the Americans are seeking negotiated nuclear solutions in Iran instead of succumbing to Saudi pressure for military action. And American self-reliance on shale gas is the first definite step against continued dependence on Saudi oil. On the heels of the Saudi VVIPs now comes the King of Bahrain to Islamabad. The PMLN government claims that foreign investment deals are in the offing. But the small print betrays the real motive behind "renewed manpower exports." The Bahraini Emir wants well-trained and equipped Pakistani military mercenaries to beef up his police and security forces to repress the rising democratic impulses of the majority Shia populations. It is as simple as that.[2]

Farhan Bukhari viewed Saudi Arabia's growing engagement with Islamabad as suspicious as Riyadh wants Islamabad's support to bolster itself on two fronts; the Southern frontline along the border with Yemen, and to the north to face internal security challenges, as well as tackling any possible spill over from conflict-stricken Syria. On 20 March 2014, writer Dr. Muhammad Taqi warned that Pakistan's involvement in sectarian conflicts in Middle East can harm internal stability of the country:

> By aligning Pakistan with the Saudis in a conflict that might rip the Middle East along sectarian seams, Nawaz Sharif seems to be making a conscious decision to set this country up to formally becomes a Wahabi confessional state eventually. Mr. Sharif, personally beholden to the Saudis like Ustad Sayyaf, may be signing on to a not just a

---

1 "Leasing out Pakistan," Najam Sethi, *The Friday Times*, 21 Mar 2014. http://www.thefridaytimes.com/tft/leasing-out-pakistan/, Zarif says Iran not worried about revealing content of Geneva talks, *Tehran Times*, 18 October 2013, *The New York Times*, 16 October 2013
2 Najam Sethi, *TFT Issue*: 21 March 2014,

personal name change but to changing the country's already abysmal confessional outlook for the worse. What are deeply disconcerting are not the small arms that Pakistan has agreed to provide the Saudis, destined for Syrian rebels in all likelihood, but the bigger doctrinal mess that Mr. Sharif might be dragging the country into. It seems like Nawaz Sharif just picked up on doing the Saudi's bidding exactly from where he left off in 1999.[1]

Both traditional Islamic terrorists and the new breed have filled ranks with militants, who receive support from Saudi Arabia. By receiving Saudi financial assistance, extremists in both Pakistan and Afghanistan learned the value of violence, in defeating security forces of the states. They are well funded with an eye on Pakistan nuclear weapons, and developed sophisticated international networks that allow them to successfully attack Pakistani security forces.

Charities from Saudi Arabia and the United Arab Emirates financed a network in Pakistan that recruited children as young as eight to wage "holy war." A US diplomatic cable published by WikiLeaks said financial support estimated at $100 million a year was making its way from those Gulf Arab states to an extremist recruitment network in Pakistan's Punjab province.

In February 2015, the Saudi embassy issued a statement saying that all its donations to seminaries had government clearance, after a minister accused the Riyadh government of creating instability across the Muslim world. The Pakistani Foreign Ministry responded by saying that funding by private individuals through "informal channels" would also be scrutinized closely to try to choke off funding for terror groups. While the statement avoided mentioning Saudi Arabia specifically, it was widely interpreted as a rebuke. In March 2015, Saudi King Salman Bin Abdul Aziz summoned Prime Minister of Pakistan Nawaz Sharif after unveiling of the covert aid to Wahhabis-allied Deobandis who promote violent extremism and takfiri terrorism in all over Pakistan.

---

1 "The confessional state and its secret Santa".Dr. Mohammad Taqi, March 20, 2014, *Daily Times.Pravda*, 2013, "China urges solutions on Iran nuclear issues." *China daily*, 15 October 2013, *Tehran Times*, 15 October 2013, "China to give Pakistan two more nuclear reactors, India protests." *Indian Express*, 15 October 2013, "Window for diplomacy with Iran 'cracking open'": *Kerry Tehran Times*, 14 October 2013, "Iran to Offer Proposal and Speak of Peaceful Aims at Nuclear Talks in Geneva." *The New York Times*, 13 October 2013, "Iran nuclear talks return to Geneva with better prospects": article *Tehran Times*, 13 October 2013.

Federal Minister for Inter-Provincial Coordination (IPC), Riaz Hussain Pirzada accused the Saudi government of creating instability across the Muslim world, including Pakistan, through distribution of money for promoting its ideology. Addressing a two-day 'Ideas Conclave' organized by the "Jinnah Institute" think tank in Islamabad, the federal minister said 'the time has come to stop the influx of Saudi money into Pakistan. Mr. Pirzada and the Jinnah Institute were calling for Pakistan to pay careful attention to the consequences of accepting Saudi funds at a time when opinions on the attendant issues are being reinforced on both sides.

Before many young radical Muslims take up arms with jihadist groups such as the Islamic State (ISIS) and al-Qaeda, they receive their first lessons on radical Islam from madrassas, Islamic schools that serve as an alternative to government or expensive private schools. "They create a sensibility among children that later turns into a big support base for extremist and sectarian views," said A. H. Nayyar, a Pakistani physicist and nuclear activist, who has also researched and written on madrassa education. Saudi Arabia greatly appreciated the capacity of Pakistan Defense industry, while cooperation in the field of Defense production also came under discussion. Defense Minister, Khawaja Asif reiterated that Saudi Arabia held great importance for all Muslims across the world, and said it is the first visit of Prince Salman Bin Abdul Aziz, after assuming the charge of Defense Minister. He expressed hope that the visit would further enhance ties and give boost to relations.

In a country like Pakistan, one difficulty with a high level act of nuclear terrorism is that of credibility; Taliban terrorists have to prove to the government that they are capable of acts that are being threatened. Now they also succeeded in persuading Pakistani government that the settlement of the ongoing conflict is impossible without the cooperation of their forces.

To destroy or retrieve nuclear weapons, Taliban and extremist groups are trying to reach nuclear installations, or infiltrate the country's nuclear forces. Nuclear, chemical and biological weapons compared to nuclear weapons are cheap. Conventional wisdom in Pakistan holds that nuclear weapons are fundamentally different from conventional weapons. They are essentially viewed as weapons of deterrence rather than warfare. Nonetheless, because they are weapons of mass destruction, their proliferation is dangerous for international security.

Pakistan's nuclear weapons are constant threat to world peace. If Pakistan provides nuclear bomb to Saudi Arabia, it will create misunderstanding between Iran and Pakistan. Russia's English newspaper, Pravda (2013) reported the Saudi financial aid to Pakistan's nuclear program:

Saudi Arabia's foreign policy is undergoing some significant shifts, as evidenced by the decision not to accept the UN Security Council seat, so the situation has become more unpredictable. It is conceivable that Saudi Arabia planted some of the evidence for this story as a means of putting pressure on the United States to be firm in dealing with Iran.[1]

The present policy adopted by Obama administration enraged all Arab rulers. According to American Thinker (2013), there is no more strategic commodity than gulf oil to the entire world economy. Iran is the winner and Arabs are the losers. Arabs and Pakistan will face the consequences of their interventionist policies. Saudi Arabia has interfered in Bahrain, Syria, Iraq and Yemen, while Pakistan army is interfering in Kashmir, Waziristan, FATA and Afghanistan. Saudi has also said that it will unleash a pre-emptive war in the Middle East in response to the pro-Iranian policy of the Obama administration.[2]

A new story emerged when secret documents exposed Pakistan's involvement in nuclear smuggling. The documents revealed that two senior Pakistani generals have been involved in the sale of Uranium enrichment technology to North Korea in return for millions of dollars in cash. In 2004, Dr. Abdul Qadir Khan confirmed the sale of high speed centrifuges to Libya, Iran and North Korea. The Guardian reported, both generals denied the allegations.

On 07 September 2012, George Washington University posted a document of US counter terrorism efforts from National Security Archive Electronic Briefing Book No. 388, which warned that eleven years after the terrorist attacks of September 11, 2001, how concerned Americans should be over threats of nuclear terrorism remains a subject of vigorous debate.[3]

Experts fear that Saudi may possibly provide these weapons to Pakistani Taliban based in Syria, or it will deploy these weapons on its borders? Because, Saudi's recent diplomatic ruction with the United States has been a demand of stern military action against the Assad

---

1 "Saudis to Obama: We Will Not Tolerate a Nuclear Iran," By Karin McQuillan, *American Thinker*, 10 December, 2013.
2 "Deconstructing the Pak bomb," *The Hindu*, 13 October 2013
3 "India, Australia seeks early closure of civil N-deal." *Hindustan Times*, 11 October 2013,

regime. The Saudis will not wait more to receive Pakistani nuclear bomb, because they have already paid for it. Libya, Korea and other Muslim states have already received their share.[1]

Since 1980s, Pakistani business men and members of the army were travelling across the world secretly to establish contacts, in various states for retrieving sensitive materials. As we read about the danger of Pakistan's nuclear weapons, and its security in print and electronic media worldwide, the country wants to endanger the stability of neighboring states, by providing weapons to terrorist groups. Recent terror attacks on Pakistan's nuclear installations confused international community about the safety and security of the country's nuclear assets. No doubt, Pakistan has deployed more than 25,000 nuclear forces on its 15 nuclear sites, but military establishment continues to create enemies by killing the children of Pashtun in FATA and Khyber Pakhtunkhwa. In 2014, politician Mahmood Khan Achakzai criticized military establishment that it has killed more Pashtuns than the remote control drone. Recent terror attacks in various cities of Pakistan triggered concerns in international community about the security of the country's nuclear weapons.

This perception has wide-ranging strategic, diplomatic, political and economic implications for Pakistan. Today's precarious situation in Pakistan comes in a world where terror groups are actively seeking nuclear weapons. Uyghur Islamic front looks towards Pakistan for its assistance against communist China. Taliban, Al Qaeda and the ISIS group wants nuclear weapons. Syrian rebels need weapons of mass destruction; Haqqani and Mullah Omar also need these weapons to use it in Afghanistan. Can Pakistan meet their demands? Yes, there are speculations in intellectual circles that Pakistan may possibly provide these weapons to Chinese dissidents or Taliban insurgents in near future.

About 1,000 Chinese jihadists received military training in a secret base in Pakistan, while an unclear number of Chinese nationals are already fighting in Syria, Jacques Neriah, a Middle East analyst at the Jerusalem Center for Public Affairs (JCPA) told a high-level delegation from China. The Chinese delegation was made up of 10 representatives, several of them members of the Central Party School,

---

1 *Daily Times*, 3 October, 2013.2- 3-" Space Policy in Developing Countries: The Search for Security in Development on the Final Frontiers." Robert C. Harding. Routledge, 2013. *Atlantic Magazine*, December 2011, 9- *The Guardian* 9 November, 2012, 20- *The New York Times*, 9 August, 2013, 21-*The Hindu*, 2 February 2013.

which trains future senior officials. As the country has already warned that in case of Indian military intervention, it would use nuclear weapons against it, we can understand the intentions of Pakistan military establishment, and its secret dealing with CIA and Strategic Clandestine Intelligence (SCI).

The continued ties of Deobandi, Barelvi, Ahl Hadeith and Salafi groups and their sympathizers within the army of the country, poses considerable threat to the nuclear installations. According to the recent report of National Crisis Management Cell of Pakistan (NCMC), more than 400 sectarian and extremist groups operate alongside Punjabi Taliban in Southern Punjab, which receive supports from various civilian and military quarters. Punjabi Taliban control dozens of villages in Southern Punjab and receive funds from the Punjab government. Punjabi Taliban has established a strong network in Army and police forces.

As we have already discussed the networks of extremist and terror groups in the country, the globalization of world industry and transport, containerization of trade, diffusion of nuclear weapon technology, and the availability of the weapons of mass destruction in Pakistani black market, present a bigger threat to the national security of Afghanistan, China and India. Terrorist groups and, specifically, Islamic State (IS) and Taliban are planning to acquire these weapons and, with their ability and financial resources to purchase, steal and make these weapons from fissile material. In its report, weapons of mass destruction commission, initiated by the Swedish Government on a proposal from the United Nations warned that:

Acquiring weapons of mass destruction and usable materials directly from a sympathetic government would significantly simplify the requirement for the terrorists, obviating the need to defeat security system protecting such materials. During the civil wars, violence or instability in a country like Pakistan, terror groups can gain control of fissile materials. Insurgent groups, like Taliban or sectarian groups of can make a safe penetration with the cooperation of inside contacts.[1]

Even if such an insurrection were unsuccessful, however, nuclear sites could fall behind "enemy" lines, before fissile materials could be removed permitting their transfer to terrorists or their allies. Pakistan is the center of nuclear jihad where Islamic Atom Bomb has received a lot of investment from the Muslim world. Islamic Atom Bomb also inculcate other Muslim states the right and religious obligation to

1 *Report of Weapons of Mass Destruction Commission*, initiated by the Swedish Government on a proposal from the United Nations.

acquire weapons of mass destruction (WMD) and use them against non-Muslim states. Since Gen Musharaf came to power, relations between Pakistan and North Korea further developed, while Pakistan paid for North Korea's missiles and related technology, with dollar and wheat purchased from the US and Australia, and diverted to it.

According to an Indian scholar, the late B. Raman, Pakistan is the original birthplace of the concept of the nuclear jihad, which highlighted the need for an Islamic bomb and advocated the right and the religious obligation of Muslims to acquire WMDs and use them, if necessary, to protect their religion.

Chapter 6. Pakistan's Army: Jihadism, Ethnic and Sectarian Affiliations

The sixty-six-year journey of Pakistan army is full of controversies, atrocities, humiliation and torture. The army defended the country from external aggression, created insurgencies and terrorist networks, and ousted civilian governments unconstitutionally. The army still continues to support terrorist and extremist groups and their networks inside Afghanistan and India. This direct and indirect involvement of the armed forces in neighboring states raised serious concern about the future of Pakistan.

On 25 September 2014, Daily Times reported the promotions and changes in the command of the Pakistan armed forces caused controversies. Five serving Lieutenant-Generals retired on 01 October 2014, who wanted their term to be extended, but denied. There were speculations that these generals were tacitly helping political forces to impose Martial Law in Pakistan. The change at the ISI also became the center of debate in international forums. A Ranger Commander, and a friend of the Army Chief General Raheel, Lt Gen Rizwan Akhtar became the Director General of Inter Services Intelligence (ISI). Mr. Rizwan Akhtar had relinquished charge as Sindh Rangers Director General in 2014, and was replaced by Maj Gen Bilal Akbar. The new Chief of ISI, Gen Akhtar's counterterrorism policies in Karachi and South Waziristan were failed as he could not defeat insurgent forces. Prime Minister Nawaz Sharif also denied the promotion of 14 army officers whose record was found controversial.

The 14 major generals who were denied promotions are: Naveed Ahmed, (Artillery), Sector Commander, ISI Sindh, Sohail Abbas Zaidi, (Signals), DG (Technical) at ISI Directorate, Islamabad, Shahzad Sikander, (Engrs) DG Works and Chief Engineer (DG W&CE), Tariq Javed (Infantry), DG Personnel Administration (DG PA), Nadir Zeb, AC, DG Human Resources Development (DG HRD), Iqbal Asi, (Infantry), GOC 19th Infantry Division, Swat, Jamil Rehmat Vance, (Army Services Corps-ASC), DG Remount, Veterinary and Farms Corps (DG RV&FC), Ejaz Shahid, Artillery, IG Frontier Corps (IG FC Baluchistan), Amir Azeem Bajwa, (Signals), DG C&IT Branch, Tariq Ghafoor, (Infantry) GOC 14th Infantry Division, Okara, Muhammad Junaid, (Electrical and Mechanical Engineers-EME), DG Defense Science and Technology Organization, Iftikhar Ahmad Wyne, AC, Chief of Staff, Central Command (COS CC), Salim Raza, (Air Defense-AD), DG Air Defense (DG AD), Abid Nazir, (Infantry) Commander, Logistics Area (Comd Log Area), Peshawar.

On 27 November 2013, Prime Minister Nawaz Sharif appointed Lieutenant General Raheel Sharif as an Army Chief, who later on resisted his government pressure to reform Inter Services Intelligence (ISI). This change of face didn't make effective war against Taliban.[1] His appointment as an Army Chief further complicated the prospect of cold war within the headquarters. General Haroon Aslam resigned in protest, when he was superseded by his two juniors. General Aslam also skipped the farewell dinner of General Ishfaq Kayani, arranged by Prime Minister. Some of his colleagues inveighed against the decision of the Prime Minister. In army headquarters, the pace of ethnic antagonism adversely affected civil military relations.

Military experts do not expect any radical shift under Gen Raheel, who has been deeply involved in counterinsurgency operations during the last 13 years in war against terrorism. He needed to adapt a new military strategy as defined in the Green Book, but his ethnic role raised some important questions. He ruthlessly killed Pashtuns in North Waziristan and FATA. His army raided the houses of Pashtuns in the night, killed women and children, and kidnapped other women. Gen Raheel intended to complete the transfer of purchased nuclear weapons plus ballistic missiles to Saudi Arabia, under the Defense pact between the two states signed in 2004, but it became impossible when Prime Minister Nawaz Sharif decided to bring the army and spy agencies under democratic control.

---

1 *The Frontier Post*, 27 November 2013, and also, the *Express Tribune*, *Dawn* and *the News International*, Islamabad Pakistan. "Raheel has already failed to counter insurgency in a traditional way".

Mr. Nawaz Sharif was reluctant to deliver the bomb to Saudi Arabia. He and his party leaders were deeply anxious about the consequences. They were in trouble that if they delivered the bomb, it will make Pakistan a major contributor to the evolving Middle East nuclear arms race, boosted by six powers nuclear deal, which recognizes Iran's nuclear rights. Some experts concerned that the appointment of Pakistan's new military Chief may also relevant to the covert war waged by Saudi against Iran. The Saudis are using Pakistani Baluchistan against Iran, while Iran uses its own Baluchistan against Pakistani Baluchistan. Gen Raheel and his army needed to decide whether to support Saudi intelligence operation against neighboring Iran in Baluchistan or not.[1]

When Gen. Raheel became the army Chief, he ordered armed forces into North Waziristan, and killed thousands innocent Pashtun Children and women there. More importantly, the army has long association with jihadists and terrorist groups around the world. Now it fights sectarian and ethnic war within its barracks. Generals, commanders and low ranking officers view each other with scorn since the extra-judicial killings of thousands innocent Pashtuns in Swat, Malakand and Waziristan. Pashtun officer and commanders are under surveillance when they refused to fight against the Taliban. In North Waziristan Operation (2014), the army shifted Afghan Taliban commanders to safe houses, and bombed the houses of innocents Pashtuns. After the Swat operation, and the killing and kidnapping of civilian there, the army now faces sharp criticism for its non-professional way of talking insurgency.[2]

The challenge to Pakistan's sovereignty in Swat and Buner was addressed with brute force only after the Taliban appeared to be on a triumphant march to Islamabad. The insurgency in South Waziristan was tackled on a war footing after years of procrastination, but the writ of the Tehrik-e-Taliban Pakistan (TTP) still runs in North Waziristan. The issue of ethnic representation within the armed forces raised serious concerns. Some experts say this is not a national army and view it as the club of Punjabi generals.

The army has failed to develop a true ethnic representation process or motivate Baloch and Sindhis to join the ranks of armed forces, but gained a good experience in killing of innocent civilians. In 1971, during the liberation war in Bangladesh, Pakistan army generals, officers and soldiers raped more than 450,000 young girls and women, and killed

---

1 *Ibid.27 Nov, 2013.*
2 *Daily Times*, 03 October 3013.

hundreds of writers, journalists and men of letters. In March 1971, in Dhaka, Pakistan army killed 50,000 Bengalis in a two days military operation (Operation Searchlight).

In Baluchistan, thousands Balochs men and women disappeared in military operations during the last 13 years, while bodies of hundreds of missing people began turning up on roadsides. Since the killing of Akbar Bugti in 2006, more than 18,000 Balochs men have been abducted or forcefully disappeared by ISI and military intelligence, in which of them 1500 were students and teachers. On 29 November 2013, nineteen personnel of Paramilitary force, who had allegedly taken away 35 detainees, were directed by the Supreme Court to appear before the CID office in Quetta.[1]

In February 2015, after learning that 4,557 bodies were found in the country over the past four years, the Supreme Court asked the federal government to effectively address in a coordinated manner the handling of unclaimed bodies as well as the issue of missing persons. A two-judge Supreme Court bench, headed by Justice Jawad S. Khawaja, took up an application of Nasrullah Baloch, chairman of the Voice for Baloch Missing Persons, who invited attention of the court towards lack of a proper system for handling of mutilated or unclaimed bodies found at different places in Baluchistan.

The detainee men, women and young children were abused, raped, humiliated and then killed in secret prisons. Soldiers and officers of Pakistan army kidnapped beautiful girls and women from Swat, Momand and FATA as well. Minor children were killed in front of their parents. Moreover, Supreme Court of Pakistan ordered law enforcement agencies to arrest those army officers responsible for the enforced disappearance, but they didn't arrest them because of their affiliation with ISI and military intelligence. The army has been facing many difficulties in conducting effective counter-insurgency operations, even though, it has deployed more than 150,000 soldiers in the Khyber-Pakhtunkhwa and FATA, and has suffered over 15,700 casualties, including over 5,000 dead since 2008. Total casualties including civilians numbered 50,000 since 2001.[2]

This brutal and aimless war against their own people caused officers and soldiers of the army deep frustration and mental-illness. Their desertion greatly disturbed military leadership. There are reports that more than 3000 soldiers joined Taliban while a good number

---

1 *South Asian Terrorism Portal*, 29 November 2013.
2 "Pakistan Army: Coping with Internal Security Challenges," Issue Brief: By Brigadier (Retd) Gurmeet Kanwal, *Journal of Institute of peace and Conflict Studies*. September 2013

of soldiers and officers deployed in Waziristan, FATA, Mohmand, Dir, and Swat refused to fight against their own people. In South Waziristan agency, journalist Amir Mir reported, more than 400 Pakistani soldiers joined Taliban in 2007. Many of the army officers do not want to fight against the Taliban. Army Chief, Gen Raheel Sharif has never been succeeded to address this issue immediately.

After the killings of 2,500 innocent Pashtun children by the army in Red Mosque in Islamabad, majority of militant groups pulled out of peace treaties. Military spokesman Maj. Gen. Waheed Arshad once confirmed the desertions in the army in large number. The number of army soldiers killed at the hands of Taliban and sectarian groups in FATA, Waziristan, and Swat crossed the number of those killed in the wars (1965 and 1971) against India.

An intelligence report presented to top military brass in Islamabad confirmed the desertion of 900 soldiers who join the Taliban network. There are reports that Pashtun and Punjabi officers do not want to see each other, while the reports of infighting are more heartbreaking. Moreover, cases of soldiers killing their own colleagues in FATA, Kuram and Waziristan agencies are on the rise. Interestingly, mutiny has also been reported in three infantry brigades; Parachinar Brigade, Kohat Brigade and Turbat Brigade, with at least six recent fratricide cases in the army formations. In 2013, Times of India reported, number of Pakistan army officers belonging to Medical Corps, including Lt Colonel deserted in the US. These officers recorded interesting statements about the brutality of warlords against the people of Baluchistan and Khyber Pakhtunkhwa.[1]

Pakistani journalist, Saleem Shahzad (2011) also revealed about the army officers resigns to join their Taliban colleagues. He even named the officers who joined the Taliban ranks now fighting their country army. Pakistani scientist, Dr. Parvez Hoodbhoy depicted a transmogrified picture of Pakistani armed forces:

> The moral of a fine fighting force plummet still further when its soldiers are ordered to fight those coreligionists who claim to be fighting for Islam. The reported refusal of some military unites to confront the Taliban during the operation of South Waziristan is said to have shocked senior officers and severely limited their battle options in North Waziristan. The military's internal difficulties come at a time when its public esteem has hit near a new low, approaching that which existed in 1971. Today, it is the object of scorn and open

---

1 *Times of India*, 2013, "Pakistan army officers belonging to Medical Corps, including Lt Colonel deserted in the US".

profanities. The military's woeful inability to defend its own personnel and assets has tarnished its image still further.[1]

Inter Services Intelligence (ISI) has so for been badly failed to counter the Taliban insurgency. ISI played contradictory role of espionage, tortured civilians and supported anti-democracy campaigns in Pakistan. The ISI killed and tortured Bengalis in 1971, and ruined Afghanistan through its proxies (Gul Baddin Hekmatyar Burhanuddin Rabbani, Dostum, Haji Deen Muhammad, Sayyaf, Mujaddidi, Pir Gailani and Taliban terrorist groups) from 1992 to 2014. The agency looted Afghan museums, libraries, houses, arms depots and kidnapped Dr Najeebullah and killed him in his own country.

In 25 September 2014, Dr. Mohammad Taqi quoted ambassador Tomsen who noted that four Taliban, including, a Pakistani ISI officer, drove directly to the UN compound. Their mission was to lure the former Afghan President out of the diplomatically protected UN premises." Mullah Abdul Razzaq, according to Dr. Taqi, was the Taliban ringleader who carried out the torture, killing, mutilation and desecration of the corpses —a war crime by any definition—at the behest of his Pakistani minders. Interestingly, in 2009, former President Asif Ali Zardari admitted in an Islamabad conference, that Pakistan had, in the past, created extremist and terrorist networks to destabilize India and Afghanistan.

India and Afghanistan have long been accusing ISI and its religious proxies for interfering in their territories. The ISI provides weapons to Afghan Taliban, war criminals and Kashmiri fighters to destabilize both the states. In October 2010, former President Musharraf said that Pakistan army recruited extremist groups to fight India and Afghanistan. The ISI has often been accused for terrorist attacks in Indian Parliament in 2001, in Mumbai, in 2006 and 2008, Varanasi bombing and in Hyderabad.[2]

In FATA and Waziristan, the army is in an extremely embarrassing position. An army that cannot fight internal war supplied tanks and military personnel to Sri Lanka against the Tamil rebels. By supplying high military tech to the Sri Lankan army, Pakistan lost the trust of

---

1 "Pakistan Army: Divided it Stands." Pervez Hoodbhoy, Middle East Research and Information Centre, 11 July, 2011.
2 *Daily Times*, October 2010, "former President Musharraf said that Pakistan army recruited extremist groups to fight India in Kashmir and Afghanistan." *However, in 2009, President Asif Ali Zardari admitted in an Islamabad conference, that Pakistan had, in the past, created extremist and terrorist networks to destabilize India and Afghanistan.*

India. The army is uneasy about the Indian presence in Afghanistan and its relations with the country are in strain. Gen Raheel needs to craft a strategy that would save his country from another civil war in Afghanistan after the withdrawal of US force in the end of 2014.

There are Sunni, Shia and Tablighi brigades in the army, represent the Saudi and Iranian version of Islam. Tablighy, Salafi, Ahmadi and Deobandi affiliations are on the rise. The Northern Light Infantry (NLI) is composed of Sunni and Shia sectarian elements which promotes sectarian conflicts in four provinces. In 1990s, army officers supplied weapons to both Sunni and Shia groups in Punjab and Khyber Pakhtunkhwa provinces. NLI is based in Gilgit Baltistan which represents several sects. The Sunni-Shia conflict in Pakistan, Afghanistan and the Arab world has further divided Pakistan army, while sometimes; war of words or physical clash between Shia and Sunni officers is reported by insiders.

However, will Gen. Sharif give Prime Minister Sharif the freedom to do what he wants? Will Gen Raheel scrutinize Mr. Nawaz Sharif policies towards India or not, but if Generals want to follow the instruction of the Green Book, they will support Prime Minister in his friendly policies towards India. But, this is impossible for an army that shamelessly surrendered to the Indian army in 1971. Mr. Nawaz Sharif is cautious and moving slowly towards India. He wants peace with India and civilian control over the military command. In May 2014, when Prime Minister Nawaz Sharif invited Indian Prime Minister Narender Modi to Pakistan, General Raheel Sharif and his colleagues refused to honor him.

Prime Minister Nawaz is not sure about the army commitment to protect democracy and sovereignty of the country. He, however, openly criticize the armed forces for their inability to counter insurgency in a traditional way. A report of the Institute for Defense Studies of India analyzed the army links with extremist organization and Taliban:

> The PML-N openly questioned the army's capabilities to protect Pakistan's sovereignty. Both Nawaz Sharif and Choudhry Nisar raised questions about its accountability. Even on the Ideological turf, anti state insurgent forces like the Tehreek-e-Taliban Pakistan (TTP) openly challenged the army commitment to Islamic principles, which has led to an ideological conflict between moderate and conservative elements within its ranks. Many of these, especially at the lower echelons of the army, are reported to be sympathetic to the cause of TTP. The virus of religious radicalism has also affected the officer class,

as demonstrated by the arrest of Brigadier Ali affiliated to the Hezb-ut-Tehreer in the aftermath of the Mehran attack.[1]

Prominent Pakistani journalist, Najam Sethi argued: "Fortunately, it is dawning on the generals that the existential threat comes from internal Muslim non-state actors rather than external Hindu India. But the problem is that they are still unable or unwilling to fashion a comprehensive new doctrine to replace the old one."[2]

1 *Pakistan on the Edge, Pakistan Project Report-2013*, Institute for Defense Studies and Analyses, India. http://www.idsa.in/system/files/book_Pakistanonedge
2 "Afghan key to India and US." *The Friday Times*, 06 December 2013

Chapter 7. The Military and Nawaz Sharif in Pakistan

Rana Banerji

Much is being read between the lines about the inclinations of the Nawaz Sharif regime to improve relations with India. However, several potential conflict areas remain, especially in civil military relations, which may hamper Nawaz Sharif's capacity to move too fast. No doubt, former Army Chief Gen Ashfaq Pervez Kayani's gesture to call on the Prime Minster designate seemed a refreshingly "correct' departure from the past, acknowledging a significant democratic mandate. However, it may have been intended to provide a sobering perspective on security imperatives which face the new government. It could also be seen as a move to disarm, given the history of past suspicions.

It should have become amply clear that new threats to domestic security from Islamic radicals notwithstanding, the Army's abiding priorities have not changed. It will not countenance interference in charting the course of key security and foreign policies, especially those pertaining to India, Afghanistan and nuclear issues.

Down Memory Lane

If history is taken as a guide, whenever buttressed by a strong mandate, Nawaz Sharif has shown a penchant to take on the "Deep State,' flaunting his "Punjabi' credentials and claimed support within Army "Other Ranks (OR s)' or even the "Officer' class at the middle level. During his first premiership, between November,'90 to July'93, when Gen Asif Nawaz was the Army Chief (16 August1991–8th January1993), several issues of discord came up. When Asif Nawaz transferred Lt Gen Hamid Gul from the II Corps Command in Multan, as he was not confident of his loyalties as second in command when travelling abroad, the latter demurred against moving to a non-command post (POF, Wah). He tried to use political influence to stall his transfer. He was retired by Asif Nawaz.

Later, the Chief had to sometimes cater to unwarranted recommendations on postings and promotions of senior officers. Apprised about rumors circulating that the Ittefaq Group was distributing BMW cars as gifts from Abba ji's (Nawaz Sharif's father, Mian Mohd Sharif) to cultivate gullible generals, the Army Chief confronted Nawaz, who did not deny the allegation, rather he offered the keys of a new BMW to Asif Nawaz, urging him not to keep driving his old Toyota Corona as it was not 'befitting' for the Chief! Asif Nawaz politely returned the keys and walked away.

Quoted in a vernacular publication, Ghaddar Kaun, Nawaz Sharif described Asif Nawaz as "a headstrong individual who did not give him due regard as PM." The PM and the Army Chief were not on the same page over handling of the situation in Sindh and the splintering, infighting between Mohajir Quami movement factions(Altaf vs Haqiqi). Nawaz brought in his father's tablighi acolyte, Lt Gen Javed Nasir as the new DG, ISI without consulting Asif Nawaz.

When the latter died suddenly after a heart attack in January 1993, and there were allegations of arsenic poisoning. Begum Nawaz received anonymous letters from Nawaz Sharif's Raiwind house claiming use of special cloth to polish plates on which the Chief was served refreshments. Though Asif Nawaz's body was exhumed and an inquiry held by US forensic experts, these allegations could not be substantiated.

When Gen Abdul Waheed Kakar was appointed the next Army Chief, Nawaz Sharif did not agree with President Ghulam Ishaq Khan's choice. Relations between the two soured further, leading to Nawaz's dismissal in April'93 with the President using his powers under Art 58(2) (b) of the Constitution. Nawaz challenged this in Court and Supreme Court Chief Justice, Nasim Hassan Shah deemed the dismissal illegal. Later, the Army Chief, Gen Kakar had to mediate, leading to a situation where both Ghulam Ishaq Khan and Nawaz Sharif were made to resign and Pakistan went into fresh elections, which brought Benazir Bhutto back in for her second tenure as PM.

Nawaz's Authoritarian Streak

In the 1997 National Assembly elections, Nawaz Sharif's PML (N) received a massive mandate- 45.9% votes and 155/207 seats, with PPP getting only 18 seats. This brought to fore Nawaz's authoritarian streak—he introduced the 13th Amendment, doing away with the President's powers to dismiss the PM and dissolve Assemblies. A new chapter of confrontation was opened up with the Supreme Court Chief Justice, Sajjad Ali Shah, whose court was stormed by PML (N) supporters. The Army Chief, Gen Karamat refrained from responding to Justice Shah's call for assistance from the Army.

More differences surfaced over political demands for use of the Army in non-military functions. Lt. Gen Khwaja Ziauddin Butt was brought in as the new DG, ISI, once again without approval of the Army Chief. Karamat criticized profligacy of certain grandiose civilian government schemes and demanded setting up of a National Security Council in a speech at the Naval Staff College, Lahore in October,'98. This incensed Nawaz Sharif and he called in the Chief to remonstrate. Karamat quit as Chief.

Musharraf—The Love-Hate Relationship

When Musharraf was appointed COAS over the heads of two seniors—Chief of General Staff Ali Kuli Khan Khattak, and Lt Gen Khalid Nawaz Malik, ostensibly, because he was a Mohajir. Nawaz was advised by his close confidants that he could reach over a Mohajir Chief's head to Punjabi ORs and officers, to keep Musharraf quiescent. These pious hopes proved short lived. As claimed by Musharraf in his book, *Line of Fire*, he sympathized with Karamat after taking over as new Chief, assuring that "never again would he allow a Chief to be ill-treated" thus.

Kargil

Though Musharraf claims Nawaz Sharif was taken on board and kept informed of the Kargil incursion plan, before Indian Prime Minister Vajpayee's Lahore bus yatra (February 1999), the operation remained a closely guarded secret. In later Pakistani post-mortems, it was seen as the handiwork of "the Gang of Four," a coterie of generals close to Musharraf—Maj Gen Javed Hassan of the Force Command, Northern Areas, CGS Lt Gen Mohd Aziz, X Corps Commander Lt Gen Mehmood Ahmed and the Chief himself. Even the DGMO, Lt

Gen Tauqir Zia was "odd man out' and the DG, ISI Ziauddin only sensed something grave was brewing, much later. Distrust increased between the civilian executive and the military leadership, to the spectacular extent of the DG, MI bugging the ISI chief and the latter returning the compliment.

In September 1999, matters came to head as Musharraf sacked XII Corps Commander, Lt Gen Tariq Pervaiz, a close relative of Raja Nadir Pervaiz, Communications Minister in the Nawaz Sharif Cabinet and a 1965 war hero, on charges of leaking minutes of Corps Commanders' meetings to the political executive. Nawaz sent brother Shahbaz as emissary to the United States to focus on apprehensions of a coup attempt, urging US mediation. A last minute attempt was made to appease Musharraf by appointing him conterminously to the vacant four star slot of Chairman, Joint Chiefs of Staff Committee.

After the 12th October 1999 coup, Nawaz Sharif was taken prisoner, hauled in chains on a seven hour flight from Islamabad via Multan to Karachi and back, before being lodged in solitary confinement first in Adiala and later in Attock jail. Saudi intervention and a commitment not to return to politics for 21 years led to his exile in Jeddah. The banishment was reduced to 10 years. Nawaz was able to finally return to Pakistan after 8 years, taking advantage of the burgeoning civil society/lawyers' agitation on the issue of restoration of the judges, which caused the ground under President Musharraf's feet to disintegrate quickly.

Though Nawaz remained carefully reticent on the judicial fate befalling Musharraf on his return and during the election campaign, presently he may have to contend with a growing demand from a resurgent PML (N) to begin impeachment proceedings against the former Army Chief under Art 6 of the Constitution. Already, Musharraf has had to face the wrath of the Courts in the Judges' dismissal case, the Benazir Bhutto murder enquiry and the Akbar Bugti killing. Petitions implicating him in the Lal Masjid case are also pending. Though one option could be to let the tortuous legal procedures in various cases take their own course, Nawaz will have to think twice before humiliating Musharraf beyond a point, lest the constituency of senior Army officers takes umbrage. Already Gen Kayani has admonished the higher Judiciary to set limits to "retribution' for mistakes of the past

A More Mature Nawaz Sharif?

There are reports to suggest that adversity and exile may have metamorphosed Nawaz Sharif into a more patient and mature leader, capable of listening to differing points of view and eschewing rash decisions. Though originally a creation of the Army, Nawaz Sharif's three decades long political journey indicates he has managed to successfully move away from their apron strings and cast himself as a "mass based' politician, roping in Punjabi feudals and businessmen in an alliance for power sharing.

Yet questions persist about his political sagacity and attention span to face up to complex issues like how to deal with the Tehrik-e-Taliban, appointment of the new Army Chief, Afghan policy and relations with India. He will have to tread warily on all these issues, taking care not to cross the Army's path. This article published in the Institute of Peace and Conflict Studies, has been taken with a written permission of writer Rana Banerji. [1]

CHAPTER 8. CIVIL–MILITARY RELATIONS

On 04 February 2014, in the presence of top military commanders, Prime Minister Nawaz Sharif delivered an important speech in National Defense University, Islamabad, in which he emphasized on constitutional order and friendly relations between the GHQ and the government. After that speech, Mr. Nawaz Sharif received mixed signals from GHQ, including warnings of the commander of armed forces, Gen Raheel Sharif. In response to these signals, government reacted with its own style, while two cabinet Ministers, Mr. Khwaja Asif and Mr. Saad Rafiq severely criticized the nefarious designs of military establishment against the elected government. In Corps Commanders conference, Army Chief expressed displeasure on these statements and said the army to preserve its dignity.[1]

Mr. Nawaz Sharif wanted more central policymaking role for civilians in areas that the Army had traditionally dominated. However, Sharif publically stated that the Army and the civilian government are "on the same page." Mr. Nawaz Sharif, whose sympathies were clearly with the Pakistani wing of Taliban emerged as a strong political leader, the new commander was known for his anti-Taliban views; he lost no time ordering the air force to bomb Taliban's bases in North Waziristan for its operations across the border in Afghanistan. The difference was clear, and the resentment of civilian population against the illegal business of military general was also clear. Mr. Nawaz Sharif's resolve was strong. He

---

1 "Nawaz links state's survival to respect of constitutional order," *Dawn*, 04, February 2014.

wanted to control the army and its intelligence agencies, by providing huge funds and technology to Intelligence Bureau (IB).

On 19 June 2013, a high level meeting at the Prime Minister office over the evaluation of security situation in Pakistan agreed on the point, that an effective mechanism is a must to improve cooperation among intelligence agencies. The meeting was chaired by Prime Minister Nawaz Sharif. Meanwhile, Interior Minister informed the army Chief about the conflicting reports of ISI and military intelligence, regarding terror-related incidents in Baluchistan province. Interior Minister provided evidence of the incoherent approach of intelligence agencies to the new wave of terrorism in Baluchistan.[1]

Pakistan has a strong network of intelligence, while ISI is considered the most professional and patriotic intelligence organization, but the way these agencies operate in Baluchistan, FATA, Swat, Dir and Waziristan, is an un-professional. The ISI runs, fosters and supports numbers of terrorist groups in Afghanistan, India and Pakistan. The army does not help people in countering Taliban insurgency; they even alienated citizens from the state. The Wall Street Journal published a news story about Pakistan's military operation in Swat, Momand and Orakzai areas, where numerous people were killed:

> The army's operations in FATA drive unbelievable numbers of people from their homes. 300,000 people from the Bajaur and Momand Agencies were driven out from their homes by Operation "Sher Dil" in 2008-2009.[2]

Military operations in Kurram, Orakzai, and Momand agencies "caused nearly two hundred thousand people to flee from their homes." Momand Agency had already suffered previously. On 23 March, 2010, armed forces launched military operation against the Taliban to clear Orakzai Agency. A search operation in the area later resulted in the seizure of large amounts of foreign currency, night vision goggles, communication equipment, various small arms and heavy weapons, rocket launchers, and anti-aircraft guns.

Since the Army's campaigns in FATA never permanently dislodge the Taliban, the people of each tribal agency get killed and uprooted again and again. Rural areas, like Kalat, Khuzdar-Wadh, Panjgur, Turbat, Bolan Pass and Dera Bugti, are in the grip of insurgency. Baloch

---

1 *Daily Times,*19 June 2013
2 *Ibid,* 2009, and also, "Pakistan & Afghanistan: Domestic Pressure and Regional Threats: The Role of Politics in Pakistan's Economy." Dr. Ishrat Hussain. *Journal of International Affairs*, Vol. 63, No.1, winter 2009.

insurgents have established camps across the province and send small groups to fight against Pakistan army. Kidnappings and car-lifting are profitable business. Besides criminals, there are politically influential people being involved in money-making crime.[1]

In Baluchistan, the United Baloch Army operates with full swing, Tehrik-e-Taliban Pakistan carry out attacks under fake names, Punjabi Taliban openly collect taxes from local landlords in Southern Punjab, and Mullah Abdul Aziz of red-mosque again wants to wage jihad against the army. These new developments raised serious questions about the credibility of intelligence agencies that, either they tacitly support anti-state forces, or failed to positively respond to the looming threatening clouds across the country. The gap still exists. Military intelligence agencies, field intelligence units, and even ISI do not sincerely cooperate with the police and civilian intelligence agencies in countering militancy, terrorism and extremism in Pakistan.

No institution in Pakistan is willing to address the wrongly designed counterterrorism strategy and the policy that alienated citizens from the state. Journalist Najam Sethi noted that the counterterrorism unit idea is directly linked to civilian military relations, and there is no denying the fact that the army is not ready to give even a little bit space to civilian as far as the national security and country's foreign policy are concerned. A statement of the Army Chief was an eye-opener as he warned both the government and journalists on their criticism against the military and its private business.

Before his statement, two journalists were allegedly attacked by the agencies. "Pakistan Army upholds the sanctity of all institutions and will resolutely preserve its own dignity and institutional pride," Chief of Army Staff Gen Raheel Sharif said, while speaking to Special Service Group (SSG) commandos at Ghazi Base near Tarbela. His statement was taken as a stern warning to the civilian government against its negotiation with the TTP leaders who killed, injured, and humiliated the army. The ISPR statement noted that the army chief had made the remarks in response to "the concerns of soldiers on undue criticism of the institution (army) in civilian circles. Gen Raheel's statement came a week after Mr. Musharraf was indicted by the Special Court on five counts of high treason, a charge that potentially carries the death penalty.[2]

---

1 *Daily Times*, "The Civilian-Military Conundrum," Lal Khan, 08 December 2013.
2 *Dawn*, 07 April 2014, and also, *the News International*, 08 April 2014. And also, *Daily Times and Daily Outlook Afghanistan*, 07 April 2014.

Lawyer Babar Sattar viewed Musharaf's case in the context of civil military relations in Pakistan:

> If Nawaz Sharif was convinced that the Musharraf trial is the right thing to do and is a key to fixing the civil-military imbalance, shouldn't it have been conducted in the most solemn manner? The army chief could have been candidly advised that there would be no deal-making on the Musharraf issue. It could be ensured that the trial comes to be seen as one related exclusively to the rule of law, devoid of controversy and lacking manifestations of revenge—and is not used to engage in bravado or to draw political mileage. The army chief's posturing at Ghazi camp was essentially cathartic. Notwithstanding any sense within the military high command of being cheated by politicos post-indictment, the ISPR statement was essentially meant to vent the collective anger of the khakis.[1]

In 2013, Defense Minister Khwaja Muhammad Asif severely criticized GHQ and its intelligence infrastructure on the floor of National Assembly. The Defense Minister demanded a thorough investigation into the power abuse and illegal business of military generals. Mr. Khwaja Asif raised the killing in Afghanistan by ISI and its cronies. From 1992 to 1993, various mujahedin factions supported by ISI and Iran battled over Kabul, and committed countless atrocities against the innocent civilian population. During this conflict, tens of thousands of civilians were brutally killed and injured amidst the fighting. Thousands of people were disappeared or abducted by private militia groups, and most were never seen again.[2]

According to Human Rights report, Pakistan's government failed to act against abuses by the security and intelligence agencies, which continued to allow extremist groups to attack religious minorities. Human Rights Watch in its World Report for 2013, criticized the authorities for their inabilities to address attacks against journalists and human rights defenders, and committed serious abuses in counter-terrorism operations. In its 665-page report, Human Rights Watch assessed progress on human rights during the past year in more than 90 countries, including an analysis of the aftermath of the Arab Spring.[3]

---

1 "Small men with big egos," Babar Sattar, *Dawn and Pakistan Affairs*, 14 April 2014.
2 "*Express Tribune*," 10 April 2014.
3 *Dawn*, 02, February 2014, *Huffington Post*, 04 February and *Human Rights Watch*, 05 February 2014, and its previous report of 2013, also, Mr. *Ayaz Amir wrote that Pakistan was losing war not because the Taliban were strong but his country's position is weak. Also, Daily the News International,* Islamabad. On 21 January 2014

On 9 April 2014, Dunya News reported Corps Commander Conference presided by Army Chief General Raheel Sharif, expressed displeasure over the statement made by Defense Minister Khawaja Asif. Other matter that came under discussion included; review of internal and external security, terrorist attack in Rawalpindi, and determination to strengthen democracy. According to Dunya News sources, Army Chief decided to meet Prime Minister upon his return from China.[1]

In his special commentary, prominent Indian scholar and commentator, Mr. Rana Banerji highlighted the crisis of civil military relations in Pakistan: "It should have become amply clear that new threats to domestic security from Islamic radicals notwithstanding, the Army's abiding priorities have not changed. It will not countenance interference in charting the course of key security and foreign policies, especially those pertaining to India, Afghanistan and nuclear issues".[2]

Though, the 2013 elections in Pakistan marked a significant watershed, establishing a civilian government in the country, but civil military relations still remains troubled. As a Prime Minister, Mr. Nawaz Sharif tried to reduce the influence of military generals in policy making process, but failed and faced tough resistance from the GHQ. Finally, he was forced to promulgate Pakistan Protection Ordinance (PPO) to provide legal status to the forceful disappearance. The new ordinance states that:

> Security of life, property and dignified living of our own people shall be the prime goal for all functionaries of the state...writ of the state shall be restored with full might of the law; those to pursue fruit of terror and fear, regardless of nationality, color, creed or religion shall be treated as enemy aliens and dealt with strictly without any compunction." Now intelligence agencies including ISI are free to kidnap, torture, forcefully disappear and kill civilians. As the law clearly stated that suspects shall be treated as enemy, they will not spare any journalist, lawyer, newspaper editor and writer who criticize their policies of alienating citizen from the state.[3]

---

1 On 9 April 2014, *Dunya News reported* ,"Corps Commander Conference presided by Army Chief General Raheel Sharif expressed displeasure over statement made by Defense Minister Khawaja Asif."
2 *"The Military and Nawaz Sharif in Pakistan,"* Rana Banerji, Institute of Peace and Conflict Studies, 05 June 2013.
3 "Nawaz asks political parties to support Pakistan Protection Ordinance." On 26 October 2013, *Such TV reported.* "Prime Minister Nawaz Sharif wrote to all political parties." On January 16, 2013, *BBC* reported "hundreds of protesters in Khyber Pakhtunkhwa displayed the bodies of at least 14 people who they said were victims of extra-judicial killings outside government office in Peshawar".

The involvement of Pakistani armed forces in politics and their humiliation of civilian government became the center of debate in international media. Writer Attar Rabbani criticized the military ruler's offensive policy towards civilian government:

> Politically speaking the military in Pakistan has been disproportionately politicized like no other. Pakistan's army and its intelligence wing, the Inter-Services Intelligence (ISI) has long been at the helm of affairs in the country. They have directly or indirectly held onto power using coups, religious extremists/militants and weakness of the existing political parties and have been at the center of decision making since its creation in August 1947.[1]

In fact, the military including its intelligence wing, the ISI, over the decades, have come to occupy central position in political calculus, to the extent that now it has profound business/economic interests well beyond permitted precincts. In 16 April 2010, Wesley C. Jenkins developed a thesis on the issue of civil military relations, in which he discussed Pakistan army in a historical perspective. From 1971 to 1998, Wesley summarized civil-military conflict and the complicated task of Pakistani Armed Forces:

> During the government of Zulfiqar Ali Bhutto (1971-1977) and the second government of Nawaz Sharif (1997–1999), Pakistan experienced relatively strong—though temporary—civilian control of the military. Both cases support the hypothesis that periods of greater civilian control have been associated with a single locus of civilian political authority, a strong popular support base, and limited threats to military core interests. Sharif was less successful, however, in containing threats to military core interests in late 1998 and 1999.... By late 1998, official sources reportedly observed that Pakistan's top military commanders were increasingly concerned about the country's security situation.... When COAS Karamat complained of Sharif's indifference toward the military's concerns, the prime minister made matters worse by unceremoniously forcing him into early retirement. Their task is complicated by the fact that the top brass are loath to surrender the power and privileges that they enjoyed during the years of military rule.[2]

---

1 "The Prospect of Civilian Rule in Pakistan," Attar Rabbani, This article was published in a journal of Qurtuba University, January-March 2012. www.qurtuba.edu.pk. http://www.qurtuba. edu.pk/thedialogue/The%20Dialogue/8_1/Dialogue_January_ March-2012-1-16.pdf.
2 Mr. Wesley C. Jenkins thesis on the issue of civil military relations, in which the author discussed Pakistan army in a historical perspective. *An Elusive Balance: Explaining Pakistan's Fluctuating Civil-*

In an Asia Society meeting, it was agreed that the military has long been a powerful political player; the people of Pakistan witnessed dramatic changes in the relationship between the military and the civilian government. The government and courts are unable to prosecute a general who killed innocent children in the Red Mosque, Islamabad. Writer Amir Zia takes the case of Mr. Musharaf as a serious issue:

> Sharif in his rare statement vowed that the military will "resolutely preserve its own dignity and institutional pride," the two ministers also appear unrepentant for their harsh remarks ridiculing General Pervez Musharraf. This apparent tiff between the government and the army certainly serves as an ominous sign for the country's fragile democratic process even if it has not become alarming at this stage. The fundamental question that remains is: what forced the army chief to issue this stern warning that reflects the collective sentiment of the armed forces? Certainly a couple of irresponsible statements by the two federal ministers alone could not have triggered this reaction. This highlights the problem within civil-military relations and the feeling of distrust that seems to be growing between these two important institutions at a time when the Pakistani security forces and agencies remain the prime target of various anti-state political and militant groups as well as foreign powers.[1]

The issue became more complicated as Nawaz Sharif refused to compromise on some institutional reforms within the army and ISI. On 17 April 2014, Mr. Sharif called a meeting to discuss dialogue process with the Taliban and relations with Iran. The National Security Meeting was attended by the country's top military leadership. Army Chief Gen Raheel Sharif, Chairman Joint Chiefs of Staff Committee General Rashad Mahmood, Director General Inter-Services Intelligence (DG ISI) Lieutenant General Zaheerul Islam and Director General Intelligence Bureau (DG IB) Aftab Sultan were present in the meeting. On the other hand, PM's Advisor on Foreign Affairs Sartaj Aziz, Defense Minister Khwaja Asif, Interior Minister Chaudhry Nisar and Information Minister Pervaiz Rashid were present from the civilian side.[2]

Military Relationship. A Thesis submitted to the Faculty of the Graduate School of Arts and Sciences of Georgetown University By, Wesley C. Jenkins, B.S.F.S. Washington, DC, 16 April 2010.

1 "Brinkmanship won't pay," Amir Zia. *The News International,* 14 April 2014

2 "On 17 April 2014, Mr. Sharif called a meeting to discuss dialogue process with the Taliban and relations with Iran." *Daily news.* "The

Before this meeting, Prime Minister Nawaz Sharif discussed the political situation with former President Asif Ali Zardari and his party leaders. On 17 April, 2014, the Nation reported the two main political forces' message of unity. The meeting was followed by delegation-level consultations between the PPP and Pakistan Muslim League-Nawaz. Interior Minister Ch Nisar Ali Khan and Defense Minister Khwaja Asif were conspicuous by absence. Premier Nawaz himself received Zardari, on his arrival at PM House by helicopter.[1]

On 03 January 2015, Dawn reported, Prime Minister Nawaz Sharif addressed All Parties Conference held at PM House in Islamabad. In the conference, political leadership proved unable to defend the constitutional and democratic roots of the system or resist the generals' demands. In fact Pakistan needs a coherent strategy to fight militancy and political and military leaders to work together. But military courts were not the answer. All Parties Conference (APC), chaired by Prime Minister Nawaz Sharif, reached a consensus to bring amendments in the constitution for the establishment of special courts for speedy trial of the terrorists. The political and military leadership of Pakistan, after a 5-hour-long meeting, agreed over the formation of military courts to expedite terrorism related cases. Moreover, it was also decided that Operation Zerb-e-Azb should be extended to the cities so that the miscreants hiding amongst the citizens could be apprehended with the help of the local people.

In the first week of January 2015, the experts working group of the Anti-Terrorism National Action Plan (ATNAP) Committee forwarded 17 recommendations to ATNAP, which was discussed in Islamabad within the fold of the All Parties Conference (APC). The National Counter-Terrorism Authority (NACTA) was made effective. A special task force was set up for the fight against terrorism. It was proposed that it number 5,000 strong, including retired military personnel, 1,000 to be deployed in Islamabad and 1,000 each in all the provinces.

On 06, 01, 2015, Dawn reported the National Assembly adopted the 21st Constitutional Amendment unopposed after 247 Members of National Assembly voted in favor of the law aimed to set up constitutionally protected military courts to try civilian terrorism suspects. Pakistan People's Party (PPP) Senator Raza Rabbani was in tears after voting in the upper house on the 21st Constitutional

case of Pashtun Genocide in the Country," Kahar Zalmay. *Asian Human Rights Commission*, May 2013.
1 *The Nation*, 17 April, 2014.

Amendment for setting up military courts in the country. Rabbani said that he voted on the amendment against his own conscience, adding that he had never felt more ashamed in his life. "I have been in the Senate for more than 12 years, but have never been as ashamed as I am today and I cast my vote against my conscious," said the PPP leader. Two leading Islamist parties, the Jamaat-e-Islami and the Jamiat Ulema-e-Islam faction led by Fazal-ur-Rehman, abstained from voting on the bill,

Military courts are part of the political response to the massacre of more than 500 schoolboys in the city of Peshawar in December 2014, which shocked even a country that has grown accustomed to militancy. The country's radical religious parties are also uneasy about measures to tackle militants who claim to be fighting in the name of Islam. The 21st Constitutional Amendment Bill and the Army Act (Amendment) Bill 2015 were approved unanimously by both houses of parliament within a matter of hours to provide constitutional cover to summary military courts. On 07 January 2015, Dawn reported amendment in the Pakistan Army Act (PAA) 1952 was added which stated that civilians can now be tried by military courts.

The amendment in section 2 (d) of the PAA empowered military courts to try civilians facing charges of terrorism or abetting terrorist activity. Individuals illegally crossing national boundaries can now be tried by military courts, and those convicted by military courts have no right of appeal before civilian courts. Another amendment to subsection (IV) also empowered military authorities to take action against those who "belong to any terrorist group or organization using the name of religion or sect" and waging "war against Pakistan" if they commit an offence that has been mentioned in the Protection of Pakistan Act (PPA). The bill, however, is silent about section 133 of the PAA, which deals with the right of appeal against the judgment of military court in the superior courts. Dawn reported. National and international rights organizations have vociferously opposed the idea of setting up the military courts and said they would only perpetuate a cycle of violence. The Human Rights Commission of Pakistan (HRCP) termed the courts against the law and the Constitution.

Chapter 9. Military Operations and the Killing of Pashtuns and Balochs

During the last 6 decades troublesome history of its wrongly designed policies, Pakistan army deposed, arrested and elected several Prime Ministers. The army is a strong and well established force. The army came into existence in 1947, to defend the territory of the newly independent state. In April 2013, a London based International Institute for Strategic Studies (IISS), estimated Pakistan's Armed Forces as an active force of 725,000 personnel. Since 1947, it has been engaged in various military operations in and outside the country, including border skirmishes with neighboring Afghanistan. According to the article 243 of the Constitution of the Islamic Republic of Pakistan, the President is the Chief Commander of the armed forces, and the Chief of Army Staff is appointed by the President with the consent of the Prime Minister of the country.[1]

In 1958, the army took over power when Muhammad Ayub Khan came to power. Mr. Ayub Khan, later on, in 1965, attacked India and captured parts of the border areas inside the country. In 1968 and 1969, Mr. Ayub Khan lost the confidence of the people and relinquished office to his colleague, Muhammad Yahya Khan. General Yahya and his colleagues dismembered the country.

In 1965, a strong and well-trained military commando force, "Special Services Group" (SSG) was established. That year, war between Pakistan and India created fear and harassment in South Asia. Pakistan army

---

1 April 2013, London based International Institute for Strategic Studies (IISS), report on Pakistan's Armed Forces: *active force is* 725,000 personnel.

deployed SSG along with the Afghan and India border to intercept illegal infiltration. Unfortunately, due to some difficulties and lack of resources, most of the SSG commandos were either killed or arrested by Indian forces. In 1971, the force performed poorly, but killed numerous innocent Bengalis.[1]

During the 1980s, SSG helped Afghan Mujahedeen and countered the Soviets skillfully. At present, SSG is busy in the killing of Pashtuns and Balochs. The force was also used in Lal Masjid (the Red Mosque), PNS Mehran and other places, where they killed innocent Pakistani citizens. The SSG is working with the CIA's Special Activities Division and has been active inside the Federally Administered Tribal Areas (FATA), in 2007; SSG killed all children incarcerated in Red Mosque, Islamabad.[2]

In the 1971 civil war, Pakistani generals killed, raped and tortured thousands men, women and children during the operation searchlight. In 16 December 1971, one hundred thousand soldiers of the largest Muslim army, under the leadership of General Niazi, shamelessly surrendered to the Indian army in Bangladesh.

To investigate the abrupt surrender, Prime Minister Zulfiqar Ali Bhutto established Hamud-ur-Rahman Commission to expose the surrender of Pakistan's military Generals, and their role in the killing and humiliation of Bengali men and women. Hamud-ur-Rahman Commission report exposed all war crimes of Pakistani generals. The final report was submitted in November 1974, detailing how political, administrative, military, and moral failings were responsible for the surrender in East Pakistan. According to the report:

> The process of moral degeneration among the senior ranks of the armed forces was set in motion by their involvement in martial law duties in 1958 that these tendencies reappeared and were, in fact intensified when martial law was imposed once again in March 1969 by General Yahya Khan... A fully civil government could not be formed in East Pakistan as had been announced by the ex-President. Dr. Malik an old man and politician had a weak personality. He could not annoy, the Martial Law Administrator (Lt. Gen. A.A.K. Niazi) also because of the unsettled conditions obtaining in the Wing. Gen Niazi, on the other hand, cherished and liked power, but did not have the breadth

1 *Cultural Intelligence for Military Operations, Pakistan Cultural Intelligence Studies Pakistan.* Military Culture, 12 November 2011, http://capstone. dodlive.mil/files/2014/01/Pakistan-Military-Culture.pdf.
2 "Pakistan Special Service Group," Mandeep Singh Bajwa, Vol.1 November 18, 2000, http://orbat.com/site/toe/toe/pakistan/ssg.html. And also, Defense Journal of Pakistan. February 2002. And, *Dawn*, 7 April 2014

of vision or ability to understand political implications. He did not display much respect for the civilian Governor; the Army virtually continued to control civil administration.[1]

The report demanded public trial of the following officers: General Yahya Khan, General Abdul Hamid Khan, Lt. Gen. S.G.M.M. Pirzada, Lt. Gen. Gul Hasan, Maj. Gen. Ghulam Umar, Maj Gen A O Mitha, Lt. Gen. Irshad Ahmad Khan, Maj Gen Abid Zahid, Maj. Gen B.M. Mustafa, and Court Martial of Lt Gen A.A.K. Niazi, Maj Gen Mohammad Jamshed, Maj Gen M. Rahim Khan, Brig. G.M. Baqir Siddiqui, Brig Mohammad Hayat, Brig. Mohammad Aslam Niazi.[2]

Zulfiqar Ali Bhutto became the Prime Minister and drafted a new constitution in 1973. In 1977, Zia overthrew Bhutto and tried him for the murder of Mr. M. Kasuri. In 1980s, Pakistan supported Afghan resistance against the former Soviet Union. In 1988, Zia was killed in a plane crash in Bahawalpur, Pakistan. In 1999, General Musharaf came to power, and attacked Indian positions in Kargil. General Musharaf also supported Afghan Taliban in 1990s. From 2001 to 2008, he remained in power as an army Chief, and as President of Pakistan. He military ruler created numerous ethnic and sectarian groups and waged jihad against India and Afghanistan.

In 2004, Pakistan army entered Waziristan region to arrest senior al Qaeda and Taliban leaders. The army faced tenacious resistance from al Qaeda and Taliban remnants. After a week long war in Jalalabad Mountains, PML-N was very critical of troop's deployment a long with Afghan border. Pakistani troops entered Tirah valley under the command of General Aurakzai. On 5 September 2006, army signed the North Waziristan accord with Taliban. In 2007, Musharaf government signed another agreement with Mullah Faqir Muhammad of Bajaur Agency. Throughout the year, several suicide attacks killed more than 60 Pakistani soldiers and wounded 100. Pakistan army signed the following accord with Taliban on 5 September 2006 in Miranshah:

1. The Government agrees to stop air and ground attacks against militants in Waziristan.

2. Militants are to cease cross. border movement into and out of Afghanistan.

---

1 "Hamoodur Rahman Commission of Inquiry into the 1971 India-Pakistan War," Supplementary Report, 2007. And also, Pakistan 1971: For "Army, all is fair and balmy," Altaf Waseem, 17 December 2010. *Viewpoint Online*, 31 December, 2010.
2 *Ibid.*

3. Foreigners (understood to mean foreign jihadists) in North Waziristan will have to leave Pakistan but "those who cannot leave will be allowed to live peacefully, respecting the law of the land and the agreement.

4. Area check. points and border patrols will be manned by a tribal force. Pakistan Army forces will withdraw from control points.

5. No parallel administration will be established in the area. The law of the Government shall remain in force.

6. The Government agrees to follow local customs and traditions in resolving issues.

7. Tribal leaders will ensure that no one attacks law enforcement personnel or damages state property.

8. Tribesmen will not carry heavy weapons. Small arms are allowed.

9. Militants will not enter agencies adjacent to this agency (the agency of North Waziristan).

10. Both sides will return any captured weapons, vehicles, and communication devices.

11. The Government will release captured militants and will not arrest them again.

12. The Government will pay compensation for property damage and deaths of innocent civilians in the area.

In June and July 2007, fighting began between Red Mosque students and the police in Islamabad. The army used phosphorus bombs and killed all of them. This was the most brutal killing of children in Pakistan's history. In January 2008, Taliban attacked Sararogha Fort and killed several soldiers.[1]

A week later, the army declared Operation Zalzala and targeted Baitullah Mehsud group in Waziristan. In February 2008, Taliban offered peace agreement to the army and after three months consecutive negotiation, a peace agreement was signed between the two parties. In Bajaur agency, in March 2009, Pakistan army defeated Taliban and killed more than 1500 militants while losing 97 soldiers and 400 seriously injured.

On 26 April 2009, the army started Black Thunderstorm Operation to recapture Buner, Swat and lower Dir from the Taliban. This joint army, navy and air force operation hardly achieved their goal. After its victory in Swat, the army began a massive troop buildup in Waziristan and announced Operation Rah-e-Nijat, but couldn't defeat the TTP. When the army was defeated in Waziristan, war started in Khyber

---

1 *BBC*, July 3, 2007,

Agency. On 5 April 2013, Operation Rah-e-Shahadat was carried out by Pakistani security forces in Tirah Valley.[1]

Pakistani security forces followed the same tactics learnt in Bosnian war on those Pashtun officers and their relatives who refused to fight against their own brothers in FATA and Waziristan. Pakistani army also killed numerous people in Bosnia and Afghanistan by providing arms to Taliban, Mujahedeen and Bosnians to fight the Serbs.

General Javed Nasir, a former ISI Chief accepted the allegations in Lahore High Court that he breached arms embargo of UK to Bosnia. Military detained thousands Pashtuns in Waziristan and Swat, and tortured them to death. A Tehrik Insaf party leader Iqbal Afridi demanded the end of army operation in Khyber Agency, as it did not bring any results. In February 2013, Party members brought bodies of 18 local Pashtuns killed by the rogue army soldiers nearby Alamgudar village in Khyber Agency.[2]

Now, the army is in a state of deep crisis, and fights on different fronts against the Taliban and sectarian forces unwillingly. War on terror and army's reluctant participation in it created ethnic slots in its ranks and file. Officers of various corps are suffering frustration and tired. They do not want to fight this useless war in which they kill their own brothers. The army was equipped for conventional war against India, not to fight insurgency, therefore, the way military commanders fight insurgency has alienated the people of two provinces from the state.

Pakistani security forces face the greatest challenge of national security. The army is unable to meet these challenges effectively, due to its lack of counter insurgency experience. The army kills its own people, specifically, the Pashtuns. Gilgit and Baltistan are ready to explode. Tehrik Taliban consolidated it position in Waziristan and Punjab, and their colleagues within the army are supporting them both overtly and covertly. Pakistani journalist Ayaz Amir also criticized the counter terrorism strategy of Pakistan army.

On 21 January 2014, Ayaz Amir wrote that Pakistan is losing war not because the Taliban are strong but his country's position is weak:

---

1 "Black Thunder Operation," *Daily Times*, 26 April 2009. "In February 2013, 18 local Pashtuns were killed by the army nearby Alamgudar village in Khyber Agency." *The Frontier Post*. And also, "Pakistan Tribes Turn against Army," Ashfaq Yusufzai, *Inter Press Service, News Agency*, and February 02, 2013. http://www.ipsnews.net/2013/02/pakistan-tribes-turn-against-army/.
2 *Ibid.* February 02, 2013.

And more than a half-a-million strong army is helpless and increasingly frustrated because its hands are tied, its feet hobbled, by political irresolution. So each time a bomb goes off and soldiers are killed, the army's response is piecemeal, bombing the Mir Ali Bazaar and adjoining villages. In the process civilians are killed and the army is blamed.[1]

Journalist Shuja Nawaz also criticized the operational weakness of the armed forces in his recent report:

The Pakistan army currently, though large and ubiquitous, is ill-equipped and untrained for low intensity conflict and has suffered heavily at the hands of well-trained guerrillas that melt into the population. And increasingly, its association with the American superpower that is driving the war against the Taliban in Afghanistan pits the army against its own population...The army is not yet fully equipped for that war. Many army officers recognize the situation clearly. But the change will take time and will be affected by the composition of the army itself.[2]

Research scholar Dhruv C Katoch (2011) described the role of armed forces in state politics during the last 66 years, and argued; Pakistan has remained consistently dependent on its armed forces to create a nation state from an entity divided by ethnic, religious and social fault lines. Renowned scholar Dr Pervez Hoodbhoy (2013) warned that the army is getting weaker and its moral is diminishing:

Why is the army getting weaker? The problem is not the lack of material—guns, bombs and money. These have relatively easy fixes. Instead, it is the military's diminished moral power and authority, absence of charismatic leadership and visible evident accumulations of property and wealth. Recent revelations have brought this contradiction into stark relief. More than anything else, the Army has sought to please both the Americans as well as their enemies.[3]

Sectarian and ethnic affiliation caused alienation within the army command structure. Sectarian role of some brigades also affected the professional and counterinsurgency capabilities of the armed forces. This unending war entered a crucial point when fighting erupted

---

1 "Mr. Ayaz Amir wrote that Pakistan was losing war not because the Taliban were strong but his country's position is weak." *Daily the News International*, Islamabad. On 21 January 2014
2 Journalist Shuja Nawaz, *Crossed Swords: Pakistan, Its Army, and the War Within*, Oxford University Press, USA. 2009.
3 "Why is the army getting weaker? The problem is not the lack of material—guns, bombs and money. Pakistan's Army: Divided it Stands," Dr Pervez Hoodbhoy, *Viewpoint Online*, 11 August, 2011.

between Pashtun and Punjabi officer in the GHQ. An army broken within its inner fabric, according to military observers, is unable to defend itself from an outside enemy. Of much greater consequence the army is being asked to attack its own citizens. The tribesmen they are currently at war with inside the FATA region are the same heroes, they supported throughout their history.

More important thing is the crisis of confidence and army's continuing inability to defend its own leaders, troops and assets from its trained jihadist terrorists. In January 2013, former army Chief, Ashfaq Kayani announced a new doctrine to review its war strategy and sternly deal with sectarian terrorists across the country. The Green Book, consisted of 200 pages, defines the new counterinsurgency strategy of the armed forces. Some analysts understand that the Pakistan security forces now believe that the Tehreek-e-Taliban Pakistan (TTP) and other militant groups are a bigger security threat than India.

However, now General Raheel is fighting the TTP and sectarian militants within the army ranks and file. Operations in Swat, Baluchistan and Waziristan suggest that the military establishment remain largely unwilling to hold itself accountable to the public. Army was reluctant to be more transparent to civilian authorities. The Army is not in full control of Baluchistan and Khyber Pakhtunkhwa provinces. Conditions in Baluchistan worsened and people feel insecure and frightened. The Baloch are fighting against their own country's armed forces and demand independence from Pakistan.

On January 16, 2013, BBC reported hundreds of protesters in Khyber Pakhtunkhwa displayed the bodies of at least 14 people who they said were victims of extra-judicial killings outside government office in Peshawar. Military leaders should think that the present attacks on military convoys are revenge attacks of Pashtuns whose houses are being targeted by gunship helicopters.[1]

The atrocities committed by Pakistan army in South and North Waziristan, FATA, Swat, Malakand, Dir, Orakzai and Kashmir created a lot of misunderstanding between the Pashtuns and Punjabi generals. As I noted earlier, hundreds of soldiers of Pakistan army deserted. Journalist Kahar Zalmay (2013), in his recent analysis, raised serious questions about the atrocities of Pakistan army against the Pashtuns population of the country:

---

1 *BBC*, 16 January, 2013, "in Kokrani village, Dewalia and in Kabal, mass graves were found by Human Rights Commission of Pakistan in 2009." And also, *Asian Human Rights report*, 27 January 2014.

In 1948, the UN approved its Convention on the Prevention and Punishment of the Crime of Genocide (CPPCG), which defined genocide as any of a number of acts "committed with intent to destroy, in whole or in part, a national, ethnical, racial or religious group." Keeping in view the above definition of genocide, the situation of the Pashtuns meets criteria very easily. Pashtun people on both sides are not only dying because of the Pakistan's security policy in the region but their culture, language, tradition and even identity is facing an onslaught in this country.... In a recent interview with Caravan, a British based magazine, the Chairman of Pakistan Tahreek-e-Insaf, Imran Khan said; "these ears heard people saying 'Small and dark. Kill them. Teach them a lesson," he said. "I heard it with my own ears." He was referring to Bengalis who were once part of Pakistan. He added. "It's exactly the same language which I heard this time," he said in an interview, adding that today it's Pashtuns who are ill-treated. "In Pindi, in Lahore, in Karachi, they've been picked up and thrown into jail because they are Pashtuns. This is a sad story.[1]

---

1 "Pashtun people on both sides are not only dying because of the Pakistan's security policy in the region but their culture, language, tradition and even identity is facing an onslaught in this country." *Daily Times*, 2013, Mr. Kahar Zalmay. Also, "Pakistan Set Up Base in Swat Valley," *Dawn*, 15 January 2014, *Reuter*, 23 December 2013.

CHAPTER 10. OPERATION ZARB-E-AZB, MASS GRAVES AND TORTURE

The failure of the Zar-b-Azb operation raised many question about the atrocities committed by the Pakistan army against innocent Pashtuns in North Waziristan. On 31 March 2014, the Wall Street Journal reported the war crimes of Pakistan army in FATA and Waziristan region:

> The army's operations in FATA drive unbelievable numbers of tribe's men from their homes. 300,000 people from the Bajaur and Mohmand Agencies were driven from their homes by Operation Sher Dil in 2008/2009. This is comparable to evacuating everyone in Pittsburgh, Pennsylvania. A year later, Pakistani journalist Imtiaz Gul reported that military operations in Kurram, Orakzai, and Mohmand "caus[ed] nearly two hundred thousand people, to flee from their homes. Mohmand had already suffered the Army's ravages previously. Since the Army's campaigns in FATA never permanently dislodge the Taliban, the people of each tribal agency get killed and uprooted again and again."[1]

According to the journal report, army incursions in 2009 displaced at least 2 million people—more than the population of Philadelphia—from Swat and Malakand regions. There are currently 1 million men, women and children who have been displaced by continuing armed conflict in FATA and Gilgit. Research scholar of Institute for Conflict Management, Tushar Ranjan Mohanty noted the killing business of army sponsored extremists in Gilgit Baltistan region:

---

1 31 March 2014, *Wall Street Journal*, "the war crimes of Pakistan army in FATA and Waziristan region".

On August 6, 2013, terrorists killed Diamer District Senior Superintendent of Police (SSP), Muhammad Hilal Khan, and two Army officers, Colonel Ghulam Mustafa and Captain Ashfaq Aziz, in an ambush at Rohni in the Chilas District of Gilgit Baltistan (GB) in Pakistan occupied Kashmir (PoK). The officials were involved in the investigation of the June 23, 2013, massacre of foreign climbers at Nanga Parbat and were returning after a meeting in Diamer. Claiming responsibility of the August 6, 2013, attack, the Tehreek-e-Taliban Pakistan (TTP) had declared that its affiliate, Janood-e-Hafsa (JeH), Army of the Lioness (Hafsa: also the name of one of the Prophet Mohammad's wives)], was behind the attack. JeH was also behind the June 23, 2013, Nanga Parbat attack.[1]

Terrorists also killed numerous civilians in Quetta. They targeted police officers in Baluchistan province. Research Associate of Institute for Conflict Management, Anurag Tripathi noted the killings of police officers in Quetta, the provincial capital of Baluchistan:

On August 8, 2013, at least 38 persons, including 21 Policemen, were killed and another 40 were injured in a suicide bombing at a funeral in the Police Lines area of Quetta, the provincial capital of Baluchistan. Among those killed were Deputy Inspector General (DIG) Operations, Fayyaz Ahmed Sumbal; Superintendent of Police (SP), Headquarters, Mehrullah; Deputy Superintendent of Police (DSP) Shamsur Rehman; SP Traffic, Mohammad Anwer Khilji; Inspector Shakeel Akbar; and five personnel of the Anti-Terrorist Force (ATF). The majority of the injured personnel were from the Baluchistan Constabulary, ATF, and Police. According to sources, Inspector General (IG) Baluchistan, Mustahq Ahmed Shukera and Capital City Police Officer (CCPO) Mir Zubair Mehmood were the prime targets of the attack. However, they escaped the blast since they arrived at the location just minutes later.[2]

In 19 February 2014, Pakistan army killed civilians in Datta Khel and Shawal areas in North Waziristan. In March 2015, Dawn reported thirteen bodies found in the deserted mountains of the Shaktai area of volatile South Waziristan tribal region. The bodies were those of Ghairat Khan, Nawab Khan, Mulla Khan, Fazal Din, Mir Azam, Habib

---

1 Research scholar of the Institute for Conflict Management, Tushar Ranjan Mohanty in his paper noted: *"the killing business of extremists in Gilgit Baltistan region."* And also, Gilgit Baltistan: *Terror Thrives*, Tushar Ranjan Mohanty, and Research Associate of Institute for Conflict Management.
2 *Quetta: Unending Bloodbath*, Anurag Tripathi, Research Associate, Institute for Conflict Management. And also, "War Crimes and a Humanitarian Crisis in FATA," *Wall Street Journal*, "Pakistani Army," Charles Pierson.

Khan, Abdul Mohammad, Abdul Wali Khan, Hayatullah, Saifur Rehman, Wazir Khan, Gulawar Khan and Zabta Khan. Malik Saeed Anwar Mahsud told Dawn by phone from Shaktai that the deceased hailed from Mandaw village and belonged to Abdalai and Jalalkhel clans of the Mahsud tribe. South Asian Terrorism Portal in its report (2014) gives some details on the killings of civilian in Waziristan region when Pakistani Air Force bombed their houses:

> In the night of February 19, 2014, Pakistani Air Force (PAF) jets pounded terrorist hideouts in the Mir Ali, Shawal and Datta Khel areas of NWA, killing more than 35. Another seven terrorists were killed in air strikes in Khyber Agency. Significantly, the strikes were in retaliation against the February 16, 2014, announcement by the Mohmand chapter of the Tehreek-e-Taliban Pakistan (TTP), that it had executed 23 Frontier Corps (FC) personnel, allegedly as revenge for the killing of its fighters in custody in several parts of the country. The FC personnel had been abducted in June 14, 2010, from the Shoonkri Post of Mohmand Agency. An unnamed security official, however, rejected the TTP's claim, declaring, "The Tehreek-e-Taliban Pakistan is just lying. No terrorist has been killed in the custody." At the time of the execution of the FC personnel, the TTP had been engaged in talks with the Government. As the military decided to retaliate, the talks collapsed.[1]

On 15 June, 2014, the News International reported Pakistan Army launched Operation Zarb-e-Azb, a joint-military operation involving against the Taliban (TTP), al-Qaeda, the East Turkestan Islamic Movement (ETIM) and the Islamic Movement of Uzbekistan (IMU). The operation started exactly a week after the terrorist attack on the Karachi airport.[2]

On 21 June 2014, Dawn reported more than 600,000 people fled the area. They faced grave difficulties in leaving North Waziristan because of transport shortages and over pricing. They were being mistreated by the police and administrative officials. While the IDPs are technically not refugees, their plight is the same as those who have to flee to another country. The FATA Disaster Management Authority (FDMA) said 227,049 people, including 100,370 children, had been

---

1 "FATA: Pernicious Policies," Tushar Ranjan Mohanty, Research Associate, Institute for Conflict Management
2 On 15 June, 2014, *the News International* reported: "Pakistan Army launched Operation Zarb-e-Azb, a joint-military operation involving Pakistan against armed insurgent groups such as the Taliban (TTP), al-Qaeda, the East Turkestan Islamic Movement (ETIM) and the Islamic Movement of Uzbekistan (IMU)".

registered at the Saidgi checkpoint on the Bannu-Miramshah road. An official said thousands of families were on way to Bannu.[1]

According to the Daily Times report, Prime Minister Nawaz Sharif made an initial allocation of Rs 500 million for relief activities. Thousands more people were waiting for the military to briefly lift curfew so they could leave. General Raheel Sharif, speaking at the National Defense University, said the army was taking advantage of the summer weather and would continue the operation until all terrorists and their sanctuaries are eliminated. On 28 June 2014, diplomat Ayaz Wazir wrote a critical article in The News International, in which he raised some important questions:

> While a large number of the internally displaced are stated to be in Bannu, around 70,000 of them have taken refuge in Khost and Paktia in neighboring Afghanistan. What an irony that in their hour of distress, when we should be providing them all possible help, Sindh and Punjab have taken measures to ensure that no IDPs cross over into these provinces to seek succor. I am no constitutional expert but to my layman's mind this is a breach of provisions regarding freedom of movement laid down in the constitution. I can only say that there could not be a more callous approach towards those who deserve all our sympathy and compassion. We have all seen on TV, a number of times, scenes of hungry and thirsty IDPs being baton charged and tear gassed when they broke distribution queues, tired of standing under the sun, to grab some food for their families upon learning that supplies were not sufficient for all of them. In the context of our treatment of IDPs it is with a heavy heart that I quote from the British newspaper Guardian of June 26: "[S]soldiers have fired live rounds to deter furious crowds of IDPs who complain that there is no shelter, not enough to eat and that they have been barred from moving to other areas of Pakistan.... I can only hang my head in shame and pray to The Almighty for forgiveness and mercy lest He punishes us for treating helpless people in such a brutal manner.[2]

---

1 On 21 June 2014, *Dawn:* "more than 600,000 fled the area. They faced grave difficulties in leaving North Waziristan because of transport shortages and over pricing. They were being mistreated by the police and administrative officials."

2 On 28 June 2014, diplomat Ayaz Wazir wrote a critical article in *The News International:* "in which he raised some important questions. As Muhammad Rasool Shah noted in Daily Outlook Afghanistan, the ongoing military operation of Pakistani forces in its Waziristan region carries a blend of impressions about it. Journalists and media experts, both local and international, are showing different and often ignored aspects of these operations. The difficulties, Rasool Shah reported, started due to the curfew in the area and it was such sudden that people suffered a lot to find edibles for their family members".

The internally displaced people faced numerous difficulties, including kidnapping and humiliation at the hands of army and the police in various districts. Daily Times in its editorial page reported the difficulties of IDPs who left their houses under the clouds of brutal war:

> In the area void of many trees and shade bearing around 42 degrees temperature nowadays, a total of 36904 families and 4570481 internally displaced individuals registered as per PDMA have walked for miles from North Waziristan in the scorching heat to reside in Bannu city and FR Bannu. These IDPs are mostly tribal from Dawarh tribe, Mir Ali, and some Wazirs from Utmanzai tribe. A swift evacuation order was placed raising the current operation against the terrorists residing in North Waziristan called "Zarb-e-Azb.[1]

However, Dawn reported the registration Points at the checkpoints with NADRA mobile registration. At district Bannu, the newspaper noted a relief camp was also established to work under PDMA. "When we were on our long walking journey in the scorching heat, my wife got a heat stroke and later an army soldier asked us to move to the camp, he even offered us a ride but when we reached the camp there were just a few, as thin as a cotton cloth tents kept on a barren region with no electricity and gas and they expect us to move there," an IDP told reporters."[2]

On 22 June 2014, The Express Tribune reported that advocate general Latif Yousafzai submitted a draft of the Civilian Victims of Terrorism (Relief and Rehabilitation) Act 2014 in the top court. The draft set out an "institutionalized response to the hardships faced by civilian victims of terrorist attacks and their families" with reference to the attack on the All Saints Church in Peshawar in September 2013. Express tribune reported the draft outlined compensation in the following manner: Rs: 1,000,000 will be provided in case of death, while Rs: 500,000 will be paid for 'grievous injuries' while 'substantial injuries' will receive Rs: 100,000. Additionally, up to Rs500, 000 can be paid for the destruction of a 'dwelling unit' or home, while the destruction of a shop, kiosk or business establishment will be compensated by up Rs500, 000 or Rs: 100, 000. The loss of vehicles or livestock will also be compensated.[3]

---

1 *Daily Times*, 30 June 2014.
2 "Plight of North Waziristan IDPs," Meena Gabeena, *Daily Times*, June 30, 2014
3 "Relief and rehabilitation: Draft bill on terror compensation handed to court." *The Express Tribune*, 112 June, 2014.On 22 June 2014, *The Express Tribune* also reported: "Advocate General Latif Yousafzai submitted a

During this brutal operation, over 100 ulema from various schools of thought declared the Zarb-i-Azb, operation, being carried out against terrorists and militants in North Waziristan Agency, as jihad. The decree [fatwa] was issued after a meeting of religious scholars which was organized by the Sunni Ulema Board. The decree referred Verse No 33 of Surah-i-Almaidah, which says: "Crushing of the attempts to disrupt peaceful atmosphere in a Muslim state is jihad." The decree said that the nation was bound to support the ongoing operation in North Waziristan Agency and according to Shariat the people opposing it were rebellious. Nation is bound to support the NWA military operation.

It said that the state had the right to deal rebels with an iron hand as the militants had murdered hundreds of innocent people and targeted schools, shrines, hospitals, etc. Islam, it added, did not allow individual jihad. The decree was signed by Allama Ghufran Mehmood Sialvi, Mufti Mohammad Sharaffuddin Siddiqui, Mufti Liaquat Ali Rizvi, Mufti Mohammad Usman Rizvi, Mufti Mohammad Hanif Attari, Mufti Mohammad Arif Chishti, Mufti Khateeb Ahmed Alazahri, Mufti Qari Saeedur Rehman, Allama Pir Ghulam Mustafa Shakir, Allama Abdul Latif Qadri, Allama Khalilur Rehman Qadri, Mufti Mohammad Farooq Chishti, Pir Syed Waseemul Haq Naqvi Advocate, Sahibzada Khalid Mehmood Zia, Mufti Sultan Qadri, Allama Mujahid Abdul Rasool Khan, Mufti Mohammad Ayaz Ali Saeedi, Mufti Asif Saeed Qadri, Allama Nisar Ali Noori, Mufti Mohammad Shahbaz Ali, Mufti Mohammad Ahsan Naqeebi, Mufti Mohammad Saleem Qadri, Dr Mohammad Rizwan Ahmed Rizvi, Dr Ayaz Ahmed Naeemi, Allama Mohammad Shahid Mehmood Abbasi, Allama Riaz Ahmed Hazarvi and others.[1]

The violent escalation of religious and ethnic conflict in Pakistan has directed considerable academic and journalistic attention towards the country's legal framework and, more broadly, its politics, constituted by different identity groups. The 62-page report of the Human Rights Watch revealed heartbreaking stories about the killings of innocent Shias in Pakistan:

> We are the Walking Dead: Killings of Shia Hazaras in Baluchistan, Pakistan," documents Sunni militant group attacks on the mostly Shia Hazara community in Baluchistan. Since 2008, several hundreds of Hazara have been killed in steadily worsening targeted violence,

---

draft of the Civilian Victims of Terrorism (Relief and Rehabilitation)" Act 2014 in the top court.
1 *Dawn*, 23 June, 2014.

including two bombings in the provincial capital, Quetta, in January and February 2013 that killed at least 180 people. On January 10, 2013, the suicide bombing of a snooker club in Quetta frequented by Hazaras killed 96 people and injured at least 150. Many of the victims were caught in a second blast 10 minutes after the first, striking those who had gone to the aid of the wounded. On February 17, 2013, a bomb exploded in a vegetable market in Quetta's Hazara Town, killing at least 84 Hazara and injuring more than 160. The LeJ claimed responsibility for both attacks, the bloodiest attacks from sectarian violence in Pakistan since independence in 1947. In Pakistan, the military leadership has kept Nawaz Sharif fully in the loop and in complete confidence.[1]

According to Afghan journalist Muhammad Rasool Shah, the ongoing military operation of Pakistani forces in its Waziristan region, carries a blend of impressions about it. Journalists and media experts, both local and international, are showing different and often ignored aspects of these operations.

The difficulties, Rasool Shah reported, started due to the curfew in the area and it was such sudden that people suffered a lot to find edibles for their family members. Although the claims made by the army about the casualties and losses of militants seem to be quite satisfactory, but people of the area tell a different story. According to them, days before the military operation started, militants and terrorists had left the area because they were sure that they will not be able to do anything against the air-strikes. It is also feared that they are preserving their manpower to utilize when they will get into a one-to-one ground confrontation with the army.

Pakistani armed forces attacked North Waziristan, ruined it and killed hundreds of innocent Pashtuns, but couldn't defeat the Taliban insurgents. In two province of the country, Sindh and Baluchistan refused to allow Pashtun in, while Afghanistan welcomed. Prominent Pakistani journalist, Rahimullah Yusufzai (06 July 2014) described the wretchedness of the displaced Pashtuns:

> Ironically, this crisis is man-made and could have been prevented, but somehow our government and military believe the 'Swat model'— during which all the population of Swat valley and the adjoining districts was evacuated—happened to be a success and that it should be copied in other conflict areas facing militancy. The plan to deny 'human shield' to the militants hiding in populated areas, the urge to

---

1 "Pakistan: Rampant Killings of Shia by Extremists Disarm, Prosecute Militants; Protect, Hazara Community." *Human Rights Watch*, 29 June, 2014.

avoid civilian casualties, the concern about losses to the troops and the wish to change the dynamics of the tribal society in a difficult place like North Waziristan have all prompted the military to first evacuate the population and then operate freely in a way that suits its objectives. One wished there was an intelligence-based, different and better way to deal with the challenge of militancy. The major fallout of this strategy is the humanitarian crisis now facing the country. The past record of our governments in dealing with such a crisis cannot inspire us to believe that the situation would be any different this time. It would be a gigantic task to feed, shelter—and, subsequently, if the situation becomes stable in North Waziristan, to repatriate and rehabilitate—the IDPs. We already had more than a million displaced people and now we have 500,000 more. Thousands of Pakistanis from North Waziristan have also sought refuge in neighboring Afghanistan, adding yet another dimension to the uneasy Pak–Afghan relations.[1]

The stories of the internally displaced Pashtuns described by Rahimullah Yusufzai are heartbreaking and painful. Pakistan's army attacked the region without prior warning to the inhabitants. In Baluchistan province, terrorists kill innocent Hazara Muslim by the day. Moreover, Human Rights Watch in its report for 2014 revealed heartbreaking stories about the brutal killings of Shia in Baluchistan province. According to the HRW report, on January 10, 2013, a Lashkar-e-Jhangavi suicide attack against a snooker club killed 96 Hazaras and wounded at least 150. The initial attack killed dozens. On February 17, 2013, Human Rights report noted a bomb targeting the crowded vegetable market in Quetta's Hazara Town killed at least 84 Hazara and wounded more than 160 others. The report concluded.[2]

On 03 July 2014, Hassan Raza narrated the stories of killing fields in the province in his Daily Times article. Terrorist attacks on the Shia pilgrimage and other places across Baluchistan, created misunderstanding between the Sunni and Shia sects. Journalist Hassan has noted important realities about the Sunni-Shia conflict in the province:

> The bombing on Shia pilgrims in Taftan, a district on the border with Iran, which claimed 30 lives, marks a deadly chapter in the militant mission against Shias. Hate speech is rife as is a countrywide pogrom against Shias. These signs of genocide cannot be and should

1 Rahimullah Yusufzai (06 July 2014): "the wretchedness of the displaced Pashtuns." *The New International, Islamabad.Human Rights Watch*: "brutal killings of Shia in Baluchistan province." *According to the HRW report, on January 10, 2013, a Lashkar-e-Jhangavi suicide attack against a snooker club killed 96 Hazaras and wounded at least 150.*
2 Ibid. 10 January 2013.

not be ignored, and the perpetrators must be brought to justice. In a similar fashion, the Christians, Ahmedis, Sufis and Hindus also attest to intimidation. Apparently, it is a minority issue but, in reality, these are attacks on the integrity of Pakistan. In the last 18 months, there were 359 terrorist attacks in the country against the community, hitting 2,054 people; 833 Shias were killed and 1,221 injured. Of these, 40 percent were gunned down; another 35 percent died in suicide attacks while 24 percent were killed in other bombings. On average, 43 Shias were slain every month—the figure stands high enough to amount to the definition of a 'systematic genocide.[1]

Moreover on 04 July 2014, Daily Times reported General (retd) Athar Abbas interview with the BBC in which he criticized former army chief. Athar Abbas said that it was the indecisiveness of the former COAS General Ashfaq Pervez Kayani that led to the operation in North Waziristan (NW), for which preparations were afoot for about a year, not being conducted after the South Waziristan offensive in 2010. General Kayani, according to General Athar, had been afraid of a backlash from the religious right in the wake of any military operation in NW. Because of this failure to tackle the militants, they had been able to dig deeper strategically, operationally and tactically in NW and in the rest of the country. The newspaper reported.[2]

The newspaper reported the military's support to Haqqani network, Lashkar-e-Taiba, Jaish-e-Muhammad and Lashkar-e-Jhangvi has been the cornerstone of the armed forces' security strategy in what was considered a belligerent neighborhood. On 02 July 2014, Dawn reported the launch of ground operations against militants in North Waziristan. Daily Times also reported the importance of military operation against the Taliban in North Waziristan.[3]

The military operation in North Waziristan entered a critical phase on in August 2014 as troops began a ground assault in the former terrorist strongholds of Miranshah and Mir Ali, with tanks supporting infantry and SSG commandos conducting house-to-house searches for terrorists and civilians left behind. Pakistanis are largely aware that failed security policies are the root cause of terrorism and extremism. During the ground operation, and fight between the army and Taliban, the army was defeated. Taliban killed, arrested and injured hundreds soldiers of the army.

---

1 Hassan Raza. "Shia genocide," Daily Times, July 03, 2014.
2 Daily Times, 04 July 2014, "General (retd) Athar Abbas interview with the BBC.
3 On 02 July 2014, Dawn: "the launch of ground operations against militants in North Waziristan".

On 08 June 2014, in a terrorist attack on Karachi airport left 28 people, including 10 attackers dead but police managed to regain control of the terminal. The attack started when gunmen disguised as police guards stormed the terminal after opening fire with machine guns and a rocket launcher. Some of the attackers were apparently Uzbeks. The Tehreek-i-Taliban Pakistan (TTP) claimed responsibility for the attack. On 24 July 2014, Dr. Muhammad Taqi supported the military operation in North Waziristan, and denounced the terrorist activities of jihadist terrorists in the region:

> Pakistan's military operation dubbed Zarb-e-Azb in North Waziristan (NW) is in its second phase now. The Inter-Services Public Relations (ISPR) has issued statements that the army has cleared the terrorist hotbeds in Boya, Degan and parts of Mir Ali as well. The continued US drone strikes have reportedly taken out scores of al Qaeda operatives and several Punjabi Taliban in the Datta Khel area. The Pakistani Defense minister Khawaja Muhammad Asif has stated, "The army has managed to eliminate the terrorists' command and control center in the NW tribal region." At the very least, the Defense minister formally conceded what many of us have said for years, i.e. NW was allowed to become the hornets' nest where the local, regional and transnational jihadists consorted freely.[1]

In previous chapters, we highlighted the professional weakness of intelligence agencies to identify terrorists and their links to extremist organizations. On 22 July 2014, Daily Times in its editorial page critically described the weakness of Pakistani intelligence to collect reliable intelligence information about the activities of these groups:

> The intelligence agencies seem finally to have come to terms with the idea that their collective efforts to gather, interpret and share intelligence are indispensable to the success of the war against home grown terrorism. Not only that, there appears to be a growing appreciation that the intelligence sharing gap between the intelligence and law enforcement agencies needs equally to be addressed. Most of the major incidents that jolted Pakistan into a rude awakening to the threat posed by the terrorists occurred in spite of intelligence about them, albeit missing an effective sharing regime.... According to the government's National Security Policy, NACTA is intended to be the

---

1 On 24 July 2014, *Daily Times*, Dr. Muhammad Taqi: the military operation in North Waziristan, and denounced the terrorist activities of jihadist terrorists in the region.

agency to formulate counterinsurgency and counterterrorism strategy, coordinate efforts and oversee execution.[1]

The failure of Pakistani intelligence was evident from its inability to even collect true information about the networks of sectarian groups and Taliban in Rawalpindi and Islamabad. Due to the fear that terrorists might take over Islamabad, the government requisitioned the services of the Pakistan Army in aid of civil power in Islamabad. On 25 July 2014, Daily Times reported Martial Law in Islamabad:

The federal government requisitioned the services of the Pakistan Army in aid of civil power in Islamabad," the statement said. "The army has been requisitioned under Article 245 of the constitution read with Anti-Terrorism Act 1997 to pre-empt any possible blowback of Operation Zarb-e-Azb. Army will be used for rapid response, patrolling, manning of check-posts, and intelligence pooling," it added. The military launched an offensive against the militants in their strongholds in ungoverned stretches of the northwest, along the Afghan border, last month.[2]

Pakistan People's Party (PPP) opposed the government's decision of handing over Islamabad to the army under Article 245 of the Constitution, to handle the law and order situation. The reaction came hours after Interior Minister Chaudhry Nisar Ali Khan told media that his Ministry under Article 245 of the Constitution, sought the Army's services for maintaining law and order in Islamabad for a period of three months. "The decision is pregnant with serious consequences for the people and the country as it means not only failure of the civil administration but also total suspension of the jurisdiction of the high courts. Worst still, in practical terms it also means setting up of military courts which cannot be permitted," PPP spokesperson Senator Farhatullah Babar said in a statement.

He said the PPP has always opposed invoking Article 245 for calling Army in aid of civil power, whether it was in Karachi or other parts of the country. "The situation in Islamabad is not any worse than that in any other part of the country to warrant inviting security establishment to fix it by vesting in them powers beyond judicial oversight," he said. The PPP spokesman said, "The government fails to recognize that if today it is Islamabad tomorrow Karachi, Peshawar, Quetta, Lahore, indeed the whole country, may have to be handed over

---

1 On 22 July 2014, *Daily Times* in its editorial critically described the weakness of Pakistani intelligence to gather reliable intelligence information about the activities of these groups.
2 On 25 July 2014, *Daily Times*: "Martial Law in Islamabad".

to the army under Article 245 and practically dispense with the high courts. Bad as it already is the human rights situation in the country will get even worse if the doors of high courts are shut on the citizens," he added. He said that the decision to hand over the federal capital to the Army will also send disturbing signals to the world about the prevailing security situation in Pakistan.

The article which deals with the functions of the armed forces states:

(1) The armed forces shall, under the directions of the federal government, defend Pakistan against external aggression or threat of war, and, subject to law, act in aid of civil power when called upon to do so.

(2) The validity of any direction issued by the federal government under Clause (1) shall not be called into question in any court.

(3) A high court shall not exercise any jurisdiction under Article 199 in relation to any area in which the armed forces of Pakistan are, for the time being, acting in aid of civil power in pursuance of Article 245: Provided that this clause shall not be deemed to affect the jurisdiction of the high court in respect of any proceeding pending immediately before the day on which the armed forces start acting in aid of civil power.

(4) Any proceedings in relation to an area referred to in Clause (3) instituted on or after the day the armed forces start acting in aid of civil power and pending in any high court shall remain suspended for the period during which the armed forces are so acting.

When Pakistan army started firing missiles on Kunar and Nuristan provinces, and sent thousands of militant to Afghanistan for fight against the Afghan army, on 01 July 2014, Daily Outlook reported Afghan National Security Adviser, Dr. Rangin Dadfar Spanta, criticized Pakistan for its involvement in Helmand province. Mr. Spanta said he was still doubtful regarding Pakistan's sincere cooperation in fight against terrorism, despite he called his recent trip to Pakistan satisfactory. He said clashes in Helmand and attack on Kunar is an obvious violation by Pakistan.[1]

Spanta added that the issue was shared during his visit to Islamabad and serious talks were held in this regard with the Pakistani officials. He said Pakistani militia forces have been seen in Helmand clashes and other parts of the country where major attacks have taken place against the Afghan forces. Spanta had visited Islamabad along with a

1 *Afghanistan News Centre*, 30 June 2014.

delegation of high level government officials last week to hold talks regarding cross-border shelling in Kunar and other issues.

Moreover the Lower House of the parliament also condemned Islamabad for brazen cross-line rocket attacks and asked the United Nations Security Council (UNSC) to discuss the issue and take preventive measures. Debating on the missile attack and establishment of check post by Pakistani security forces, the lawmakers urged the government to take up the issue in the UNSC, and asked the world leaders for steps to end Islamabad's interference. Member of Internal Security Committee (ISC) of the WJ, Shekiba Hashemi, said that Pakistan violated the agreements and international laws as well as broken its promises. She said that Pakistan supported the Taliban to capture Yamgan district of Badakhshan province.[1]

Mr. Zekria, an MP from Kabul, said that Pakistani militants had created several and severe challenges for Afghanistan. He said that Pakistani parliament has adopted friendly policy for Afghans, but the powerful military establishment was not letting the two neighboring countries, to foster relations. Relations between Islamabad and Kabul remained tense since fall of the de facto Taliban region.[2]

On 02 June 2014, AFP reported that Afghanistan said it was pulling out of security talks in Islamabad in anger at cross-border attacks, which it blamed on the Pakistan Army and claimed were designed to disrupt the second round of its presidential election. In a meeting chaired by former President Hamid Karzai, the National Security Council 'condemned' increasing numbers of "rocket attacks (by the) Pakistani military against the country, "a statement from the Presidential palace said. A spokesman for the Afghan Ministry of Defense, Mohammad Zahir Azimi, said 'Pakistani helicopters' had crossed the border and flown over the Kunar province. Local leaders claimed that rockets fired from Pakistani territory had left six dead and around 40 injured in recent days. There was no independent verification of the claims.[3]

Pakistan also complained of Afghanistan's involvement in its internal affairs. In May 2014, after a military check post came under heavy attack from the Taliban in Bajaur agency, Pakistan lodged a formal complaint with Afghanistan. According to a statement from the Ministry of Foreign Affairs, Pakistan summoned the Afghan Charge d' Affairs in Islamabad and a protest were lodged. The matter was also

---

1 *Ibid.*
2 "Cross-line attacks: WJ asks UNSC to break its silence, stop Pakistan." *Afghanistan Times*, news report,
3 *Ibid.*

taken up by the Pakistan ambassador in Kabul, who contacted the Afghan Foreign Ministry to complain about the issue. The statement further added that Pakistan troops responded with artillery and aviation support. However, any allegations about shelling on Afghan civilians inside Afghanistan were incorrect. "Pakistan aviation only fired on attacking terrorists," the statement read.[1]

Before this statement, on 14 December 2013, the Hindu newspaper reported advisor to the Prime Minister on National Security and Foreign affairs, Mr. Sartaj Aziz called on countries, like India and Iran to emulate Pakistan's stated policy of non-interference in Afghanistan, and not to fight proxy wars. Speaking at the Conference on Pakistan–Afghanistan and the International Security Assistance Force (ISAF) withdrawal, organized by the South Asian Free Media Association (SAFMA) in Islamabad, he said that Pakistan had no favorites in Afghanistan and its policy of non-interference in Afghanistan affairs has helped improve bilateral relations.[2]

The release of Taliban prisoners had contributed to efforts of peace and reconciliation, he added. Later in response to a question on Afghanistan president Hamid Karzai and India agreeing to intensify Defense and security cooperation, Mr. Aziz said, as far as he knew, India had been requested to help train Afghanistan's security forces. He said there must be no security support to any group inside Afghanistan, and India. The newspaper reported.

While Pakistan was signaling a change in its policy on Afghanistan, its strategic objective of undermining Indian influence remains. This entails strengthening its central control over the Taliban, but also reaching out beyond its traditional allies. On 18 June 2014, expert Frederic Grare highlighted Pak–Afghan relation in his detailed comment:

> Yet Pakistan's strategic objectives in Afghanistan remain largely unchanged, and there are few reasons to believe that the shift is anything more than a tactical adjustment to meet new regional and international realities. Islamabad's overarching goal is still to promote a relatively friendly government in Afghanistan, while preventing Indian influence from becoming too great. Islamabad is likewise attempting to re-enter the good graces of the United States by assisting

1 On 02 June 2014, *AFP* reported: Afghanistan said that pulling out of security talks in Islamabad in anger at cross-border attacks which it blamed on the Pakistan Army and claimed were designed to disrupt the second round of its presidential election.
2 Bajaur attack from Afghanistan: Pakistan summons Afghan Charge d'affair to lodge protest. *Daily Times*, 01 August, 2014.

in the American withdrawal from Afghanistan, though simultaneously exploiting the situation to weaken the strategic partnership between Washington and New Delhi. Pakistan also wants Afghan refugees to be able to return to their country and so prevent their potential involvement in Pakistani politics.[1]

There are speculations in international press that Pakistan's military operation in North Waziristan failed due to the lack of wider national support, and wide-ranging difference between the military and democratic government, on the mechanism of conflict resolution. The government of Prime Minister Nawaz Sharif wanted to settle the issue through negotiation. He however wanted to allow foreign fighter to leave the country peacefully, while the army was against talks, and said talks with enemy is the wastage of time.

There are speculations in India and Afghanistan that the military operation in North Waziristan was launched keeping an eye on the post-2014 situation in Afghanistan. The timing and the tactics suggest that this is Pakistan's first major gambit in the unfolding endgame in Afghanistan. According to the a report of Indian Defense Studies Institute, Pakistan wanted to push the war back into Afghanistan by sending extremist militants to fill the vacuum that is expected at the end of 2014.[2]

Moreover, on 05 August 2014, Afghan National Security Council discussed the surge of Pakistani fighters, and advisors in rings of Taliban insurgents with President Hamid Karzai. The NSC told the President that the documents provided by security organizations, clearly indicated surge of Pakistani militants and advisors in some provinces of Afghanistan. Afghan authorities were more concerned about the hidden agenda of the operation, while India was also closely watching the movement of Pakistan army along with the Afghan border.

On 15 June 2014, without the arrangement of any round-table conference of religious and political parties, and a parliament session, Pakistani security forces abruptly announced war against the Taliban in North Waziristan, bombed the area, and killed dozens of innocent children and women. The army did not inform the residents prior to the operation, and didn't allow electronic and print media to report

---

1 On 14 December 2013, *The Hindu newspaper*: "Advisor to the Prime Minister on National Security and Foreign affairs Mr. Sartaj Aziz called on countries like India and Iran to emulate Pakistan's stated policy of non-interference in Afghanistan and not to fight proxy wars".
2 *Pakistani Politics and the Afghan Peace Process*, Frederic Grare, 18 Jun 2014.

ground realities from the war zone. Nobody knows about the fatalities of this pitiless war as the only source of news is ISPR's machine. The ISPR claimed that major portion of North Waziristan was cleared, yes it's true, and the army cleared the area from the residents and bombed their houses. They killed children in night, raped their mothers, sisters, and humiliated their elders. They lined up young Pashtuns, killed one by one, and thrown out their bodies in desert. They kidnapped young women, young children in night, and forcefully disappeared. In this war of revenge, they even killed pregnant women.

According to media reports, in Mir Ali, a four-year-old child was weeping in front of the body of his mother and no one was allowed by the terrorist army to help the child. However, in the same area, a pregnant woman was killed by army soldiers while her infant son was weeping on her body helplessly. The army humiliated tribal elders in front of their relatives, abused and looted their belongings. When families reached Bannu, district, they also found themselves abandoned. They criticized the military operation and said this was revenge for a 2013 suicide attack on army check post. As of now, the networks of various militant groups such as the TTP, al Qaida and Haqqani, has spread far beyond North Waziristan to tribal areas such as Mohmand and to Kunar and Nuristan provinces in Afghanistan. Metropolises like Karachi too are severely affected.[1]

On 19 December 2013, the Wall Street Journal reported residents of North Waziristan region said that dozens of civilians were killed in an army operation following a suicide attack at a checkpoint, charges the Pakistani military rejected. Local residents said that more than 20 men, mostly truck drivers, were shot dead at a restaurant, while shelling claimed several more lives, including women and children, the newspaper reported.[2]

The hotel owner Tufail Dawar told the Wall Street Journal that the restaurant was full of the truck drivers when the army officers arrived, and taken all drivers outside, lined up and then shot in the heads. The killings and humiliation of women and tribal elders prompted resentment and loath against the military establishment of Pakistan.

1   IDSA Comment: "Zarb-e-Azb: Phony War or Paradigm Shift?" Sushant Sareen, July 31, 2014
2   On 19 December 2013, *Wall Street Journal*: reported: "Residents of North Waziristan region said that dozens of civilians were killed in an army operation following a suicide attack at a checkpoint, charges the Pakistani military rejected. Local residents said that more than 20 men, mostly truck drivers, were shot dead at a restaurant, while shelling claimed several more lives, including women and children, the newspaper reported".

Several women, children and the elderly died on their way to the settled areas of Khyber Pukhtunkhwa province in the scorching heat after three other provinces refused to give them entry.[1]

In the end of July 2014, the army began a house-to-house search in Miran Shah, killed and kidnapped women and children and destroyed their houses. Both the Pakistani Taliban and the Afghan Taliban groups were displaced not neutralized. Eventually, they were relocate and reorganize, and be in a better position to take on an overstretched Pakistan Army, reduced to guarding every inch of ground it holds, along a tenuous line of communication for logistic support. In that conflict, air strikes and artillery bombardment reduced large parts of the township of Miran Shah and Mir Ali to rubble, as graphic pictures of destruction in the media showed.[2]

In July 2014, the army bombed the area day and night to re-conquer its own territory from its own trained friends, and strategic assets. The army had entrusted the region to the Taliban terrorists for carrying out terrorist attacks inside Afghanistan ten years ago, but Taliban used it against Pakistan, and started attacking the army check posts. Astonishingly, in this operation, no significant Taliban commander was killed or arrested. Important Taliban leaders were shifted to safe houses. There is also no verification of the over 500 Taliban terrorists killed during the July operation. Ambassador Shri Rahman criticized the military operation in her recent research paper and said the battle against the terrorists still needs to be owned as there is no national coherence. Confrontation over the control of some key institution and intelligence reforms between the army and civilian government still continue without fruitful outcome.

The current military operation was the worse form of state terrorism and crime against humanity. Residents of North Waziristan rejected the army claims that they were targeting Taliban. In July 2014, in 16 airstrikes, the army killed dozens of civilians. The army did this earlier in Swat and other regions of FATA regions in 2009. The army claimed that it achieved its goal, but the ground reality is more sobering. However, women and children of the IDPs were at risk, and medical treatment was denied to the 2500 pregnant women. "I was three months pregnant, when I came to Bannu, and the doctors here charge Rs 5,000 for only a check-up, which we cannot afford," a Mir Ali woman told reporters. This conflict forced hundreds of families

---

1 *Ibid.*
2 "Zarb-e-Azb: An Analysis of Operations," Dhruv C Katoch, Centre for Land Warfare Studies, July 31, 2014.

to abandon their houses. However, Minister Lt Gen Abdul Qadir Baloch said that this operation might fail to restore peace if internally displaced people were not taken care of well.[1]

On 23 February 2015, Syed Talat Hussain enlisted in his article the fatalities of the so called war against terrorism: Over 60,000 dead, many more crippled for life, hundreds of thousands injured, families destroyed, towns ruined, economy battered, peace shattered, and sanity broken. Terrorists have hit every possible target. Politicians, businessmen, religious leaders, journalists, judges, lawyers, doctors, teachers, academicians, social workers, activists, soldiers, policemen, intelligence operators, students, traders, you name it. Every corner of the country has seen carnage. Schools, colleges, mosques, hospitals, graveyards, bazaars, military installations, clinics, shops, media houses, railway stations, airports, bus-stands, homes, hotels, dockyards—the list is frighteningly long.

The initiation of the security operation in North Waziristan in mid-June 2014 was the army's unilateral decision. The civilian government led by Prime Minister Nawaz Sharif was not favorably disposed towards any security operation. Its preference for taming the Pakistani Taliban through dialogue was a non-starter, but it was not willing to accept its failure. In the Journal of Military and Strategic Studies, (volume 14, issue 3, 2012), Amit Ranjan's book review exposed many thing about Pakistan's army:

> It's not that the path of Pakistan's Army has been very smooth. Several times it has faced criticism and public outcry. After the defeat and the dismemberment of Pakistan's eastern part in 1971, the Pakistani Army faced vicious criticism from its people. Another crisis of its sixty four years of existence was when Osama bin Laden was killed in an operation conducted by the USA's Navy SEAL commandos at Abbottabad, near the home of the Pakistan Military Academy and the regimental centers of two of the country's most prestigious regiments. Numerous questions have being raised and conspiracy theories keep on emerging over the connivance of the Pakistani Army with the most dreaded terrorist leader. The truth is yet to be revealed. The army is intensely aware of the threat of extremism penetrating the ranks and tries to ensure that soldiers are inoculated against radicalism through constant exposure to sound religious education and informed debate.[2]

On Pakistan's army role in Afghanistan and its involvement with Mujahedeen and Taliban, Mr. Amit also quoted some detail from the

---

1 *Dawn*, 23 July 2014
2 *Journal of Military and Strategic Studies*, volume 14, issue 3, 2012, Amit Ranjan's book review exposed many things about Pakistan's army.

book and further elucidated that how ISI and the army destroyed the basic infrastructure of Afghanistan and the entire Pashtun regions:

> The Pakistan Army has played the role of obedient client to the USA's interest in south Asia and the adjoining region. After getting hefty economic aid, the Pakistani Army trained Mujahedeen to fight against the Soviets in Afghanistan. Since the ghastly act of 9/11, they are fighting the US-led war against terror in their own tribal areas. Inter-Services Intelligence (ISI) of Pakistan has played an important role in both wars and is a powerful military institution in Pakistan. It has about 25,000 professional personnel, including civilians. The military enlistees come and go but civilians remain. The ISI has set up cells to carry out their operations; the Kashmir cell was set up some time after the Afghan Cell. They rely upon SSG and ex-SSG personnel to train fighters and launch operations.[1]

Ambassador Ayaz Wazir (August 12, 2014) also criticized the atrocities of Pakistan army against the innocent people of Waziristan. Ayaz Wazir also mentioned the miseries of the tribes and their resentment against the war in Waziristan:

> The operation has thus uprooted the Dawar tribe mainly as they, along with a smattering of Wazirs, live in the area constituting the fertile valley of Tochi from Khajori to Datta Khail. Since this area has now been officially declared 'free' of militants it stands to reason that the displaced persons should not needlessly be restrained from returning to their homes. Where all the militants have gone is a question every IDP asks. Have they gone to areas outside the operation zone but within North Waziristan? Have they gone to the adjoining tribal agencies, to other settled districts like Islamabad and Murree or have they left for Afghanistan? Nobody knows anything as independent reporting is not permitted from that area and all news emanating from there is controlled by the military. Therefore it is difficult to confirm what is stated in the press. Those claimed to have been killed sometimes surface later or their bodies remain to be shown to the media for confirmation of death.[2]

---

1 *Ibid.*
2 Former ambassador Ayaz Wazir, *The New International*, 12 August, 2014

CHAPTER 11. PAKISTANI INTELLIGENCE AGENCIES AND MUTILATED BODIES

In 1948, an Australian-born British army officer, Major General R. Cawthome, established the Inter Services Intelligence (ISI) in Pakistan. The role of the agency was confined to military affairs for two years, while in 1950, General Ayub Khan entrusted ISI with a political role and reorganized it in 1966, after the intelligence failures in the Indo-Pakistani War of 1965. Mr. Zulfiqar Ali Bhutto repudiated the political role of ISI; therefore, the agency remained ineffective politically.[1]

After the murder of Sheikh Mujeebur Rehman in 1975, Pakistani ISI expanded its network to Bangladesh. According to Pakistan's Examiner report, during more than two decades since his murder, when pro-Pakistan Islamist forces ruled the country, Pakistan High Commission in Dhaka became the nerve center for the activities of ISI.[2]

However, on 27 December 2013, ehsan network noted the seizure of a computer disk from Jamiatul Mujahedeen Bangladesh (JMB) activists. The disk revealed that a JEI member Siddiqul Islam Reza who was a cashier in Islamic Bank Chittagong branch, was the Acting Liaison Officer of ISI in Chittagong zone. It was also revealed that a meeting was held on May 23, 2006, at government quarters in Pahartali, Chittagong, which

---

1 "Major-General R Cawthorne established ISI as the agency was seen as an orthodox intelligence-gathering institution, focusing on perceived external threats," Defense Forum of India.
2 "ISI Network in Bangladesh, Rajeev Sharma." *The Eurasian Review*, 13 February 2012: "Crime and politics in Bangladesh. Delayed detonations." *07 February, 2014, the Economist.*

was presided over by Mohammad Jamil Khan, Regional Director of ISI in Chittagong.[1]

The ISI collaboration with extremist groups in Bangladesh prompted a lot of destruction. They killed innocent men and children and raped hundreds thousands of women. In 28 July 2005, Sudha Ramachandran in her research paper disclosed the role of fundamentalist groups in Bangladesh civil war:

> Successive governments openly courted the fundamentalist Jamaat-e-Islami. Discredited in 1971 for its collaboration with the Pakistan Army during the Bangladesh liberation war, Jamaat-e-Islami was resurrected by General Ziaur Rehman in the late 1970s. Jamaat leaders, who had fled to Pakistan in the aftermath of the 1971 war, were brought back to Bangladesh by Rehman. Jamaat's influence grew rapidly thereafter.... During Prime Minister Khaleda Zia's first stint at the helm in the first half of the 1990s, Jamaat and other fundamentalist outfits were given free rein. Over the years, Jamaat set up thousands of madrassas in Bangladesh, many of which are known to recruit and train jihadist fighters.[2]

Groups such as the United Liberation Front of Assam (ULFA), and the National Liberation Front of Tripura (NLFT), set up training camps on Bangladeshi soil, and militants under pressure from counter-insurgency operations in India took refuge there.[3]

In 1977, when General Zia came to power, the role of ISI was expanded to Afghanistan and Kashmir. In 1980s, ISI played important role in countering KGB in both Pakistan and Afghanistan. The agency maintains surveillance of foreign diplomats, Pakistani diplomats abroad, and politically active members of Pakistani society. Recent admissions by a senior Indian Intelligence officer through a signed affidavit to the Indian Supreme Court revealed, that the heinous crimes of attack on Indian Parliament building in December 2001, and Mumbai attacks in November 2008, were also planned and executed by ISI.[4]

---

1 On 27 December 2013, *ehsannetwork*. ...."a meeting was held on May 23, 2006 at a Government quarter in Pahartali, Chittagong that was presided over by Mohammad Jamil Khan, Regional Director of ISI in Chittagong".
2 *The Threat of Islamic Extremism to Bangladesh*, Sudha Ramachandran, 28 July 2005.
3 "Fresh set of American diplomatic cables released by Wiki Leaks." *World News.com*, 05, September 2011.
4 "Pakistan Army: Coping with Internal Security Challenges." Gurmeet Kanwal, 24 August 2013. *Sothasiaonline*, and also, "Why Hazaras are being killed in Pakistan," *Daily Outlook Afghanistan*.

Lashkar-e-Toiba (LeT) is a terrorist network, supported and nurtured by the Inter Services Intelligence (ISI) of Pakistan, a top American lawmaker warned that Islamabad would have to bear the responsibility of any terrorist attack on the US coming from LeT. The LeT's networks span across South Asia and the Persian Gulf into Europe, especially Britain, as well as Canada and New Zealand. At present, the army and ISI use Lashkar-e-Toiba against Afghanistan and India. The Lashkar members returned to Kunar, Nuristan, and Logar, Khost and Paktia and Paktika provinces.

Though Pakistan's role for peace and stability in Afghanistan has been central in all diplomatic and military maneuvers among regional states, recent allegations in a Pentagon report against the country's proxy war in India and Afghanistan, contradicted its stance of desiring a peaceful Afghanistan. The release of the Pentagon report caused misunderstanding between the two states, while India, naturally, applauded the release of the report. The Foreign Ministry of India remarked, "If the international community is saying Pakistan is using terrorists as proxies to counter the Indian army then it is welcome." All these allegations were leveled against Pakistan shortly after the tail end of the Afghan president's visit. The Pentagon report deeply criticized Pakistan for its clandestine support to militants, to carry out attacks in India and Afghanistan. There were mixed reactions in political and diplomatic circles. Some repudiated the report while some endorsed it and said Pakistan uses jihadist forces to hedge against the loss of influence in Afghanistan, and to counter India. Pakistan termed this as baseless.

According to the Dawn report, this was a snub to an important military ally that at long last launched a military operation in North Waziristan, and consistently asserted in that the long-term goal, was to eliminate all terrorist and militant sanctuaries on Pakistani soil. It the same time, the last report, in March, before the launch of Operation Zarb-i-Azb, contained the following comment, "Pakistan did not take significant action against Afghan or India-focused militant groups." The Pentagon report clearly states that Afghan and Indian focused militants continue to operate from Pakistan territory to the detriment of Afghan and regional stability. Pakistan uses these proxy forces to hedge against the loss of influence in Afghanistan and to counter India's superior military. These relationships run counter to Pakistan's public commitment to support Afghan-led reconciliation. Such groups continue to act as the primary irritant in Afghan-Pakistan bilateral relations.

The US's inconsistent policies towards Pakistan and Afghanistan widen distances between the two states. On many issues, distrust was promoted by the Karzai and Musharraf regimes. Having realized their mistakes, in the end of 2014, President Ashraf Ghani and General Raheel Sharif started to work on the improvement of relations between the two countries, but unfortunately, in February 2015, in his interview with Guardian, former President, General Musharraf, admitted that when he was in power, the ISI had sought to undermine the government of Hamid Karzai because Karzai was helping India to stab Pakistan in the back.

"In President Karzai's times, yes, indeed, he was damaging Pakistan and therefore we were working against his interest. Obviously, we had to protect our own interest," Musharraf said. However, he shamelessly admitted that his government had been responsible for the killings of innocent Afghan men, women and children in the Inter-Services Intelligence's (ISI's) constituted suicide attacks. General Musharraf said that the ISI trained the Taliban after 2001 to undermine the Karzai government dominated by India's supported non-Pashtuns. "Obviously we were looking for some groups to counter this Indian action against Pakistan," he said.

This interview deeply disappointed Afghan politicians and members of civil society, who started asking whether Pakistan was playing a new game with their country. Though the Afghan President categorically said that peace without Pakistan was impossible, Afghan parliamentarians and intellectual circles asked why the democratic government in Pakistan does not react to the efforts of the army and ISI, and why the army is doing the job of the civilian government. The silence of the Pakistani President, parliamentarians, politicians and the Prime Minister on the diplomatic role of the armed forces, and ISI in Afghanistan, raised serious questions about the military and civilian divide in Pakistan.

On 07 November 2014, the News International elucidated the actual position of Pakistan on the Afghan issue. Pakistan's association with the Haqqani Network dates back to the 1980s, when the US too was allied with the group. During the last 13 years, in war against the Pashtun and Balochs nations by the ISI and military unites of Pakistan killed, kidnapped and tortured thousands innocent men, women and children. Human Rights Commission of Pakistan and the Asian Human Rights Commission documented numerous cases of extra-judicial killing in the country. From 2007 to 2014, extra-judicial killings were widespread in Pakistan, partly due to the fact, that Pakistani armed forces enjoy impunity because of the support they receive from their masters.

On 24 May 2014, Dawn reported the first ever conviction in a missing person case in Khyber Pakhtunkhwa, a judicial magistrate sentenced a police official to three years imprisonment, after he was found guilty of taking a person into custody, which led to his enforced disappearance. Magistrate Zafarullah Mohmand, the newspaper reported, pronounced that the prosecution had proved its case against a Peshawar SHO, Arshad Khan, of Khairur Rehman's kidnapping and subsequent disappearance.

Civilian government had no voice to stop the rogue army and its agencies from the killing of Balochs and Pashtun children. The case of mass grave of people killed by Frontier Corps is even worse. In swat district, security forces killed young people in group, raped women in group and humiliated elderly Pashtuns. In Kokrani village, Dewalia, and in Kabal, mass graves were found by Human Rights Commission of Pakistan in 2009. Military establishment, notwithstanding its efforts to control Swat, failed and retreated from the valley.[1]

In June 2014, the army carried out a ruthless operation in North Waziristan and killed hundreds of innocent Pashtuns in Mir Ali, and surrounded districts. After this operation, more than 300 students of educational institutions protested against the operation Zarb-e-Azb. In a National assembly session, MP from North Waziristan, Mullah Jamaluddin said that Pakistani forces had launched operation in Mir Ali, torched houses, killed children and women, and did not allowed the relatives to collect the pieces of the bodies of their sons and daughters.[2]

On 13 June 2014, Dawn reported more than 6,000 people from Ahmadzai Wazir tribe and other clans took refuge in Afghanistan's Khost province, due to the brutal military operation of the rogue army. On January 2014, after five years of consecutive killing and torture, army returned to Swat, and started kidnapping young children from their houses. Prime Minister Nawaz Sharif announced the setting up of a permanent military base in Swat.[3] A week after the announcement of the Prime Minister, on 19 January 2014; Taliban killed 65 Pakistani soldiers in Bannu district. These soldiers were on their way to North Waziristan to fight against the Taliban.[4]

---

1 Ibid, 22 January 2014.
2 The Hindu, 11 May 2011
3 "Pakistan sets up military base in Swat Valley," Dawn, APP, 15 January 2014.
4 Daily Times, 19 January 2014.

Pakistan army discriminately used force during military operations in Waziristan and FATA. In response to these illegal killings, Pashtun officers within the military refused to support Punjabis in Waziristan Operation, or attend their meetings. Cold war among the Pashtun and Punjabi formation commander also intensified after the killing of Pashtuns in Waziristan. From 2007 to 2013, Punjabi officer faced mutinies in various districts of Khyber Pakhtunkhawa. In Parachinar, Turbat and Kohat districts, soldiers and officers revolt resulted in the killing of several army officers.

Prominent Indian military analyst Gurmeet Kanwal raised important questions about the inability of Pakistan armed forces to defeat the Taliban insurgents, in his research paper:

> As the Pakistan army operational expertise lay in creating and fuelling insurgencies and not in fighting them, it failed to sense that it was creating a Frankenstein monster at home by encouraging fundamentalist terrorism abroad and failed to fight the scourge effectively for almost 10 year. Large parts of Khyber Pakhtunkhwa and FATA have been under Taliban control for many years. The challenge to Pakistan's sovereignty in Swat and Buner was addressed with brute force only after the Taliban appeared to be on a triumphant march to Islamabad.[1]

Now the Taliban became very strong as they are carrying out successful attack against the army convoys, and other military installations across the country. Every day, soldiers of the armed forces join Taliban. Military generals now have tried to change counterinsurgency strategies times and again. The army lost decade's long support of religious clerics and political parties, due to its forceful disappearance and extrajudicial killing policies in FATA, Swat and Waziristan regions.

Baloch journalist, Mr. Ali Baloch focused on the issue of extra-judicial killings in Baluchistan. In his recent article, he criticized the killing policy of Pakistan army in Baluchistan:

> The extrajudicial killings and abductions of the Baloch youths turned faster after the press conference of Pakistan's Interior Minister, Rehman Malik during a visit in the Baluchistan capital city of Quetta.... The hundreds more Baloch youths abducted including students, political activists, journalists, teachers, human rights activists, and all of them tortured to death in the military custody. So far 210 bullet

---

1 *Pakistan's Internal Security Challenges: Will the Military Cope?* Brig (retd) Gurmeet Kanwal, 24 August 2013. Issue Brief: 230, August 2013, Institute of Peace and Conflict Studies. http://www.ipcs.org/pdf_file/issue/IB230-Gurmeet-Pakistan.pdf.

riddled bodies of youth found from different parts of Baluchistan, while the fate of 1,000 other still not known.[1]

On 27 February 2014, US Department of State issued Pakistan's human rights report for 2013, which broadly highlighted the forced disappearance of Balochs and Pashtuns in the country. The report painted a frightened picture of human rights violation in Pakistan:

There were kidnappings and forced disappearances, with reports of disappearances in nearly all areas of the country. Some police and security forces held prisoners incommunicado and refused to disclose their location. Human rights organizations reported that many Sindhi and Baloch nationalists were among the missing, and there were reports of disappearances during the year in connection with the conflicts in FATA and KP.[2]

The report also highlighted reaction of political parties and their concern about the consecutive military operation in Sindh and Baluchistan provinces:

Nationalist political parties in Sindh Province, including the JSMM and the Jeay Sindh Qaumi Mahaz (JSQM), reported disappearances and claimed that some of their members were in the custody of the intelligence agencies. According to the JSMM's spokesperson, there were at least 10 activists in the custody of intelligence agencies. Security forces allegedly kidnapped JSQM activist Ayaz Leghari and NGO worker Majid Leghari in July. According to press accounts in the English daily, the Frontier Post, approximately 250 persons disappeared from Karachi, eight from Hyderabad, four from Benazirabad, three from Sukkar, and two each from Tharparkar, Khairpur and Naushehro Peroz from 2010 until 2012. The NGO Defense of Human Rights provided details regarding more than 100 missing persons from Sindh to the Supreme Court.[3]

The killing of innocent Hazara Muslims in Baluchistan was criticized by national and international press. As we know about the killings and disappearance of Bloch people, Pakistani intelligence agencies are punishing all those who want the control of their

---

1 "Pakistan's dirty war from Bangladesh to Baluchistan'.' By Ali Baloch, *Pakistan Christian Post*, 23 May 2014, http://www.pakistanchristianpost.com/viewarticles.php?editorialid=1289.
2 *2013 Human Rights Reports*: "Pakistan, 27 February 2014, US Department of State issued Pakistan's human rights report for 2013," http://www.state.gov/j/drl/rls/hrrpt/2013/sca/220402.htm.
3 *Ibid.* 27 February 2014.

province resources.[1] There are numerous stories of women raped by Pakistan army soldiers in Baluchistan and Khyber Pakhtunkhwa provinces, which painted an ugly image of the Muslim army. In May 2011, The Hindu Post and Hindustan Times reported cases of women sexually abused by the officers of Pakistan army.[2]

According to newspapers and NGOs reports, Pakistan army officers assaulted and sexually abused non-Muslim women and girls, and used them as sex slaves in Punjab, Baluchistan and Khyber Pakhtukhwa provinces. In a prayer-cum demonstration held at the United Nations, participants complained about the attitude of the army officers toward Christian and Hindu women. More than 100 women from different faiths complained that women are being raped and killed by officers of Pakistan army. According to the NGOs report; army officer in Baluchistan and Gilgit took women as a sex slaves, tortured and then killed. "One such case of that Zarina Marri, a 23-year-old school teacher from Quetta, was being used as a sex slave by the Pakistan army," the EOPM said in a statement.

Women and young girls from Christians, Sikhs, Hindus and other minority communities are the constant target of the army officers. On 28 July 2005, BBC reported the family of a young woman of Kashmir raped by three Pakistani soldiers. These three soldiers were from Mujahid Battalion. Moreover, on 02 February 2014, the News International reported an anti terrorism court remanded an army soldier involved in Uzma Ayub kidnapping and rape case into police custody, for an additional two days. Miss Uzma Ayub, a single mother was kidnapped by an army officer and three police men. She was repeatedly raped. She became pregnant.[3] In another important case, Shazia Khalid was raped and tortured by Pakistan army captain in Baluchistan. Elders of Bugti tribe saw a rape in their heartland as being a breach of their code of honor, especially when the alleged rapist was a captain in the army.

In Baluchistan province, the demand for an independent state has grown as thousands well trained Baloch are fighting army and FC in towns and cities. Pakistan's failing state is no more interested in bringing Baluchistan back to its control, because the writ of the

---

1 *The Asian Human Rights Commission report (2013):* "recorded army's atrocities in Baluchistan, however, On 27 January 2014, *Asian Human Rights Commission* (AHRC) reported 100 dead bodies of killed Balochs in three mass graves in Baluchistan province".

2 *The Hindu,* 11 May 2011

3 02 February 2014, *The News International:* "an anti terrorism court remanded an army soldier involved in Uzma Ayub kidnapping and rape case into police custody for an additional two days".

state is no more existed in more than 90% area of the province. There are reports that thousands men, women and children are still missing from Baluchistan. According the Human Rights Commission of Pakistan report, in 2010 and 2011, in many instances, bodies of missing person were found on roadside in deserted areas.

On March 29 2011, Guardian reported mutilated corps in Baluchistan bearing the signs of torture, among them, were lawyers, students and farm workers:

> Bodies surface quietly, like corks bobbing in the dark. They were dumped on desolate mountains or empty city roads, bearing the scares of great cruelty. Arms and led are snapped; faces are bruised and swollen. Flash is sliced with knives punctured with drills; genitals are singed with electric pods. In some cases the bodies are unrecognizable, sprinkled with lime or chewed by wild animals. All have a gunshot wound in the head.[1]

According to the Amnesty International report, the clandestine nature of the arrests and detentions makes it impossible to know exactly how many have been subjected to enforced disappearance. Amnesty International and other rights organizations accounted for more than 100 bodies of students and lawyers. In Punjab province, hundred men and women were also missing. On 25 October, 2013, Daily Nation reported the National Commission on Missing Persons complained about the police failure to recover 29 missing persons. Punjab Home Department disclosed that NCMC had handed over the details of missing persons but in spite of joint investigation body, they cannot investigate this case.[2]

In Baluchistan, the army used helicopter gunships, bombed villages, and destroyed the houses of the poor Baloch. The Asian Human Rights Commission in its recent report (2013) recorded army's atrocities in Baluchistan:

> The main military sweep took place in Awaran, Panjgur and Makran districts of Baluchistan. Hundred of villagers were rounded up and interrogated. Many since have disappeared. Some were later found dead, with their mutilated bodies showing signs of torture.[3]

Now Baluchistan is free and the writ of Pakistani government has ended. In February 2015, Defence Minister Khawaja Asif revealed in

---

1 *The Guardian*, 29 March 2011.
2 25 October, 2013, *Daily Nation*: "the National Commission on Missing Persons complaints about the police failure to recover of 29 missing persons. *The Asian Human Rights Commission report 2013*".
3 *Ibid.*

a TV debate that some 'separatist leaders' from Baluchistan travel on Indian passports. "The separatist leaders take trips to India and get directions," said the Defence Minister while speaking in Geo News program 'Capital Talk.' Khawaja Asif said Pakistan can respond to India in the same coin and 'we can also take up the issue of the recent incidents of Indian aggression at an international forum.

This way of tackling insurgency in Baluchistan and forceful disappearances affected the credibility of the armed forces, in the eyes of the public. Pakistan has a notorious track record of committing genocide, mass murder, collective punishment and ruthless operations against any community/nation, asking for its rights. History remembers Pakistan of committing a mass genocide of Bengalis, where estimated 3 million people were massacred in a record 6 months period. Around 450,000 Bengali Women were raped by the Islamic Army of the country. In Baluchistan, 15000 Mari tribesmen were killed, and others were expelled from the country. From 1992 to 1998, some 15000 Urdu speaking Muhajirs were killed by the same army with the help and approval of dominant Punjabi elite, in Karachi.

This fame of atrocities of Pakistan taught a new lesson to the military establishment of committing selective genocide, instead of mass genocide. This time, when Baloch raised voice of their right to self-determination and independence, Pakistani establishment and intelligence agencies adopted the strategy of forced disappearances, kill and dump. Under this policy, the Guardian (2011) reported the torture victims in secret prisons, and after acquiring information or finding the victim irrelevant, they are killed, and bodies are dumped on desolate mountains or empty city roads, bearing the scars of great cruelty. According to the Guardian report:

Kidnapped Balochs are killed in similar fashion; their arms and legs are snapped; faces are bruised and swollen. Flesh is sliced with knives or punctured with drills; genitals are singed with electric prods. In some cases the bodies are unrecognizable, sprinkled with lime or chewed by wild animals. All have a gunshot wound in the head and upper torso.[1]

On 25 August 2009, IRIN reported that mass graves were found in Swat valley and Malakand. The graves were of people who were

---

1 "How many more have to die before we can stop weeping"? Khalid Hayat Jamaldini, Bloch Samachar, 05 April 2011. http://www.crisisbalochistan.com/about-us.html, and also, "Pakistan's secret dirty war," *The Guardian*, Declan Walsh, 29 March 2011, http://www.theguardian.com/world/2011/mar/29/balochistan-pakistans-secret-dirty-war. also, *Washington Post*, 22 April 2014.

killed by Pakistan army. Human Rights Commission of Pakistan reported mass graves in Banozai and Kabal districts of Swat.[1]

An addition to this, discovery of mass graves in Baluchistan created a lot of misunderstanding between the center and provinces. Express Tribune reported the central spokesman of Bloch Republican Party, Mir Sher Muhammad Bugti, who warned that the mass graves in Dera Bugti were a big question for the world particularly for the Islamic countries. Sher Muhammad Bugti stated that 19 Bloch including his brother Shah Muhammad Bugti were kidnapped by Pakistan army in 05 December 2010, after two days, he and his colleagues received their dead bodies.[2]

From 2012 to 2013, Baluchistan remained a killing field. Hundreds of Baloch political worker were killed by Pakistan security forces in custody, while their bodies were dumped across the province. Such heinous crimes by the state security forces are tantamount to war crimes and crimes against humanity. On 27 January 2014, Asian Human Rights Commission (AHRC) reported 100 dead bodies of Balochs in three mass graves in Baluchistan province. Newspapers in India and the United States also reported these mass graves and demanded a thorough investigation into death of these innocent people. Asian Human Rights Commission (AHRC) in its statement expressed deep concern over the killing of these people in the hands of Pakistan army:

> The Asian Human rights Commission (AHRC) express shock and deep concern over the discovery of mass graves in Baluchistan; it is suspected that these graves are of Baloch missing persons who were arrested and subsequently extra-judicially killed. A large number of family members gathered around the places of Tootak village; district Khuzdar to inquire about their loved ones who have been missing for many years.... On January 25, three mass graves were found after one of them was discovered by a shepherd who saw pieces of human bodies and bones.... In total 103 bodies were discovered from the graves. The bodies were too decomposed to be identified.[3]

On 09 February 2014, Provincial Heath Minister of Baluchistan confirmed that all the decomposed and mutilated bodies found in Tootak area of Khuzdar district were of those who had been missing since long. "This is intolerable and a cause of serious consternation, especially among the youths losing all hopes fast. This is a liability

---

1 22-On 25 August 2009, *IRIN*: "human rights groups saying that mass graves were found in Swat valley and Malakand".
2 *The Express Tribune*, 2012
3 27 January 2014, *Asian Human Rights Commission* (AHRC) report.

of wrong policies left out by the Musharraf regime for the helpless people of Baluchistan to suffer, that is also providing space to the inimical hidden hands to pursue their nefarious designs." the Minister told Dawn.[1]

Secret Agencies, Police and the Killing of Journalists

Pakistani and international media continues to debate the harassment of journalists by intelligence agencies and militant groups. The Taliban, sectarian groups, and the ISI are harassing journalists and have decided to translate their threat into action. Eight years ago, international community ranked Pakistan as the world's most dangerous state for journalists. Pakistani journalists have been receiving bad treatment from the state authorities since the last two decades, whenever the country became a frontline state in the war against terrorism.

Hundreds of media workers and investigative journalists received death threats, and many of them have been killed. In a latest freedom of press index, released by Reporters without Border, Pakistan dropped eight places to 158th out of 179 states. Experts believe that failure of Pakistani establishment to provide security to journalists' families is a major factor contributing to Pakistan's shameful reputation as a graveyard for journalists.[2]

Risks to the lives of media men increased during the last few years. Moreover, war in Baluchistan, Khyber Pakhtunkhwa, Waziristan, Aurakzai, and Karachi, together with sectarian and ethnic terrorism, and actions of 'murder squad' of the intelligence agencies, have also led to the killings of local journalists. Several domestic intelligence services monitored politicians, journalists, and the media. These services included the Inter-Services Intelligence, Intelligence Bureau, the police Special Branch, and Military Intelligence.

There were credible reports that authorities routinely used wiretaps, monitored mobile telephone calls, intercepted electronic correspondence, and opened mail without the court approval. In January 2013, three more journalists were killed in Quetta. In 2013,

---

1 "Khuzdar graves are of missing persons, concedes Minister." *Dawn* ,09, February 2014.
2 "Pakistan Remains Deadly for Journalists," *Voice of America*, Ayaz Gul, 30 January 2013 http://www.voanews.com/content/pakistan-journalists-press-freedom-report/1594058.html. And *Daily Times* 13 March 2013, "Pak journalists in the crosshairs, Muhammad Waqas," *Arab News*, 16 April 2013.

in Karachi, terming Pakistan as a dangerous place for journalists, speakers at a media workshop said; that 65 journalists were killed during the last six years. Speaking about vulnerability of journalists, speakers said that on an average one journalist was killed every 28 days.[1]

Intelligence agencies targeted political parties, journalists, and media outlets. Journalists and their families were harassed and abducted. Media outlets that did not practice self-censorship were often the targets of retribution. In 2013, seven journalists were killed for reporting intelligence matter. A number of journalists also reportedly were subjected to physical attack, harassment, intimidation, kidnapping, or other forms of pressure.

On 21 April 2014, Daily Times in its editorial page expressed deep concern over the ISI attacks against journalists in Pakistan:

> Attacks on the media and journalists seem to be intensifying since the start of this year and acquiring a sinister pattern. Earlier attacks on the Express group and particularly its TV anchor Raza Rumi in Lahore, in which he was fortunately relatively unscathed but in which his driver was killed, point to the slate of possible suspects. In Raza Rumi's case, the gang responsible has recently been rounded up in Lahore and identified as belonging to the Lashkar-e-Jhangvi, a banned extreme sectarian group. However, given the controversy that has arisen as a result of the revelation of Hamid Mir's allegations against the ISI, the matter assumes even more important dimensions requiring investigations that get to the bottom of the mystery.[2]

According to the international media reports, more than 55 journalists were killed in Pakistan by various terror groups, and state agencies in the last few years. Among these journalists, 14 were from Khyber Pakhtukhwa, 12 from Baluchistan, nine from Sindh and three from Punjab province. The number of incarcerated, missing, intimidated and harassed journalists is unknown. In view of these threats and harassment, dozens of Pakistani journalists relinquished their profession and moved to safe places with their families.

In 2013, from January to December, seven journalists were killed. Before these killings, in 2011, 16 journalists were killed by Pakistani intelligence agencies, and extremist groups, and continue to torture and kidnap journalists, and their families. Well-known journalist, Mr.

---

1 *Sectarian Identities or Geopolitics? The Regional Shia Sunni Divide in the Middle East*, Mari Loumi, Working Paper-2008. "In Pakistan, another journalist breaks his silence," Sumit Galhotra, Committee to *Protect Journalists*, 09 December 2013.
2 *Daily Times*, 21 April 2014

Saleem Shehzad was kidnapped, tortured and later found dead in a canal. Many people in Pakistan are confident that the ISI was behind his murder.

Another sad story of the brutal killing of a Pakistani journalist, Malik Mumtaz in North Waziristan, appeared in the last week of January 2013. According to the Geo Television report, Mr. Mumtaz came under attack near the Chashma Bridge. Mr. Mumtaz was just elected president of the Miranshah Press Club. Another senior journalist, Mr. Khushnood Ali Sheikh, the chief reporter of the state controlled Associated Press of Pakistan (APP), was killed in Karachi by mafia groups. He was killed in February 25, 2013 as he refused to pay Rs, 50,000 in extortion.

An addition to the above mentioned attitude of Pakistani establishment towards journalists, recently, another Pakistani journalist came under attack for his courageous investigative reporting. ARY Television Journalist, Mr. Saqib Raja who fled Pakistan in fear of his family's safety claimed asylum in the UK. He is the son of a mother who served as a doctor and a father who served as a high ranking police officer in Pakistan.

On 30 April 2014, Dawn reported Amnesty International concerns about the safety of Pakistani journalists. The report, said that since the restoration of democracy in Pakistan in 2008, there have been 34 documented cases in which journalists were killed due to their reporting. Pakistan's media community is effectively under siege. Journalists, in particular those covering national security issues or human rights, are targeted from all sides in a disturbing pattern of abuses carried out to silence their reporting," an AI press release quotes Amnesty International's Deputy Asia-Pacific Director David Griffiths.[1]

In another case, the Pakistan Electronic Media Regulatory Authority (PEMRA) served a show-cause notice on Geo Entertainment network for airing objectionable content in its morning show "Utho Jago Pakistan' and sought immediate explanation from the channel. The program drew a bitter reaction from viewers and religious organizations. Several political and religious organizations, including the Pakistan Tehreek-i-Insaf (PTI), the Jamaatud Dawa, Tehreek

---

1 *Dawn*, 30 April 2014: "Journalists under siege from threats, violence and killings," 30 April, 2014, http://www.amnesty.org/en/news/pakistan-journalists-under-siege-threats-violence-and-killings-2014-04-30.

Hurmat-i-Rasool, and the Majlis Wahdatul Muslimeen, staged rallies in various parts of the country.[1]

On 07 June 2014, the PEMRA banned Geo TV. The HRCP statement also drew attention to what it called "divisions among the media ranks":

> It is regrettable that competitive media houses are adding fuel to the fire, without realizing what they are being complicit in or what a dangerous precedent they are setting and that the same fire can engulf them too. It is in no one's interest to unleash forces that are neither accountable nor answerable to anyone.[2]

On August 2014, two more journalists were killed in the line of duty in Pakistan. Online news agency bureau chief Irshad Mastoi and reporter Abdul Rasool Khajak, along with their accountant Mohammad Younis, were murdered in an attack carried out by armed men in their Quetta office. Thus, more than 30 journalists reportedly fallen victim to targeted killing in Baluchistan over the last seven years, making the province the most dangerous part of what is already, according to the Committee to Protect Journalists, the fourth most dangerous country in the world for reporters.

No one has even been put on trial, let alone convicted, for any journalist's murder in Baluchistan. Reporters without Borders' issued its annual report in February 2014, which showed that four out of seven reporters killed in Pakistan in 2013, came from Baluchistan. The report also stated that none of the cases had ever been thoroughly investigated, there had been no arrests in connection with any murder of a journalist anywhere in the country, and the successful prosecution of those who murder journalists is vanishingly small. There are ruthless insurgent organizations, feuding tribes with shifting allegiances, rapidly proliferating extremist groups—many of them with overt sectarian agendas—who are allegedly being used by the state to counter the nationalists, as well as the Frontier Corps, intelligence agencies and the military that make up the heavy security footprint in the province.

On 22 April, 2014, Daily Times reported Pakistan's Army Chief hailed the sacrifices of the Inter Services Intelligence (ISI) during

---

1 *Dawn*, 20 March 2014: "The Pakistan Electronic Media Regulatory Authority (PEMRA) served a show-cause notice on Geo Entertainment network for airing objectionable content in its morning show `Utho Jago Pakistan' and sought immediate explanation from the channel."
2 *The News International*, "HRCP decries malicious campaign against Geo," 19 May 2014, http://www.thenews.com.pk/article-148187-HRCP-decries-malicious-campaign-against-Geo.

a visit to the premier intelligence agency's headquarters. It was the incumbent army chief's second visit to the ISI headquarters in over four months. On 04 December 2013, the army chief paid his maiden visit to the intelligence agency's headquarters after assuming the army's command on 29 November 2013. A team of ISI generals led by ISI Director General Lieutenant General Zaheerul Islam briefed the army chief about the peace talks with the Tehreek-e-Taliban Pakistan (TTP), that lately seen an apparent deadlock.[1]

Other generals reported to be in the briefing were ISI's DG Security Major General Sajjad Rasool, DG Counter-Terrorism Maj Gen Naveed Mukhtar, DG Counter-Intelligence Maj Gen Nasir Dilawar Shah and ISI's sector commanders in the four provinces. A statement from the Inter Services Public Relations (ISPR) said that the army chief was given a detailed briefing on the internal and external security situation of the country.[2]

1 *Daily Times*, 22 April, 2014, http://www.dailytimes.com.pk/islamabad/23-Apr-2014/army-chief-hails-isi-s-sacrifices-for-country.
2 "Army chief hails ISI's sacrifices for country." *Daily Times*, 23 April, 2014.

Chapter 12. Intelligence Cooperation and Reforms

The intelligence community of Pakistan faces numerous challenges, including a broad lack of civilian support, confidence, credibility, and sectarian affiliations, war in Waziristan, FATA and Baluchistan. The role they are playing in the forced disappearance of Pashtun and Balochs has alienated the majority of Pakistani citizens from the state. In these circumstances, the state and the citizens look on each other with scorn. The greatest challenge Prime Minister Nawaz Sharif faces is, the national security threat. Former Pakistani diplomat Ayaz Wazir (2014) warned that the killing of innocent Pashtuns in Waziristan cannot help resolve the issue:

A deeply alarming factor in military operations is the killing of innocent civilians in the recent so-called 'targeted operation,' a factor to which everybody there can testify.[1]

Marilyn Peterson in her research report for the US Bureau of Justice Assistance has defined intelligence and information, and its role in effective planning, and says that despite many definitions of "intelligence" that have been promulgated over the years, the simplest and clearest of these is, "information plus analysis equals intelligence." Intelligence is critical to effective planning and subsequent action.

Pakistani intelligence agencies have impairing approaches to counter insurgency and counterterrorism, which caused a deep distrust between the army and the civilian government. Government doesn't trust the army

---

1 "FATA operations and the evolving situation," Ayaz Wazir." *The News International*, 08 June, 2014, http://www.thenews.com.pk/Todays-News-9-254812-Fata-operations-and-the-evolving-situation.

and its intelligence agencies. The army does its own business, runs its own domestic and foreign policy. On Afghanistan and Kashmir, army doesn't share its views with civilian government. In general understanding, effective intelligence mechanism can only work if it is part of the real time decision-making process, where intelligence assessment is integrated. In the case of Pakistan military and civilian intelligence mechanisms, there is wide-ranging disagreement about the way militancy is countered. They gather intelligence information in different ways but cannot process it.

In Pakistan, intelligence information collection faces numerous difficulties as Taliban and other militant groups control parts of the country. This is one of the greatest challenges for ISI and civilian intelligence agencies. Intelligence operations have generally been unsuccessful in holding territory, although they appear to have improved over time. Some intelligence assessments indicate that militant control of territory increased during this period. Indian research scholar, Gurmeet Kanwal highlighted the ISI interference in neighboring states through proxies:

> Over the last decade, the deteriorating internal security environment has gradually morphed into Pakistan's foremost national security threat. The Pakistan army and its intelligence arm, the Inter-Services Intelligence (ISI) Directorate gained considerable experience in aiding, abetting and fuelling insurgencies and terrorism in Afghanistan during the Soviet occupation in the 1980s and in Jammu and Kashmir (J&K) and other parts of India since 1988–89.[1]

As the cold war between the government and GHQ over security reforms, and talks with the Taliban insurgents intensified, military and civilian intelligence agencies also started sword-play against each other. Intelligence Bureau received huge money and information gathering equipments from the government, while ISI faced isolation as it didn't want to hear the Prime Minister. The record of ISI is shameful as the agency forcefully disappeared and killed thousands innocent Pashtuns across the country. The Prime Minister ordered to strengthen Intelligence Bureau (IB), train its agents in a professional way, and give it more powers, to reinvent the concept of civilian intelligence mechanism in Pakistan.

---

1 *Pakistan's Internal Security Challenges: Will the Military Cope?* Gurmeet Kanwal, The Institute of Peace and Conflict Studies (IPCS), http://www.ipcs.org/issue-brief/pakistan/pakistans-internal-security-challenges-will-the-military-cope-230.html.

In February 2013, prominent Pakistani journalist and intellectual, Najam Sethi opened the Pandora box by revealing the fact, that military intelligence agencies do not permit the civilian agencies to even keep intelligence gathering equipments. "If the proposed counterterrorism unit is headed by an army officer, he will run the unit according to the army national security policy" said Najam Sethi.[1]

There are numerous stories of intelligence agencies successes and failures in South Asia, as ISI faces a modern intelligence war in and outside the country. In fact, the wrongly designed policies of the successive governments in Pakistan badly affected the professional abilities of ISI, and civilian as they were used against each other for political purposes. From 1980s, the real journey of ISI, IB, CID and MI began, when they tighten their belts to challenge KGB, and other European intelligence networks in Afghanistan. Pakistani agencies trained, recruited and brainwashed Afghans, Kashmiris and dozens other extremist and radicalized organizations from across the world.

In 1989, they forced the Soviet military machine to withdraw from Afghanistan. The credit goes to Afghans, ISI, MI6 and CIA. During the Zia military regime, the process of radicalization began in military barracks, and a major change occurred when General Zia-ul-Haq instructed Military and intelligence unites, to take on combatant mullah with them to the front line. Soldier and officers were also required to attend the Tablighi Jamaat classes. The purpose was to indoctrinate young officers. Many of those young officers later took control of higher sensitive positions, and introduced sectarian Islam in their ranks. This virus also spread in the country's intelligence infrastructure, therefore, ISI and other agencies now gather information on ethnic and sectarian lines. Inter Services Intelligence is now a pure Punjabized network. It doesn't represent Pashtuns and the Balochs.

In 1992, the decline of Pakistani intelligence agencies began when military establishment decided to directly intervene in Afghan civil war, by providing military and financial support to specific groups. This caused deep loath among Afghans against Pakistan. The intelligence of the country also divided on ethnic and sectarian bases. After the fall of Dr. Najibullah regime in 1992, a General from Tablighi Jammat became ISI's Chief. He adopted anti Wahabi and anti Deobandi policy in Afghanistan. He nominated Sabghatullah Mujaddidi (Barelvi Pir) as the two months President for Afghanistan.

---

1 "No effective mechanism to counter terrorism in Pakistan." *The News International*, 23 February 2013.

In 1994, with the support of Deobandi army Chief, Taliban emerged with their transmogrified version of religion. Pervez Musharaf, according to Mark Curtis, organized Taliban who, later on, defeated Barelvis in the Southern and Eastern provinces of Afghanistan.[1]

In 1997, Taliban entered Kabul and established Amarat Islami government (Deobandi Government) in Afghanistan. After the fall of the Taliban regime in 2001, the Deobandis were defeated, and a pure Barelvi government of Hamid Karzai was established by the United States. During the Taliban regime, Pakistan's intelligence infrastructure also became radicalized, ethnicized, and sectarianized due to their proximity with Taliban terrorist groups. In another U-turn, in 2001, the army and intelligence agencies supported CIA and Pentagon, and declared war against their Deobandi colleagues. In their third U-turn, from 2001 to 2014, the army and ISI again started supporting Barevi groups; to de-radicalize the Deobandi-dominated intelligence agencies and military command of the country.[2]

Unfortunately, all these contradictory policies of civilian and military governments left worse effects on Pakistani society. Social, political and religious institutions divided on ethnic and sectarianism bases, and violence ruined the society. The Taliban declared jihad against Pakistan army in FATA and Waziristan regions, and still continue to ruin the lives of innocent civilians.

Inter Services Intelligence (ISI) and MI has so often proved that they are stronger than the country's parliament. They can make parliament, and they can dissolve it. The case of Mr. Nawaz Sharif is not so different from the case of former President Asif Ali Zardari, who received serious threats from the country's secret agencies. He was warned that ambulance is ready to shift him to hospital.[3]

In August 2014, ISI and military intelligence supported Tahirul Qadri and Imran Khan, to force Prime Minister Nawaz Sharif to resign. They wanted to drag the Army into political controversies. However, they initiated this involvement; it is not as if the other party didn't willingly accept it. If it was the PTI, and the PAT, that insisted on meeting the Army chief, then the government could easily have rejected the request. On 19 April 2014, the News International reported journalist Hamid Mir was attacked by the ISI in Karachi. Mr. Hamid Mir was heading to the Geo News office when his car was targeted by gunmen as it left the Jinnah International Airport

---

1 *Daily Times*, 25 March 2014.
2 *Ibid*, 25 March 2014.
3 *The News International*, 19 April 2014

on Shara-e-Faisal near the Natha Khan Bridge. He was shot three times and was rushed to a private hospital where he underwent an operation. His brother told Geo News that Hamid had told him that if he is attacked in future, ISI and its Chief Lt. General Zaheerul Islam would be responsible for that.[1]

His brother Amir Mir said that the senior anchorperson had informed some visiting intelligence officials about the threat he was facing from the ISI. He said that his brother was aware of the agency's method of threatening journalists and media houses for "biased reporting" of certain national issues. He said the ISI officials were apparently unhappy about his brother's famous talk show, Capital Talk, being broadcast on Mama Qadir's long march over missing Baloch persons. Mir said the agency was also unhappy about Hamid Mir's criticism aimed at the ISI in different Capital Talk shows.

The senior journalist was concerned on the government's failure to hand over written proof of ISI's threat to his life, said Amir, adding that he was also concerned about the probe of a planted bomb underneath his car in November 2012. His fight is for sovereignty and security of Pakistan, restoration of peace, eradication of terrorism, rule of law and freedom of speech which cannot be suppressed, said Hamid Mir's brother.

The ISPR issued a statement in response to allegations that the ISI was directly behind the attack on the journalist. The ISPR spokesman said that an independent inquiry must immediately be carried out to ascertain facts. Meanwhile, Defence Minister Khawaja Asif also reiterated that a detailed inquiry would be launched into the incident to trace the culprits. The Minister said that the government would ensure foolproof protection to journalists facing security threats. Mr. Khawaja Asif said the government was "determined to find out the truth." "This is a very sad incident that should be condemned in every possible manner." "This is a very serious allegation, and I hope this is not true. Nothing can be said without a detailed inquiry. Such a serious allegation on the army's intelligence arm demands detailed and thorough probe," he said.

Pakistan's response to terrorism has not been positive during the last three decades. There is no national consensus to counter the state sponsor terrorism in the country. Meaningful action has not been possible against terrorists in the country, because of the army's reluctance to wage a conclusive battle against them, its unwillingness

---

1 *Daily Times*, 25 March 2014, http://www.dailytimes.com.pk/opinion/25-Mar-2014/pakistan-reorganization-of-intelligence-infrastructure

to target groups such as the Quetta Shura and the Haqqani network, and now the backing by a large section of the political class of dialogue.

A decade long war among civilian and military intelligence agencies deeply impacted their professional intelligence mechanism. Intelligence bureau never liked to receive instructions from ISI and military intelligence agencies. From 1977 to 1999, ISI and MI confiscated the secret record of the federal and provincial offices of Intelligence Bureau IB, and Special Branches, many times. This civilian and military intelligence war caused loathsome in police and other law enforcement agencies, as they also received bad treatment from ISI, and the army in the past. In a nine page statement before the Supreme Court, former Chief of Intelligence Bureau (IB), Masud Sharif Khatak revealed that former Prime Minister Benazir Bhutto had extensively increased the budget of IB, because ISI was not willing to report to the Prime Minister.[1]

There is an impression in Pakistani media that ISI has become state within state, answerable neither to the military establishment, nor the civilian government. Consequently, there is no real check and balance to oversee into the money circulating machine that further complicates the democratic process in the country. Kidnapping and forceful disappearance has become legalized since the promulgation of recent Defense of Pakistan Law. From 2003 to 2014, civilian and military intelligence agencies forcefully disappeared more than 18,000 people from FATA, Waziristan, Baluchistan, and Khyber Pakhtunkhwa.

In South and North Waziristan, more than 2,000 Mehsud, Mengal and Wazir tribesmen were kidnapped by the intelligence agencies during the last 13 years. The Supreme Court of Pakistan has been hearing the cases of thousands missing persons since years, and issuing arrest warrants against the ISI and military intelligence every year. The Chief Justice also urged that the military must act under civilian government, and follow the constitution of Pakistan. But the army doesn't follow the constitution of the country. Newspapers in the country recently revealed about the 33 intelligence agencies and their 600,000 personnel, while there are still 56,000 more vacancies available[2]

The issue of reform has never been touched by the civilian governments as they have often been dismissed by the military

---

1 *Ibid*, 25 March 2014.
2 "Pakistan: fixing the intelligence machine," *Daily Times*, 05 April 2014, http://www.dailytimes.com.pk/Columnist/musa-khan-jalalzai

governments. If the government wants to reform the present intelligence infrastructure, it needs the support of international community, to pressure military leaders for deep reforms. The present National Security Policy can be considered as an attempt to counter terrorism, Talibanization and sectarianism inside the country, that has ruined the lives of thousands Pakistanis over the last decades.

The Pakistani Inter-Services Intelligence Directorate (ISI) serves as the state intelligence and counterintelligence organization, but is also deeply embedded in domestic politics and foreign policy initiatives. According to a secret NATO report seen by the BBC that Taliban remain defiant and have wide support among the Afghan people. The report is based on material from 27,000 interrogations with more than 4,000 captured Taliban, al-Qaeda and other foreign fighters and civilians.[1]

The Intelligence Reforms

The failure of Inter Services Intelligence (ISI) to intercept the consecutive terror attacks on Pakistan nuclear and military installations, and its intransigency to maintain professional intelligence cooperation with civilian intelligence agencies, or even consider Intelligence Bureau (IB) as an older civilian brother, during the last four decades, forced Prime Minister Nawaz Sharif to restructure IB, and make it more effective to meet internal and external security threats. The need to reform or restructure Pakistani intelligence does not spring from any desire to ape US or Europe, this is a constant need, as there has been no broad-based exercise to restructure the country's intelligence apparatus, and make the civilian agencies more effective in the past.[2]

In Pakistan, unfortunately, different military regime suppressed political forces and strengthened sectarian mafia groups, subjugated silent majority through radical mullahs under the cover of Sharia and trained militants, to fight inside India and Afghanistan. These policies of dictators destabilized the country. The experience of military regimes has not been a positive one. The army supported sectarian mullahs and weaken democratic forces, as a result, the country has been in a state of despondency. On 03 April 2014, Pakistani newspapers published news stories about the resolve of the Prime Minister to

1 *Dawn*, 25 February 2014
2 "Making Intelligence Smarter: The Failure of US Intelligence," Report of *Independent Task Force*. Sponsored by The Council on Foreign Relations. http://www.fas.org/irp/cfr.html.

restructure his country's intelligence agencies, generated a hope that Mr. Nawaz Sharif wants to counter insurgency and extremism with a national professional mechanism, but unfortunately, the army and ISI refused to allow the government to interfere in their illegal business of war and blood.

Intelligence Bureau, (IB) that never received attention from both the civilian and military governments during the last 65 years, is now trying to stand on its feet and challenge the militarization of intelligence mechanism in Pakistan. The Prime Minister, according to his office, allocated huge funds to the IB to recruit, and employ more agents to meet internal and external challenges of the country. Intelligence Bureau is the country's main civilian agency that functions under the direct control of the Prime Minister, tackles terrorism, insurgency and extremism.

The way military intelligence operated in the past was not a traditional and cultural way. Inter Services Intelligence (ISI), MI and other military intelligence unites, mostly concentrated on countering international terrorism, and political forces within the country. They never gave any importance to the internal security threats in the past. The ISI began as the external intelligence tool of the army, supported militant groups, sent them to India and Afghanistan, and served the interests of military establishment, and the United States. These self designed strategies and policies of civilian and military regimes, isolated the country in international community. Military intelligence and ISI purveyed arms to Sunni and Shia groups in Afghanistan in 1990s, and used them against each other.

On 28 December 2014, Tehreek-e-Taliban Pakistan (TTP) released a new video accusing the Pakistani Army of attacking the 'Mujahedeen' even after using them for "blood games" and "proxy war" in Jammu and Kashmir in the name of "so-called freedom" and in Afghanistan. The video, purportedly of its senior Commander Adnan Rashid, a former Pakistan Air Force official, who was involved in an attack on ex-dictator Gen. Pervez Musharraf, called upon the soldiers of the Pakistani Army to join the TTP, listing the atrocities committed by the force including "killing of millions" and "raping of own sisters" during the Bangladesh Liberation War in 1971. Mr. Rashid said that, "you may remember when people from the tribal areas fought the war of 1948 for you, and liberated the Azad Jammu and Kashmir for you." He accused the Pakistani Army of taking a "U-turn" and labeling jihad as terrorism and mujahedeen's as terrorists. Mocking the soldiers of the Pakistani Army as the "most foolish creature," Mr. Rashid asked them not to obey the orders of the "generals and the air marshals." He also announced a general amnesty for all those Pakistani soldiers wanting to join the TTP.

The list of problems faced by Pakistani intelligence machines is long. The IB also played political rule in the past. In 2008, a case was filed in Pakistan's Supreme Court against the alleged involvement of the agency in destabilizing the Shahbaz Sharif government in Punjab. The IB also spied on journalists and politicians with a non-traditional manner, which badly affected its professional reputation.

The Prime Minister now realized that a legislative and structural umbrella is a must under which intelligence agencies must function without military and political interference, while remaining committed to their central mission. On 25 February 2014, Prime Minister Nawaz Sharif approved and published National Internal Security Policy (2014-2018), and introduced a new mechanism in countering internal and external threats.[1]

The involvement of Army and Air force in tackling insurgency in FATA and Waziristan, caused misunderstanding. Pakistan military and civilian governments relying on US drones attacks did not give any importance to the intelligence reports of the country's agencies. The use of force against its own people always sends uncomfortable signals. Intelligence relationship between the police intelligence, IB, ISI and MI, lack of trust has been a long standing concern in civilian circles. Majority members of intelligence agencies of the country belong to different jihadist sectarian groups. They support their respective sectarian mullahs and receive huge money from their networks.

This illegal affiliation also directed intelligence operations on sectarian bases. Poor data collection with regards to the activities of militant sectarian organizations and their networks across the country is challenging problem. Many criminals who joined terrorist groups are not tracked and profiled effectively. Many terrorists currently arrested have not been recognized properly, and these groups continue to propagate their agendas through their weekly, daily and monthly publications. Extremism and militancy is hardwired into the society and the country has been divided into sects. No single political force has the capacity to turn the tide.

---

1 *A Case for Intelligence Reforms in India*, IDSA Taskforce Report, Institute for Defense Studies and Analyses, New Delhi. 2012, *Pakistan's New Policy on Counter Terror-An Appraisal.* Munish Gulati Published by: Vivekananda International Foundation, http://www.vifindia.org.

The Report of Independent Task Force has outlined the basic function of an intelligence agency, intelligence collection and assessment. The report also discusses intelligence analysis and its importance for policy makers:

> The utility of intelligence collection and assessment transcends the continuing need to learn about secrets. It also involves the importance of sorting out mysteries, of analyzing events and trends. Indeed, intelligence can often be of greatest use in increasing a policymaker's understanding, rather than in trying to predict individual events. The cadre of analysts maintained by or available to the intelligence community constitutes an important resource for policymakers trying to manage an enormous stream of information.... Intelligence collection priorities, while reflecting both national interests and broader policy priorities, need to be based on other considerations. First, there must be a demonstrated inadequacy of alternative sources; except in rare circumstances, the intelligence community does not need to confirm through intelligence what is already readily available. Second, devoting resources to intelligence can be justified more easily when the efforts of the intelligence community are likely to produce a specific benefit or result for the policymaker or consumer. In short, collection priorities must not only be those subjects that are policy-relevant but also involve information that the intelligence community can best (or uniquely) ascertain.[1]

Though domestic information sharing is an important undertaking and represents a better understanding of how to combat terrorism, this approach overlooks two important points. First, states increasingly rely on other states either for their security or the necessary training, and equipment to perform security functions. Second, to combat transnational threats effectively, states must share intelligence at the international level. Monish Gulati, outlines the basic role of intelligence in a modern world in his comprehensive report:

> Intelligence agencies must be clear about the challenges to the security of the state. Their ambit will perforce need to extend the entire gamut of collecting intelligence on internal security, external security, military intelligence—both tactical and strategic, economic and commercial intelligence as well as new data in science and technology related issues. Intelligence is essential but its purpose

---

1 Report of *Independent Task Force*: "Making Intelligence Smarter: The Future of US Intelligence) has outlined the basic function of intelligence, intelligence collection and assessment".

must be to inform action. It has a broader range of applications in the context of modern day threats.[1]

In counterterrorism cooperation, as with other aspects of intelligence liaison, the services of the countries involved perceive such collaboration to be in their self-interest. Liaison relationships allow each partner to draw on the comparative advantage of the other. In view of the above mentioned established way of intelligence mechanism, Pakistani intelligence agencies now need to change their way of operation in countering extremism and militancy across the country.

The Prime Minister Nawaz Sharif's decision to restructure intelligence infrastructure received worldwide appreciation. Mr. Sharif is now in position to take stern steps and try to improve the operational capabilities of his country's intelligence agencies. The creation of an effective intelligence infrastructure to meet internal and external challenges must necessarily to be taken as a long-term policy.

1 "Pakistan's New Policy on Counter Terror-An Appraisal." Munish Gulati, Published By: Vivekananda International Foundation, http:// www.vifindia.org

Chapter 13. The Professionalization of Intelligence Cooperation

The professionalization of intelligence cooperation, or at least efforts leading in that direction became increasingly necessary, when TTP and Afghan Taliban extend their terrorist networks beyond their sphere of influence. Heightened, sustained vigilance and coherent approach to a professional intelligence mechanism is considered central in countering their way of misgovernment. Worse can emerge, when thinking in terms of the professionalization of intelligence cooperation, its counter or antithesis, namely poor intelligence sharing, can increasingly become the dominant them.[1]

The issue of professionalization of intelligence cooperation in Afghanistan and Pakistan received little attention as majority of foreign intelligence agencies in the region, do not sincerely cooperate on intelligence sharing matter. Afghan intelligence agencies operate inside Pakistan, while Pakistani intelligence agencies operate inside Afghanistan, thus, the issue of intelligence sharing just remains on paper. The activities of NDS, RAMA, and NATO intelligence in various parts of Afghanistan, particularly along with the Durand Line, have long been the subject of conjecture and supposition. These agencies usually adhere to their national interests; do not necessarily want to share their collected data with CIA, ISI and other agencies.

---

1 *Professionalization of Intelligence Cooperation: Fashioning Method out of Mayhem,* Adam, DM Svendsen. Palgrave Macmillan, 30 Aug 2012

However, British and UN diplomats once told American academics that Afghan intelligence provided weapons to Baloch insurgents in Pakistan. These statements further increased in the distrust of Kabul and Islamabad. Islamabad also complained that two of its neighbors, India and Iran, are secretly bidding to destabilize Pakistan using Afghan soil.[1]

International Security Assistance Force (ISAF) established different intelligence unites, but most of its secret operations are carried out by individual states in Afghanistan. The CIA did not share all information with its allies while German intelligence agencies have their own operational role in Kabul and Northern Afghanistan. Inter Services Intelligence (ISI) is no doubt a professional organization but its changing loyalties has made it suspicious in the eyes of most Pakistani citizens. Its involvement in the forced disappearance of 18,000 Pakistani citizens, and its changing shape of alliances with CIA, raised serious questions regarding its patriotism. Outside the Middle East, intelligence cooperation and sharing partners have been instrumental in the roundup of terror leaders in subcontinent region.[2]

With Pakistan's proximity to Afghanistan, its links with insurgent groups and its intelligence support has been critical in the war on terror in Afghanistan. As a full-fledge partner of the US, Pakistan provided an air corridor, logistic and intelligence support to the CIA. Mutual trust between the two states remained fundamental in their critical intelligence cooperation. Intelligence cooperation between Pakistan and US represents one of the most significant challenges in Afghanistan.

The exponential terrorist networks of TTP and Afghan Taliban in Pakistan, and Afghanistan, though necessitated increased cooperation among the intelligence agencies of ISAF, NATO and ISI, NDS and Iranian intelligence, but in reality, no one is willing to share its intelligence with other. The present new emphasis on intelligence sharing between CIA and ISI created new challenges. The CIA relationship with ISI has arguably been one of the most complicated intelligence partnerships in South Asia. Nevertheless, some challenges persist in fostering closer CIA and ISI cooperation on Afghanistan, but both the states appear committed to foster closer relationship in the area of counterterrorism, law enforcement and border control. On

---

1 "Chuck Hagel stirs up India-US storm over Afghanistan": *BBC*, 27 February 2013, *Dawn*, 27 February 2013, http://www.bbc.co.uk/news/world-asia-21601120.
2 *Daily Times*, 19 March 2014

14 April 2014, ABC News reported US intelligence official on strained relations with Pakistan:

> I have to be careful what I say here [Director of National Intelligence James Clapper told students at the University of Georgia]. First I'll say that Pakistan is a very important ally, partner—particularly as we draw down in Afghanistan and won't have the presence there that we've had in the past, whatever form that takes.... Many times our interests converge and sometimes they don't. Clapper added that while thousands of Pakistani citizens have been killed or injured because of domestic militant actions, for the Pakistani government and its Inter-Services Intelligence agency (ISI), neighboring India is their greatest strategic concern.[1]

For years, the United States had complex intelligence sharing relationship with Pakistani intelligence agencies. American officials have often accused the ISI of using terrorist groups in Pakistan to their own ends, even if it means targeting Americans. On 05 September 2013, in his American Thinker article, Matthew Ernest exposed Pakistan's double-edged sword in relations with the United States in Afghanistan. Pakistan wants peace in Afghanistan on one hand, and support Afghan Taliban on the other:

> Pakistan is truly a double-edged sword as both a nation where democracy has taken hold, yet still harboring Al Qaeda and countless other terrorist groups. On one hand, we need Pakistani cooperation to help locate terrorist suspects, but on the other hand, it is often Pakistani government officials that are supporting those same suspects. Since the 9/11 attacks, the U.S. has provided approximately $23.55 billion in military and economic aid to Pakistan. In exchange, Pakistani officials have arrested over 600 AQ members and 8000 terrorists are reported to be on death row. The U.S. has also received intelligence cooperation, resulting in the launching of 343 drone strikes in Pakistan since 2006.[2]

On 04 November 2013, Shahan Mufti reported in New York Times about the double game of ISI in war against terrorism in Afghanistan:

> Meanwhile, American officials keep pointing to Pakistan's "double game" for most of their failures in Afghanistan, while downplaying the fact that, without Pakistan, this war would have been impossible to wage in the first place. The real root of the dysfunction is not so much deceit between allies as the lies both governments have told their own people. Pakistani and American leaders have systematically and

---

1 *ABC News*, 14 April 2014
2 "Pakistan: Ground Zero for U.S. Counterterrorism." Matthew Ernest 05 September 2013, American Thinkers.

purposefully misled their own publics about the nature and details of their partnership. Each country has used the other as a strategic and convenient punching bag.[1]

After the Swat and Abbottabad operations in 2009 and 2011, their relationship raised serious questions. Suspicion grown, the two sides became near adversaries. The arrest of Raymond Davis in Lahore, and the US unfriendly attitude towards Pakistan, further complicated relations between the two states. However, intelligence sharing and cooperation between the two states completely stopped. As for as Afghan intelligence is concerned, in fact, extending intelligence cooperation to ISI was not in its control—some external powers had remote-control in their hands. The US intelligence officials recently disclosed that their country's intelligence network is one of the largest in the world—the agency has more than 1,000 personnel in Afghanistan, including operatives and technical staff.

Moreover, there are number of intelligence unites; like Serious Organized Crime Committee (CCSC) and Military Counterterrorism Investigation Group with 3,000 soldiers from Afghan army, work under CIA across Afghanistan. All these unites, Blackwater, NDS and other private intelligence companies have different ways of intelligence culture. Their relations with CIA are in strain. Russian intelligence experts recently exaggerated the capabilities of CIA in Afghanistan and say; it does not give any wider role to the intelligence agencies of NATO and ISAF member states.

Disagreement between EU member states and CIA also negatively affected the professionalization of intelligence cooperation. Fundamental divergences regarding the way terrorism are tackled; US unprofessional approach to the war in Iraq and Afghanistan, estranged partners and hinder the advancement of intelligence cooperation. In Afghanistan, CIA closely worked with Northern Alliance war criminals, and drug smugglers, therefore, the roots of Afghan intelligence are in Northern Afghanistan. Pashtuns were marginalized, and the Taliban who accepted the new administration were targeted. Intelligence was skewed to meet immediate operational needs, rather than directed to build up multidimensional picture of key actors, context and dynamics.

The US Commander in Afghanistan, Major General Michael T. Flynn in his report complained about the poor intelligence cooperation in Afghanistan. Military officers and civilians working with ISAF are non-cooperative and do not share a single word with

1 *New York Times*, 04 November 2013

each other. There is no common database, no common strategy and no common thinking among the ISAF allies. The Lack of digital network available to all participating states raised serious questions about their partnership in the war on terrorism in Afghanistan.

It's no secret that U.S, NATO and Afghan intelligence agencies don't always get things right, and their analysis leads policy makers and military commanders to a wrong conclusion. Their poor data, inaccurate intelligence information about the Taliban activities, their source of low quality disinformation and their misinterpretations and flawed strategies often caused civilian casualties and infrastructural damages.

In Afghanistan, intelligence is mostly retrieved from newspapers, Internet, military and law enforcement agencies, and civilian informers. Moreover, intelligence is being gathered by private intelligence and security companies, which always proved wrong and misleading. In view of their inability to provide an accurate information, in 20 Oct 2013, British intelligence, MI6, immediately called for reinforcement in Afghanistan amid fears that the country will become an "intelligence vacuum" where terrorists will pose an increased threat to Britain.[1]

As we all know, intelligence approach of the US and Afghanistan, has been incoherent during the last 13 year, as they failed to collect true military and civilian intelligence information from majority districts of Eastern and Western Afghanistan, and FATA region of Pakistan. When we study the role of NATO intelligence agencies, NDS, CIA, Russian and Chinese intelligence, Defense Clandestine Intelligence and Pentagon in Afghanistan, we come across several stories of their failure as they have never been able to stabilize the country or counter the terrorist activities of Pakistani jihadists effectively.

For the US and NATO intelligence agencies, the type of information needed by their military commanders to conduct population-centric counterinsurgency operations in Afghanistan, was very important, but they couldn't retrieve it from majority of remote districts. When intelligence is ignored then twisted to produce a desired result it is truly a failure. Since the war in Afghanistan, the failure of US foreign policy created many problems while intelligence community is resisting becoming a party to fabrication; witness and recent pushback over the issue of counterinsurgency.

The US and its allies approach to professionalization of intelligence cooperation, cooperation on civilian and military level with Afghan intelligence agencies, and Inter Services Intelligence

---

1 *The Telegraph*, 20 October 2013

(ISI) in Baluchistan, Kunar province, FATA and Waziristan has never been satisfactory. They failed to gather information about the sleeping cells of insurgence from remote mountainous areas where insurgents prepare themselves for attacking coalition forces. The role of CIA and Afghan intelligence and their strategies has been deeply contradictory, particularly, since the emergence of Taliban networks and their attacks across the Durand Line. They failed to professionalize intelligence cooperation, operations, collection and process, or provide military and strategic guidance to the US and NATO military command.

For a professional intelligence network to be relevant in counter insurgency operation, it needs to supply wide-ranging military information to the commanders and policymakers from the war zone. That information, along with much else including realistic presentation setting out the entire range of possible outcome, the time needed to achieve the objectives, and the intractable issues tied to information collection must be presented in ways so they are fully integrated into the design and planning for the intervention itself.

In January 2010, US commander in Afghanistan, Mike Flynn prepared an intelligence report which revealed about the worse intelligence failure. General Flynn complained that intelligence was hard at work but it was doing the wrong job. Later on, he suggested the separation of COIS from intelligence operations, focusing on Taliban to promote various approaches for gathering the right information. In Fixing Intel, General Flynn sought to drive home the concept that US intelligence needs to collect information about the population of Afghanistan. US military commanders admitted to having very little knowledge of Afghan culture and Taliban insurgents.[1]

They accept a predilection of military-led approaches to problems, including those that were quintessentially political. Research scholar, Matt Waldman also described flawed policies of the United States and its allies in his recent article: "In the eyes of US officials and informed observers, high level US policymaking on Afghanistan was severely impaired by fundamental, structural flaws, many of which are interrelated and reinforcing."

Another US Commander, General Eikenberry criticized counter insurgency strategy promoted by General Petraeus. The General rejected the COIN strategy as applied in Afghanistan, in his article published in Foreign Affairs. In the end of 2013, US National

---

1 *Fixing Intel: A Blueprint for Making Intelligence Relevant in Afghanistan*, By Major General Michael T. Flynn, USA, Captain Matt Pottinger, USMC, Paul D. Batchelor, DIA, Centre for a New American Security.

Intelligence Estimate (NIE) warned that the country would quickly fall into chaos as President Hamid Karzai refused to sign security deal with the US. National Intelligence Estimate report, which includes input from 16 intelligence agencies in the U.S, predicted that the Taliban would become more influential as the US forces draws down in the end of 2014.[1]

Moreover, in response to these allegations, Afghan President Hamid Karzai expressed grief concern that his country was the victim of war which served interests of the US and its Western allies. "Afghans died in a war that's not ours" President Karzai said in an interview with Washington Post. President Karzai said he was in trouble by war casualties, including those in US military operations and felt betrayed by what he described as insufficient US focus on going after Taliban sanctuaries inside Pakistan.[2]

The US and its allies should know that Chinese and Russian agencies seek influence in the country as a means of securing their borders. But in reality, the presence of US forces in Afghanistan provided China with a sense of stability. Beijing understand that now US is focusing on terrorist networks in the country, and it is in China's interest to engage NATO and US forces there rather than stirring up trouble in China. However, China gives cause for optimism on this matter as it so far has succeeded in avoiding any linkage between its friendship with Pakistan and its interest in Afghanistan. China is seeking ISI's role in stabilizing Afghanistan. The country knows that ISI has influenced in Kabul in many ways but wants to deal with Afghan security as a separate issue altogether.

An addition to ISI and Saudi intelligence designs, Iran pursues a policy of its own, shaped by its national security interests. Iranian intelligence supports non-state actors and some groups of Taliban as well. In reality, all Afghan neighbors are busy in provoking ethnic and sectarian groups to strengthen their position in the country. Pakistan wants to maintain its influence in Afghanistan and also trying to stabilize the country to secure its own territory but, unfortunately, Afghanistan has been in trouble due to its complicated ethnic politics since decades.

1 "Afghanistan gains will be lost quickly after drawdown, U.S. intelligence estimate warns," By Ernesto Londoño, Karen DeYoung and Greg Miller *Washington Post, 28 December 2013.* And also, *Daily Times,* 11 March 2014.

2 "Interview: Karzai says 12-year Afghanistan war has left him angry at U.S. government," By Kevin Sieff, *Washington Post,* 02 March 2014, http://www.washingtonpost.com/world/interview-karzai-says-12-year-afghanistan-war-has-left-him-angry-at-us-government/2.

The sad incident of Kunar province in which 20 soldiers were killed is considered an intelligence failure, because Afghan civil and military intelligence agencies unnecessarily focused on targeted killings in Baluchistan province. The KHAD and NDS operations in Khyber Pakhtunkhwa and Waziristan regions only bring instability to Afghanistan. The NDS started targeting prominent political and religious leaders in these regions. This unnecessary involvement raised many questions about their killing business. The Kunar province is mostly controlled by Taliban forces; Afghan intelligence has no access to collect intelligence information about the dissidents. Speaking at the funeral ceremony, Defense Minister Maulana Bismillah Khan Muhammadi criticized the controversial role of Taliban, ISI and his own country's military intelligence.[1]

The existing organizational structure, infrastructure and operational methodology of intelligence agencies in Pakistan are of a period, prior to the rise in incidents of terrorism. When it comes to basic sources of intelligence, i.e. human intelligence, signal intelligence, electronic intelligence, communication intelligence, imaginary intelligence and sophisticated equipment and training, Pakistani agencies are found to be lacking. There is a dire need of reforms backed by legislation.[2]

In Muhammad Ali Durrani's article, trust between the army and agencies has been stressed. The basic reason Durrani noted, is the trust that the military rulers of Pakistan have had in the ISI. In fact, an effort was made by the military rulers to militarize the IB:

> I recollect the appointment of Gen Agha Neik as the head of the IB by Gen Ziaul Haq. Because of the efficiency of the ISI, even civilian rulers placed greater reliance on the ISI. Surprisingly, a popular civilian leader gave the role of political espionage to the ISI. The IB still feels akin to MI5 and MI6 of the British intelligence system. Unfortunately, as the ISI grew in stature, the role of the IB diminished. Today the IB is a junior partner to the ISI. However, even though its external operations were curtailed, the IB still has a fairly broad role in national security. I feel these external operations need to be restored. The IB's Director General also reports directly to the prime minister.[3]

---

1 *The Nation*, (Urdu Weekly, London), 20 March 2014, http://www.thenation.org.uk/200314/opinion.aspx.
2 Hassan Abbas- "Reforming Pakistan's Police and Law Enforcement Infrastructure": *special report*, of the United States Institute of Peace, February 2011.
3 "Intelligence Reforms," Mahmud Ali Durrani. *The News International*, June 18, 2011

CHAPTER 14. THE ARMY AND PARAMILITARY FORCES

On 16 December 2014, unknown terrorists attacked the Army Public School in Peshawar. They entered the school and opened fire on school staff and children, killing more than 145 people, including 132 schoolchildren, ranging between eight and eighteen years of age. A rescue operation was launched by the Pakistan Army's Special Services Group (SSG). Chief of ISPR, Major General Asim Bajwa said in a press conference that at least 130 people had been injured in the attack.

The ISI investigated to determine the nationalities of terrorists, who the FIA determined were all foreign fighters: "Abu Shamil was a Chechen terrorist, Nouman Shah was an Afghan terrorist, Wazir Alam was an Afghan terrorist, Khatib al-Zubaidi was an Egyptian terrorist, Mohammad Zahedi was a Moroccan terrorist, and Jibran al-Saeedi was an unknown Arab terrorist." This incident changed the whole civilian and military way of governance in Pakistan. Military courts were established, but relations between Pakistan and Afghanistan did not improve.

The people of Pakistan have been experiencing a sharp resurgence in sectarian terrorism and Taliban insurgency, ever since the Soviet invasion in Afghanistan. Most frequently, sectarian terrorism involves clashes among Muslim and non-Muslim sects, but terror attacks on each other's religious places have been on the rise since the 1990s. In Pakistan, state institutions, specifically, the army and the police, have been divided on ethnic and sectarian bases. There are Deobandi, Barelvi, Shia, Ahmadi and Salafi affiliations within the armed forces, which represent their own versions of Islam. South Asia Terrorism Portal has painted a multi-faceted picture of extremism and sectarianism in its recent report:

the 'terror industry' that was established by Islamabad decades ago with the primary intention of exporting mujahedeen into neighboring countries, including India and Afghanistan, to secure Pakistan's perceived 'strategic interests,' continues to thrive. This vast misadventure, however, turned progressively against its very creators, and, since 9/11, Pakistan has itself become the increasing target of several formerly state sponsored terrorist formations that have 'gone rogue,' even as international pressure has forced Islamabad to undertake visibly reluctant operations against some of these groups. The process escalated after the creation of the Tehreek-e-Taliban Pakistan (TTP) in the aftermath of the Lal Masjid (Red Mosque) operations in 2007, causing a spiral of violence that now threatens the very existence of the country. Pakistan's undiminished tolerance for religious extremists has not just destroyed lives and alienated entire communities; it is destroying Pakistani society and the very idea and edifice of the nation.[1]

In March 2015, in two suicide attacks, at least 15 people were killed and more than 70 injured. The bombings occurred during prayers at two churches located around half a kilometer apart in the city's Youhanabad neighborhood that is home to more than 100,000 Christians. Suicide bombers attacked two Christian churches during Sunday services, killing at least 15 people and wounding dozens in the attack on religious minorities in the country. In the aftermath of the attacks, an enraged crowd lynched two people suspected of being accomplices in the bombings, one of whom was wrenched from police custody. Local news outlets reported that the mob set their bodies on fire. Sectarian attacks on Christian community in Gojra village of Punjab province in 2009, and the recent attacks on Hazara community in Quetta, Baluchistan, generated more communal fire. On 05 August 2009, Time magazine reported the brutal killing of Christian children and women by extremist and religious fanatics in Gojra:

> The intruders wore masks and carried guns. They went door to door, through the narrow and dusty alleyways, asking if there were any Christians inside. When the terrified faces inside replied yes, they poured chemicals on the small, redbrick homes of Episcopalians, and Evangelicals, setting them ablaze. In some cases, they didn't bother with the question. Instead, they opened fire and hurled rocks, forcing families to flee in a panic—moments before fresh flames consumed their homes as well. When the attackers were done, nine people

---

1 *South Asia Terrorism Portal*, Pakistan Assessment 2014http://www. satp.org/satporgtp/countries/pakistan/index.htm

had been killed and 45 homes lay smoldering and destroyed in the clustered Christian colony in Gojra, a town in central Punjab, marking the worst anti-Christian violence Pakistan has seen in recent years.[1]

The killing of Sunnis, Shia, Ahmadis, Hindu and Christians continues as terrorists infiltrated in the ranks of these religious groups. According to the Human Rights Watch report of 2011 and 2012, Pakistan minority groups Shia, Ahmadi, and Christians face persecution in the country. South Asian Portal in its 2014 assessment recorded important incidents of terrorism and target killing:

> Terrorism in Pakistan has already resulted in at least 460 fatalities, including 241 civilians, 86 Security Force (SF) personnel and 133 militants in just the first month of 2014, according to partial data compiled by the South Asia Terrorism Portal (SATP). 38 major incidents (each resulting in three or more fatalities) have inflicted at least 309 fatalities, and 70 explosions have also been recorded, accounting for 167 deaths. In one of the worst attacks of 2014 targeting civilians, at least 24 Shia pilgrims returning from Iran were killed and another 40 were injured in a bomb attack targeting their bus in the Khusak area of Kanak in the Mastung District of Baluchistan Province, on January 21, 2014. The Lashkar-e-Jhangvi (LeJ) claimed responsibility for the attack.[2]

On 09 June 2014, Daily the News International reported terrorists attack on the old terminal of the Karachi Airport, a high security area, in which seven Airport Security Force (ASF) personnel were killed, while 13 injured. The newspaper claimed that three passenger aircrafts and a cargo aircraft were damaged in the brazen attack. During the gun battle, six terrorists were also killed.[3]

According to the Dawn report, equipped with suicide vests, grenades and rocket launchers; terrorists battled security forces in one of the most brazen attacks in years in Pakistan's biggest city. Among the 14 victims were security personnel and four airport workers.[4]

Former Director General of Sindh Rangers, Maj-Gen Rizwan Akhtar, in a press conference claimed that unidentified foreign militants appeared to be involved in the attack. In another incident,

1 *Dawn*, 18 April, 2012, and also, Pakistan: "Who's Attacking the Christians"? By Omar Waraich, *Time Magazine*, 05 August 2009. http://content.time.com/time/world/article/0,8599,1914750,00.html.
2 "Pakistan: Who's attacking the Christians"? By Omar Waraich, *Time magazine*, 05 August 2009. http://content.time.com/time/world/article/0,8599,1914750,00.html.
3 *The News*, 09 June 2014
4 *Ibid*, 09, June 2014.

23 Shia pilgrims were killed in Taftan terrorist attack. The attackers entered Al-Murtaza hotel and Hashmi hotel, located in Taftan, minutes after the pilgrims arrived at the hotels. Independent sources from Taftan said that the attackers hurled hand grenades and opened indiscriminate fire with modern weapons killing 23 people on the spot.[1]

The Daily Times editorial noted an incident of a similar nature occurred in the Mastung district of Baluchistan province, where a bus carrying Shia pilgrims back from Iran was stormed, resulting in the death of 22 people, while injuring several others. Lashakar-e-Jhangavi terrorist group took responsibility for that attack. The Baluchistan government promised the Hazara Shia community, to take stern action against the LeJ. At that time, the Chief Minister Baluchistan Dr Abdul Malik Baloch announced, to launch a ferry service to Iran to make the journey safe. Several flights from Quetta to Iran and from Karachi to Iran were initiated as well.

In February 2012, more than 81 Shia Muslims were ruthlessly killed by terrorist travelling from Punjab to Gilgit Baltistan. Their bus was stopped and they were killed one by one. On 16 February 2013, however, 90 Shia Muslims were killed, and 180 injured in Quetta city market. Research scholar, Huma Yusuf has painted a true picture of Pakistan's violent society in her research paper:

Since Pakistan's is the second-largest Shia community in the world after Iran, widespread sectarian violence threatens to destabilize the country and the region. Because sectarian affiliations are ubiquitous and deeply felt this kind of violence has the potential to involve large swathes of the population and spur radicalization. Sectarian strife is also likely to further fragment Pakistan's polity, already divided by language and ethnicity. Moreover, the growing power, networks and resources of sectarian organizations will lead to an overall deterioration of Pakistan's already fragile security situation. Given this destabilizing potential, this report focuses on the resurgence of sectarian violence in Pakistan and interrogates whether this kind of violence poses one of the greatest threats to the stability of present-day Pakistan.[2]

According to the Washington Post report, on 06 January 2014, a suicide bomber tried to enter a school filled with several hundred students in a Shiite-dominated area in the northwest but was

---

1 *Ibid*, 09, June 2014.
2 Research scholar, Huma Yusuf (July 2012) painted a true picture of Pakistan's violent society in his research paper: "Conflict Dynamics in Karachi." United States Institute of Peace

stopped by a ninth-grader, who is being hailed as a national hero after he died when the bomb went off in the ensuing scuffle.[1] On 06 January 2014, The Express Tribune quoted the report of Pakistan Institute of Peace Studies, which noted militant, nationalist insurgent and violent sectarian groups carried out a total of 1,717 terrorist attacks across Pakistan in 2013, claiming the lives of 2,451 people and causing injuries to another 5,438.[2]

On 11 February, 2014, Long War Journal revealed important information about the network of Ahrar-ul-Hind militant group in Pakistan. Ahra-ul-Hind is a new extremist group which opposes the Taliban talks with Pakistan. The group was part of Taliban terrorist network, but split from the network:

> A new global jihadist group that is unwilling to negotiate with the Pakistani government has announced its formation and vowed to continue attacks in the country despite the outcome of ongoing peace talks. The group, which is calling itself Ahrar-ul-Hind, said its goal is the establishment of sharia, or Islamic law and that the Movement of the Taliban in Pakistan is still "our brothers" despite separation from the group. Ahrar-ul-Hind emailed two statements to The Long War Journal on Feb. 9: one from its spokesman, and another that outlined its "aims and objectives," according to the SITE Intelligence Group, which translated the communiqués. Ahrar-ul-Hind has also posted both statements on its Face book page. "Ahrar-ul-Hind was part of TTP [Tehrik-e-Taliban or Movement of the Taliban in Pakistan] and 'other jihadist organizations' but split from TTP due it [TTP] engaging in talks with the Pakistani government," Adam Raisman from SITE told The Long War Journal.[3]

Having commented on the article, Birbal Dhar quoted the Hadeith of Prophet Muhammad to explain the basic aim of the group:

> To them Pakistan is a nationalistic name, which they only use as a temporary phase. Also "Hind" was referred in the Hadith, where the prophet Mohammed predicted that the Indian subcontinent (comprising of India, Pakistan, Bangladesh) will be conquered by Muslims and a Muslim people from that land will fight the infidels (those who are not Muslim or not sufficiently Muslim in their eyes) in the middle east on the day of judgment and will reclaim Jerusalem for the Muslim people, with Jesus (Muslims call him Isa) coming back.[4]

---

1 *Washington Post*, 06 January 2014
2 *The Express Tribune*, 06 January 2014
3 *Long War Journal*: "Pakistani jihadists form Ahrar-ul-Hind, vow to continue attacks" February 11, 2014.
4 *Ibid*, 11 February 2014.

On 31 May 2014, RSN Singh reported Pakistan's designs against India and Afghanistan on CanaryTrap.com. Pakistan wants to disrupt the Indian efforts in Afghanistan:

> Apart from the Pakistan Military's nervousness over the uncertainty of evolving contours of Pakistan–Afghanistan–India strategic triangle due to the envisaged withdrawal of ISAF from Afghanistan, the terror attacks on Indian Consulates, therefore has also much been engendered by the internal institutional rivalry and dynamics within Pakistan.... If the TTP continues to gain further ascendance, the strategic maneuver space of Pakistan Military with regard to Afghanistan and India will accordingly shrink.[1]

The strategy of proxy war by Pakistan Military in Afghanistan and India via Afghan-Taliban and LeT respectively is now facing a formidable despoiler by way of TTP. Pakistani authorities have been accused by rights groups of turning a blind eye to the banned sectarian militant groups, and their relentless attacks on vulnerable communities, such as Shia Muslims and other minority groups. Taliban insurgencies have now openly challenged the state army, and the authority of the government. Directionless and ineffective strategies of army, and civilian government further exacerbated the precarious speed of violence across the country. There are numerous books available in the markets and libraries, which almost discuss the same problem facing Pakistan, but majority of books and research papers, have never touched the basic roots of sectarian terrorism. Some writers have poorly touched the issue and some have focused on unnecessary issues.

The Madrassa (religious schools) culture has created big problems in Pakistani society. These schools cause security challenges. Sectarian attacks against Ahmadi, Zikri and Shia sects, and attacks on Christian religious places, war among Sunni sects and the recent killing of Hazara minority in Quetta and Punjab, painted a transmogrified picture of Pakistani Islam abroad. Financial support to the Shia and Sunni communities from Iran and Saudi Arabia resulted in the outbreak of proxy war in the country.

In his Dawn article, Murtaza Haider described the scourge of sectarianism in Pakistan in detail. From Kurram to Gilgit Baltistan and from Karachi to Punjab, sectarian terrorists continue to devastate the lives of innocent people through their subversive activities:

---

1 RSN Singh, "the next attack on India from Pakistan." CanaryTrap. com, 31 May 2014, http://www.canarytrap.in/2014/05/31/the-next-attack-on-india-from-pakistan/

> Sectarian violence has spread to all corners of Pakistan. Only last week several Shias belonging to the Hazara tribe were gunned down by the Sunni extremists in a crowded market in Quetta. Later, Sunni militants called local newspapers and claimed responsibility for their murderous accomplishment. Over the past few years hundreds, if not thousands, of Shias have been murdered in Kurram Agency by Sunni extremists and Taliban factions who are reportedly aligned with Pakistan's intelligence agencies. In other parts of Pakistan Shias have been taken off buses, lined up, and gunned down.[1]

The assassination of the governor of Punjab province in 2011, and other target killings across the country, challenged the security infrastructure of Pakistan. In Kurram, Orakzai and Gilgit regions, Pakistan army killed thousands Sunni and Shia Muslims. This brutal war forced both Sunni and Shia Muslims to abandoned their houses and move to safe places. The Shia Sunni divide intensified under the military rule—used Muslim youth and enrolled them in sectarian seminaries during the Afghan war.

Jihad in Kashmir, Chechnya, Bosnia and Afghanistan has been a profitable business of Pakistan army in 1980s and 1990s. The inconsiderate policies of military establishment resulted in the reorganization of sectarian infrastructure across the country. The arrest of some members of sectarian groups along with their colleagues within the army, opened up some important revelations before the police about the future role of Pakistan army in the civil war of the country.

In 2010, police arrested a few Taliban fighters while thousands more suspected members of Jundullah, the Badar Mansoor group, Kharooj, the Al-Mukhtar group, Punjabi Taliban, Asian Tigers, Lashkar-e-Jhangvi Al-Alami, Jundul Hafsa, Al-Furqan and Al-Qataal who continue to kill innocent people, collect illegal taxes, and are involved in robbery, theft and looting. Moreover, the city became a hub of international criminal gangs, drug and arms smugglers, and these syndicates have now become a roosting ground for the private militias of the Sunni and Shia sects.

In September 2012, Pakistani newspapers quoted a secret ISI report about the activities of Blackwater. Blackwater's first known contract with the CIA for operations in Afghanistan was awarded in 2002, and was for work along the Afghanistan-Pakistan border. Pakistan's military establishment thinks that the US supports anti-Pakistan elements fighting against Pakistani security forces in the

---

1 Murtaza Haider, *Dawn*, 18 April, 2012

tribal areas as the CIA conducts its covert war in Pakistan through Blackwater or Ex. Services. The issue of the existence of Blackwater in Pakistan became clear when ex-US Defense Secretary Robert Gates in an interview with a TV channel in January 2010 confirmed that Blackwater and DynCorp were operating inside Pakistan.[1]

As far as terror finance is concerned, the UK-based Pakistani ethnic and sectarian groups channel a huge amount of money through fake IDs to their respective groups in Karachi. This illegal transaction of money plays a major role in the purchase of arms and ammunition for ethnic and sectarian terrorists. In 2011, the Sindh Assembly was told that thousands of sophisticated weapons were smuggled into Karachi. On August 2, 2011, CID officials claimed to have seized rocket-launchers, rockets, weapons and bullets from a terror group. Moreover, the Anti-Extremism Cell (AEC) in Karachi seized heavy weapons from a sectarian group.

As international security experts have already warned about the smuggling networks of Afghan, Iranian and Pakistani smugglers, who smuggle drugs and arms from Central Asia, the Middle East and Iran into Karachi. Police and security agencies have so far failed in tracking down their local connections. A secret document in Karachi recently revealed that Sri Lankan terror group, LTTE, had established an arms smuggling network in Karachi on September 14, 2009. The document revealed that LTTE had established joint arms smuggling networks with a number of international terrorist groups. Al Qaeda agent Mohammed Ali Qasim alias Abu Sohaib al-Makki was recently arrested living in the country for more than 10 years.

In February 2011, the Special Investigation Unit (SIU) arrested serial killers, including a retired army officer, involved in arms smuggling in Karachi. There are more than 35 sectarian terror groups and 25 illegal tax collecting religious and ethnic groups, who have besieged the city from all sides. Arms are being smuggled into Karachi via the Gulf and the Arabian Sea. The underground networks of Afghani, Iranian, Pakistani and Central Asian arm and drug smugglers created a warlike situation in the city.

Poverty, unemployment, sectarianism, ethnicity and arms smuggling may further exacerbate the level of violence in the city. The ruction between General Musharaf and his country diplomatic mission over their inabilities to defend the reputation of the army raised serious questions during the Kargil war (1999), when Britain

---

1 US Defense Secretary Robert Gates in an interview with a *TV channel* in January 2010 confirmed that Blackwater and DynCorp were operating inside Pakistan.

and U.S newspapers labeled Pakistan army as rogue army. On 02 January 2003, according to the Tribune article, Pakistan army killed thousands innocent people in four provinces:

> The Pakistan army has killed more of its own citizens in the past three decades that any other armed forces, except the Khumer Rouge led by the genocide's poll pot. Documented evidence of the number of Pakistani citizens killed following the carnage by the Pakistan army in Bangladesh (1971), Baluchistan (1972–1974), rural Sindh, (1983 onward) and the urban centers of Sindh against the MQM (in the 1990s) confirms this fact. Despite this record, the closest collaboration in establishing and sustaining military rule in Pakistan has been and remains the United States of America. Military dictators from Ayub Khan to Zia Ul Haq and Gen Musharaf have all been beneficiaries of American patronage.[1]

In 1979, after the Soviet Union intervention in Afghanistan, Pakistan military and ISI welcomed millions Afghans and Muslim extremists from across the globe, to join jihadist organization in war against Afghanistan. Founded in 1948, ISI employed more than 500 army officers to organize its intelligence operation in Afghanistan in 1983. In 1984, ISI agents started operating in Jalalabad, Bagram and Kabul. They were mostly Pashtun army officers who organized Mujahedeen groups inside the country. The ISI then managed to employ retired army officer in Afghanistan and advised to fight to the end inside Afghanistan. In 1986, ISI managed more than 20,000 Mujahid force along with the border of Afghanistan. Members of this force were recruited by Pakistan army officers.

After the death of Zia-ul Haq in 1988, the late General Hamid Gul continued to recruit Afghan Mujahedeen. Hamid Gul played very important role in Afghan jihad. After the fall of Dr. Najibullah regime in 1992, Pakistan supported Mujahedeen groups to establish a friendly government in Kabul. On April 2011, in his Land Warfare Paper, Christopher L. Budihas has analyzed Pakistan's political, military and economic interests in Afghanistan after the Soviet withdrawal:

> However, after the Soviet installed Najibullah regime fell in 1992, warlordism prevailed in Afghanistan. Pakistan recognized that in order to see a pro-Pakistani government in Kabul, it would have to shift its strategic approach. This anarchical environment in Afghanistan contributed to the country's increasingly negative influence on Pakistan. In the last four years of the Najibullah regime, the rise of a Pakistani friendly Afghan Pashtun Taliban force under Mullah Omar

---

1 *The Tribune*, Pakistan on 02 January 2003.

seemed the logical choice for bringing stability to Afghanistan and providing Pakistan a strategic alliance.[1]

Pakistan's support to Taliban exacerbated in the misadventures of Afghan population. After the fall of Taliban regime in 2001, all extremist and insurgent groups gathered in Pakistan to wage jihad against the country. In tribal areas, Waziristan and Swat, Taliban started attacking Pakistani armed forces. On 25 November, 2008, Professor Shaun Gregory analyzed violence and political turmoil in Pakistan:

> The heart of Pakistan's conflict is the violence in Pakistan's tribal areas, The Federally Administered Areas (FATA) and North West Frontier Province (NWFP); this in turn has a key impact on the United States-led war in Afghanistan. To understand what is happening, it is necessary to distinguish between the Afghan Taliban and Pakistan Taliban; and to grasp the relationship of each to the Pakistan military and Pakistan leading intelligence agency, the Inter Services Intelligence (ISI). Pakistan army and the ISI supported the Afghan Taliban in the government's rise to power in Afghanistan between 1992 and 1996. Pakistan army and ISI oppose the post Taliban leadership of Hamid Karzai because Karzai is antipathy to Islamabad and is permissive to Indian influence in Afghanistan.[2]

Pakistan army has been involved in many conflicts in Asia and Europe since 1990s. The army trained Afghans, Bosnians, Somali, Sudanese, Kashmiries, Chechens, and Arabs, Philippines, Tamil, Muslim groups of Chinese Turkistan, Iranians, and Islamic Movement of Uzbekistan in Central Asia, Nigerians and Americans. The military became a radicalized jihadist groups and started sending young jihadists to Chechnya, Bosnia, Kosovo, Kashmir and Afghanistan. Various Arabs marooned in Afghanistan were identified as Afghan Arabs, while the Pashtun fighters were described as Taliban—a name that had been adopted by Mullah Omar's organization. According to the Tribune report:

> The ISI also actively connived with the Taliban in supporting terrorist groups ranging from the Chechens to the Islamic Movement of Uzbekistan in Central Asia and the Abu Syyaf in the Philippines. Former ISI Chief, General Javed Nasir has now revealed that the Americans had sought his ouster in 1993, because he secretly arranged

---

1 On April 2011, "Land Warfare Paper," Christopher L. Budihas analyzed Pakistan's political, military and economic interests in Afghanistan after the Soviet withdrawal.
2 "The Pakistan army and the Afghanistan war," *Open Democracy*, Shaun Gregory, 25 November 2008

for the airlift of anti tank missiles and other weaponry to the Bosnian Muslims in violation of UN sanctions. General Nasir has also revealed how he forged an alliance of fundamentalist parties in Afghanistan to assume power under President Mujaddidi in 1992. It is no secret that it was General Nasir who organized the Mumbai bomb blasts of 1993 and remains involved in promoting separatism and terrorist violence in Punjab.[1]

Authors, Jayshree Bajoria and Eben Kaplan explore the links of ISI in terrorist incidents in India and Europe. In their joint research paper, the authors quoted some US and NATO officials accused ISI for sponsoring terrorism across the world:

Pakistan's military intelligence agency, the Inter-Services Intelligence (ISI), has long faced accusations of meddling in the affairs of its neighbors. A range of officials inside and outside Pakistan have stepped up suggestions of links between the ISI and terrorist groups in recent years. In fall 2006, a leaked report by a British Defense Ministry think tank charged, "Indirectly Pakistan (through the ISI) has been supporting terrorism and extremism--whether in London on 7/7 [the July 2005 attacks on London's transit system], or in Afghanistan, or Iraq." In June 2008, Afghan officials accused Pakistan's intelligence service of plotting a failed assassination attempt on President Hamid Karzai; shortly thereafter, they implied the ISI's involvement in a July 2008 attack on the Indian embassy. Indian officials also blamed the ISI for the bombing of the Indian embassy. Pakistani officials have denied such a connection.[2]

India also named ISI for the November 2008 Mumbai terrorist attacks, Islamabad denied allegations of any official involvement, but acknowledged in February 2009, that the attack was launched and partly planned from Pakistan. On 19 June 2013, in his India Today report, Abhishek Bhalla quoted Indian delegation visiting Norway to attend a conference of the Financial Action Taken Force (FATF) given proof of Pakistan funding terror activities, allowing its soil to be used for abetting cross-border terror, and circulating fake Indian currency.[3]

---

1 "Pakistan's rogue army: A powerful factor in all walks of life." G. Parthasarathy, the Tribune, 02 January 2003.
2 "The ISI and Terrorism: Behind the Accusations," Jayshree Bajoria, and Eben Kaplan, Council on Foreign Relations, 04 May, 2011, http://www.cfr.org/pakistan/isi-terrorism-behind-accusations/p11644.
3 India Today, 19 June 2013, writer Abhishek Bhalla: "quoted Indian delegation visiting Norway to attend a conference of the Financial Action Taken Force (FATF) given proof of Pakistan funding terror

On 13 June 2013, a top US lawmaker warned that Islamabad would have to bear the responsibility of any terrorist attack on the US coming from LeT:

We should make it clear to Pakistan that any LeT attack upon our homeland, they will bear responsibility for that because of their close relationship between ISI and LeT," Congressman Peter King said during a Congressional hearing. However, Alexander, a former ambassador to Afghanistan, said the fight against the Taliban and groups like al-Qaeda will never be won in Afghanistan alone because it is a "cross-border conflict" supported by the Pakistan government.[1]

Amidst exacerbating differences between the two states over the role of India in Afghanistan, Pakistan's army chief, General Raheel Sharif, visited the US to discuss Pakistan's future priorities in Afghanistan. After this visit, the contradictory statement by former army Chief General Musharraf caused further distrust surrounding the relationship between Kabul and Islamabad. General Musharraf's statement washed out all efforts of confidence building measures. He said that Indian influence is a danger for Pakistan: "That is another danger for the whole region and for Pakistan because Indian involvement there has an anti-Pakistan connotation. They [India] want to create an anti-Pakistan Afghanistan. If the Indians are using some elements of ethnic entities in Afghanistan, then Pakistan will use its own support for ethnic elements, and our ethnic elements are certainly Pashtuns," the general said.

The US's inconsistent policies towards Pakistan and Afghanistan widen distances between the two states. On many issues, distrust was promoted by the Karzai and Musharraf regimes. Having realized their mistakes, in the end of 2014, President Ashraf Ghani and General Raheel Sharif started to work on the improvement of relations between the two countries but, unfortunately, the recent interview of the former President, General Musharraf (February 2015), with a UK newspaper once again caused misunderstanding and distrust. Mr. Musharraf admitted that when he was in power, the ISI had sought to undermine the government of Hamid Karzai because Karzai had "helped India stab Pakistan in the back.

"In President Karzai's times, yes, indeed, he was damaging Pakistan and therefore we were working against his interest. Obviously, we

---

activities, allowing its soil to be used for abetting cross-border terror, and circulating fake Indian currency".

1 "Lashkar-e-Toiba terror proxy of ISI": *PTI: Washington*, Thu Jun 13 2013, and also, *Indian Express*. http://archive.indianexpress.com/news/lashkaretoiba-terror-proxy-of-isi-us-lawmaker/1128536/.

had to protect our own interests," Musharraf said. However, he shamelessly admitted that his government had been responsible for the killings of innocent Afghan men, women and children in the Inter-Services Intelligence (ISI) constituted suicide attacks. General Musharraf said that the ISI trained the Taliban after 2001 to undermine the Karzai government dominated by India's supported non-Pashtuns. "Obviously we were looking for some groups to counter this Indian action against Pakistan, he said.

This interview deeply disappointed Afghan politicians and members of civil society, who started asking whether Pakistan was playing a new game with their country. Though the Afghan president has categorically said that peace without Pakistan is impossible, Afghan parliamentarians and intellectual circles asked why the democratic government in Pakistan does not react to the efforts of the army and ISI, and why the army is doing the job of the civilian government.

Former Afghan President Hamid Karzai reacted angrily from New Delhi in a speech, saying; "Of course Afghanistan will not allow a proxy war between Pakistan and India," Karzai said. Pakistan supports the Afghan Taliban, thus the war in Afghanistan is causing discontent and hopelessness.

According to the Indian government officials, ISI runs forty two terror training camps in Kashmir, and nearly 270 terrorists entered into Jammu and Kashmir from across the border, through Loc in the last three years. Minister of State for Home, RPN Singh said there were 1,000 attempts of infiltration by terrorists from Pakistan, and through the Loc from 2010 to 2012. But the so-called Punjabi jihadists played an important role—the role of military police, helping main backers, such as the ISI and the CIA, to keep the jihadists on a leash.

The Indian National Security Advisor (NSA) Ajit Doval visit to Kabul was seen as an extremely significant one. From Kabul's perspective, India's role and its military deployment can help the country defeat the Pakistan-backed Taliban insurgents. The Afghan rulers want to bolster their ethnically divided army with big ticket military hardware from India and Russia. Having realized the importance of China other than India, the new Afghan President, Ashraf Ghani Ahmadzai, visited China for crucial talks. He knows the importance of neighboring states, specifically Pakistan, and within two weeks he visited the country. With the withdrawal of UK and US forces from the country, new players like China, Russia, India and Pakistan are expected to fortify their strategic interests. India's relations with Afghanistan improved steadily since the fall of the Taliban but relations with Pakistan are strained.

India needs to walk slowly into mountainous Afghanistan because the return of the Taliban or other extremist forces might pose a major threat to its interests in the near future. If Pakistan increased pressure on Afghanistan, according to Afghan military sources, India may possibly retreat from Afghanistan, and there are clear signs that it is scaling down its presence. Pakistan's Inter-Services Intelligence (ISI) and military control Afghan policy, but, unfortunately, they have failed to get a grip on the problem that now threatens to overwhelm the Pakistani state itself.

India's strategic partnership agreement with Afghanistan is of much importance. Among other things in the signed agreement, the issue of security cooperation between the two states has been underlined. The agreement states: "Security cooperation between the sides is intended to help enhance their respective and mutual efforts in the fight against international terrorism, organized crime, illegal trafficking in narcotics, money laundering and so on."

However, when Pakistan, under General Pervez Musharraf, made a u-turn in its Afghan policy, not only did the Afghan Taliban find them betrayed by their backers, but the whole Pakistani establishment was also shocked. From then, a split set in within the establishment which ultimately caused the overthrow of the Musharraf regime. Pure Punjabi generals used the lawyers' movement and got rid of Musharraf. During that period, the Lal Mosque incident also weakened Musharraf's authority and turned the Punjabi Taliban against him. These factors led to his ultimate overthrow, and the Punjabi Taliban got a package of big successes, replacing a general, a government and a regime.

The new guards at Rawalpindi GHQ were aware of this power and, when they tried to overlook it, the Punjabi Taliban reminded them of their strength by carrying out attacks on GHQ, a nearby mosque and other strategically important places. A similar attack on the Indian parliament had been seen earlier. Islamization of the army is matter of great concern. Pakistan army supports Taliban and al Qaeda against the United States and NATO allied states. In his Long War article, Mr. Jason Roach analyzes the development of Islamism in the ranks of Pakistan army:

> [The] Islamization of Pakistan army has been occurring in some form since its birth in 1947. The nation was founded on the unity of a common religion. This religious identity was ingrained in the army

as a way of distinguishing itself from its Hindu counterpart. Officials accomplished this in superficial ways initially. Shortly, following the creation of the state, Pakistan army realized that they were the disadvantaged force when engaging in direct conventional conflict with the massive Indian army. Starting with the First Indi-Pakistan war in 1947, Pakistan army used militant Islamists as a weapon against the Indian army. The army used Islamist rhetoric to mobilize Pashtun tribesmen from the Federally Administered Tribal Area (FATA) and urged clerics to issue Fatwas ordering their clans into Kashmir.[1]

The greatest challenge Pakistan army now faces are from its trained militants and Taliban terrorist groups. In January 2013, Pakistan army specified it enemy. The army published a Green Book, in which they mentioned the guerrilla war in the tribal area near Afghan borders, and armed attacks from different groups on security installations, and in cities, as a biggest security threat. In the revised edition, a new chapter of conventional warfare was included. The various actors involved in the never-ending conflicts in the Subcontinent have views so entrenched that they are unable to recognize, that the situation is fluid and the narrative changing. The US believes Pakistan aids militants to carry out attacks in India and Afghanistan, a view that is echoed in both countries. This prevailing view found itself mentioned in a report the Pentagon sent to the US Congress on the security situation in Afghanistan. Pakistan has reacted angrily to the suggestion that it harbors militants and foreign affairs adviser Sartaj Aziz told the US ambassador as much.

The inability of Pakistan army to meet internal challenges is a worrying factor. War in Baluchistan and FATA and Waziristan has become a long-term challenge for the army. Karachi remains divided and Gilgit has become the battlefield of Sunni-Shia forces. Groups like Taliban, al Qaeda and Tablighi Jamaat have established roots in Pakistan army ranks. Now, officers and soldiers of the army refuse to fight Taliban and religious fanaticism. The Nawaz Sharif government announced a new strategy of counter terrorism under which the army entered North Waziristan region.

In recent years, terrorism has become a major issue in print and electronic media. From 2001 to 2013, more than 60,000 Pakistani have been killed either by terrorists or their own rogue army. The military leaders, ISI, IB, MI and other agencies forcefully disappeared more than 20,000 innocent citizens of the country during the last 12 years.

1 "The Growth of Islamism in the Pakistan Army." Jason Roach, *Small War Journal*, 30, January, 2013, http://smallwarsjournal.com/jrnl/art/the-growth-of-islamism-in-the-pakistan-army.

Former President Asif Ali Zardari and Gen Musharaf admitted that army and ISI deliberately formed sectarian terrorist organizations to create instability in India and Afghanistan. CIA and ISI encouraged Mujahedeen, Laskar-e-Toiba and Taliban to completely destroy Afghanistan. In October 2010, Gen Musharaf admitted that Pakistan army recruited terrorists to fight against India in Kashmir.

On 15 June, 2014, Dawn reported Pakistan Army launched a comprehensive operation against foreign and local terrorists who are hiding in sanctuaries in North Waziristan Agency, a week after a brazen insurgent attack on the country's busiest airport in Karachi:

The operation has been named Zarb-e-Azb," said an Inter-Services Public Relations (ISPR) statement. "Using North Waziristan as a base, these terrorists had waged a war against the state of Pakistan and had been disrupting our national life in all its dimensions, stunting our economic growth and causing enormous loss of life and property. The statement said.

On 16 June 2014, Dawn reported the press release of Pakistan army confirmed the operation designed to strike against both foreign and local militants. Prime Minister Nawaz Sharif, during a speech delivered in the National Assembly justified the government's decision to initiate a full-scale operation in North Waziristan tribal region and said that the 'Zarb-e-Azb' operation would continue until terrorism is eliminated from the country. Sharif added that the government had tried patiently to pursue peace talks but it was unfortunate that after four and a half months of trying peace, dialogue could not be fruitful. He further said that the world knew that "On one hand we were pursuing dialogue, and on the other we were being targeted. We were pursuing talks, but from Islamabad courts to Karachi airport we were attacked."

Opposition in Senate extended full support not only to the PM but also to the military operation in North Waziristan. "The opposition supports the military operation launched in NW agency and stands fully behind the government," Opposition leader Aitzaz Ahsan told the House. According to Rizwan Asghar, both the Pakistani and Afghan Taliban have worked in the past as close associates of al Qaeda and have provided it with logistical and operational support in its areas of operation. On 11 June 2014, writer Agha Iqrar Haroon reported, some 580,000 people left the Khyber district in fear of a fuller ground offensive that has been anticipated for years.

Pakistan has established various paramilitary forces, which performs different duties. These forces protect citizens from threats that could come from inside the country. Some divisions of paramilitary forces recently became part of National Army. In 1999, Northern Light Infantry became part of Pakistan Army. In this chapter, I will try to highlight all 20 Paramilitary Forces and militias with a brief comment.

Para-Military Forces

Frontier Constabulary (FC)

Frontier Constabulary (FC), known for its brutal military operations in Baluchistan and FATA, was established in 1913. The force is governed under the Frontier Constabulary Act, 1915 and North West Frontier Constabulary Rules, 1958. Frontier Constabulary Corps Headquarters (CHQ) is in Peshawar, headed by Commandant Frontier Constabulary (CFC).[1] This force operates like a police force but receives instruction from the army, particularly, during the military operation. Frontier Constabulary various duties, like; supporting LEAs in law & order situations, assisting Federal and Provincial LEAs in conducting operations against miscreants, assisting the Pakistani Army in KPK & FATA, security of Diplomats & vital government installations, security of VIPs/VVIPs, security of Multi National Companies (MNCs), and security of Hydro Power Projects.[2]

In February 2010, on the instruction of Federal Government, Operation "Spring Cleaning" was carried out in the areas of FR Kohat, FR Peshawar, Peshawar and Nowshera to consolidate the writ of the Government, but severely failed. Taliban killed FC men and they killed innocent civilians. In Sindh, more than 60 platoons have been deployed in Karachi, Hyderabad and Sukkar. In 2010, suicide bomber killed seven FC men. In 2011, FC helped the Army & Police in relief and law order duties

Pakistan Rangers

Rangers are more effective and well-trained forces of Pakistan which play very professional role in maintaining law and order in Karachi. Prior to 1995, the Pakistan Rangers were two separate forces: the Pakistan Rangers, Lahore Punjab and Mehran Rangers in Karachi,

---

1 *The News International*, 03 December 2013,
2 "Pakistan frontier force facing arms crunch," force's chief Abdul Majeed Khan Marwat, *Indian Express*,30 November 2013

Sindh. These forces maintain two different chains of command and work under the Pakistan Rangers Ordinance 1959. In 1965 and 1971, Pakistan Rangers played important role. Rangers were receiving instructions from the Ministry of Defense. In 1995, Mehran force was merged into Sindh Rangers.[1]

In 1992, Rangers were deployed in Karachi, where MQM was targeted. In 1999, Rangers fought the Kargil war. In 1969, Sutlej Rangers was restructured and Chenab Rangers was established with its Headquarters at Sialkot in 1972. Force was renamed from West Pakistan Rangers to Pakistan Rangers. In 1974, the force became part of the Civil Armed Force under the Ministry of Interior. In 1989, Mehran Force was established with five permanent sectors and four wings; Shahbaz Rangers, Bhattai Rangers, Qasim Rangers, Sachal Rangers. On 01 Jul 1995, Pakistan Rangers was divided between Punjab and Sindh.[2]

The basic role of Pakistan Rangers is: Protection of personnel and property in the border areas, apprehension of persons unlawfully entering into or going out of Pakistan territory, organize village Defense committees in the border areas, prevention of smuggling, collection of intelligence in the border areas, coordination with police and other civil agencies in the prevention and detection of smuggling, assist police in the prevention and detection of crimes in the border areas, and reinforce the police for the maintain of law and orders whenever it is necessary.[3]

Mehran Force

In Sindh province, Pakistan army used Mehran force for maintaining internal security. In 1994, 24,000 personnel were operating under the command, and were organizationally divided into "wings" of approximately 800 men each. This force was receiving instructions from Interior Ministry and was commanded by seconded army generals.[4]

Khyber Rifles

---

1 *The News*, 26 June 2014
2 "Pakistan Ranger Blog," 2012, http://paksindhrangers.blogspot. co.uk/2012/04/history.html
3 Encyclopedia Britannica/Zhob,1911
4 *Pakistan: Army and Paramilitary Forces*, Library of Congress Country Studies, Data of 1994, http://lcweb2.loc.gov/cgi-bin/query/r?frd/ cstdy:@field%28DOCID+pk0159%29

Khyber Rifles is the most effective paramilitary force, which forms part of Pakistan Army's Frontier Corps. This force was formed by the British army in 1880. Solders of this force were recruited from Afridi tribesmen. The first commander of the force was Sir Robert Warburton. Landi Kotal was selected as the headquarters of Khyber Rifles. The main role of the force was to guard the Khyber Pass. The three main garrisons of the regiment were Landi Kotal, at the western end of the Pass, Fort Maude to the east, and Ali Masjid in the center.[1]

In 1919, during the Afghan independence war, the majority of Khyber Rifles soldiers deserted and refused to fight against the Afghans, therefore, the force was disbanded. In 1946, Khyber Rifles was re-established in Landi Kotal, under the leadership of Sharif Khan. In 1947, after independence, the command of Khyber Rifles and other forces was transferred to Pakistan. Khyber Rifles is comprised of five wings: Khyber Rifles, Tirah, Khyber Rifles, Jamrud, Khyber Rifles Bara and Khyber Rifles Charbagh.

Khasadar Force

In 1921, the British India government introduced Khasadar system in the province. This was a new security program of the British government to maintain security along the Afghan border. Khasadar security system was established in every agency. The Khasadars were enlisted from amongst the tribes who were designated by the local Maliks. Khasadar force performs different functions: Protection of roads, patrolling roads and protecting train journeys, guarding government installations, arresting anti-social elements, maintain law and order, detection and prevention of crimes; intelligence and feedback from the tribes, traffic control, recovery of government dues, and security of high level dignitaries.[2]

Levies Force

As we mentioned earlier, that Khasadar carry their own weapons, while Levies receive weapons from government. They are recruited on merit from amongst the indigenous tribes. In 1889, the Zhob levy was

1 "Pakistan Army, Pakistan Rangers," Sindh Website. https://www.pakistanarmy.gov.pk/AWPReview/TextContent.aspx?pId=141
2 FATA Administration: Law Enforcement Forces, Maqbool Wazir, 2009, http://waziristanhills.com/FATA/FATAAdministration/LawEnforcement Forces/tabid/127/language/en-GB/Default.aspx. Also, "Grave danger," Dr Ali Jan, The News International, 02 March 2008, http://jang.com.pk/thenews/mar2008-weekly/nos-02-03-2008/foo.htm.

established, and after that Malakand Levies, Dir, Kurram, Orakzai and Bajaur levies were established step by step. Main responsibilities of the Levies are: Maintain Law and Order within the territorial jurisdiction of their respective tribes, to trace and detect crimes and anti state activities, to wield the loyalties of the tribes with the Government, anti smuggling and anti sabotage work, patrolling roads, trains, protection of vital installation, railway tracks, bridges, Government buildings, telephone lines, Government offices etc, checking of traffic offences and recovery of Government dues.

Malakand Levies

After the reorganization of Swat Levies, in 1920, Saadullah Khan was promoted, and a regular force was introduced. In Chitral, Malakand and Dir, Levies was given more powers. In 1977, the Malakand levies were reorganized and come under the administrative control of SAFRON Division, Government of Pakistan. The Commandant of Malakand Levies is the commanding officer of 1325 strong force while the Subedar Major is the second high-ranking officer after the commandant.[1]

The Frontier Corps

Known as a Scout Militia, the Frontier Corps is a historical paramilitary force in Pakistan. The militia receives instructions from Interior Ministry. The force is comprised of 12 unites, known as Corps with a total of 46 Wings. The overall authorized strength of the Force is about 35,070 personnel. Unites of the force are: Kurram Militia, Tochi Scouts, Chitral Scouts, Khyber Rifles, South Waziristan Scouts, the Bajaur Scouts, Mahsud Scouts, Mohmand Rifles, the Thall Scouts, Shawal Rifles and Dir Scouts. Baluchistan has its own private militias, operating under the Interior Ministry of the country.[2]

Bloch Corps comprised of 15 Units known as Corps with a total of 41 Wings. Units of Frontier Corps Baluchistan include Zhob Militia, Chaghai Militia, Sibi Scouts, Kalat Scouts, Makran Militia, Kharan Rifles, Pishin Scouts, Maiwind Rifles, Ghazaband Scouts, Bambore Rifles, and Loralai Scouts. The main responsibilities of this force are: Defends the western border of Pakistan, provides security to the lines of communication and carrying out patrolling in tribal belt to maintain the writ of the government, conducts raids to recover

---

1 *Ibid*, 02 *March* 2008.
2 *Ibid*, 02 *March* 2008.

kidnapped personnel, stolen property and to apprehend proclaimed offenders from tribal areas, and aids civil law enforcing agencies in conduct of anti narcotics and weapons recovery operations.

Northern Light Infantry Regiment

In 1869, Gilgit became part of Kashmir, but re-established in 1889, and Gilgit Levies was established to help the British government stabilizing the region. In 1913, the force was reorganized and named as Gilgit Scouts. In 1947, the force again became an effective player in Northern Areas. This regiment is consisted of 15 units and drawn from eight ethnic communities involving, Baltees, Shins, Yashkuns, Mughals, Kashmiris, Pathans, Ladakis and Turks. The force is based at in Skardu.[1]

The Pakistan Coast Guard

In 1971, Pakistan Coast Guard was established through a Presidential order. This is a law enforcement service and one of the six uniform services of the Paramilitary command receiving instructions from the Interior Ministry of Pakistan. This guard is based in Sindh province and guards the coastal areas of Sindh and Baluchistan provinces.

1 "Pakistan: Country of Origin Information (COI) Report," COI Service, 7 December 2012. UK Border Agency ttps://www.gov.uk/government/uploads/system/uploads/attachment_data/file/310422/Pakistan_COI_report_dec_2012.

Chapter 15. Soldiers for Sale: Pakistani Blackwater

Today, the post-Saddam Hussain Persian Gulf and the entire Arab world present an ugly picture of violent sectarian conflict, in which Pakistani Blackwater, army, and sectarian mafia groups are playing an important role. The deployment of Pakistani security forces in Saudi Arabia, Bahrain, and their fight alongside the ISIS against the Shia population of the region, raised important questions. The elimination of Sunni dominated regime in Iraq, and the Shia uprising in Bahrain, Yemen, Syria and Saudi Arabia, has shattered the hope of Sunni power in the region. The political realignment along sectarian lines applies not only to Iraq, but potentially, to all states in the Middle East. Iran, Saudi Arabia, Iraq, Lebanon, Syria, Jordan, Egypt and other small Gulf states, seem to be sliding into a Sunni-Shia conflict. The present feature of this conflict indicates that one day this uncontrollable fire will caught Pakistan into its flames.

Global Research News reported the civil war in Syria opened opportunities for foreign mercenaries. Russian Foreign Ministry spokesman Alexander Lukashevich said that Syria was turning into a "center of attraction" for international terrorists in the ongoing civil war, between rebels and government forces. Pakistan's interference in Bahrain and its fight against the Shia population in Syria raised serious questions about the sectarian role of the country's armed forces in the Middle East conflict. Pakistanis in Bahrain comprise people working in government forces, and their locally born descendents.

The overseas Pakistanis Foundation estimates that the population of Pakistan's Blackwater in Bahrain is between 50,000 to 60,000. These members of private militia fight against the Shia majority of Bahrain. Majority members of Pakistani Blackwater and army work with Bahrainis army. Fuji Foundation and Bahria foundation are also recruiting retired military personnel for Bahrainis army, and sectarian groups in Persian Gulf. Fuji and Bahria Foundations recently agreed to send more Blackwater forces to Bahrain to help Al Khalifa regime against the Shia uprising.[1]

Writer Zai Ur Rehman noted the establishment of Pakistani Taliban office in Syria to fight against the country's national army:

> Recent media reports and interviews with TTP militants suggest that the Pakistani Taliban have sent militants to fight alongside rebels in Syria. Mohammad Amin, described by the BBC as the TTP's coordinator for Syrian affairs, said that the TTP have established a base in Syria with the help of Arab fighters who had previously fought in Afghanistan. The purpose of the base, Amin said, is to assess the "ongoing jihad" in Syria and coordinate joint operations with Syrian militants. He claimed that the Iranian regime is sending Pakistani Shia fighters to Syria through Iran and Iraq to join al-Assad's forces to suppress Syria's majority Sunni Muslim population.[2]

Professor Hassan Abbas recently argued that Pakistani Taliban militants offered help to radical Muslim groups fighting in Iraq and Syria, according to a statement marking the Muslim holy festival of Eid al-Adha on 04 October, 2013. Hassan also reported Taliban Chief Mullah Fazlullah called the fighters in the Middle East as "mujahedeen brothers" and vowed to support them. "Mujahedeen fighting in Iraq and Syria are our brothers and we are proud of their victories." There are speculations that these people are not Taliban militants, they are Pakistani retired soldiers and officers, (Financed by Fauji Foundation and Ex-Services men Society).

According to the Al Jazeera report, Pakistani militants in Syria fight under the platform of Katibat Muhajiroon, a Latakia-based jihadist group solely composed of foreign militants belonging to various Islamic and European countries, and led by a Libyan, Abu Jaafar al Libi. Pakistan denied the allegation that it arms Syrian rebels at Saudi Arabia's behest. Experts, however, confirmed that Islamabad

---

1 *Daily the News*, 09 June 2014, "Pakistani Fighters Joining the War in Syria," Zai Ur Rehman's research paper, 24 September, 2013, http://afpakwatch.wordpress.com/category/published-in/ctc-sentinel/
2 "Is Pakistan aiding Syrian rebels"? *Siasat daily*, 29-Mar-2014, http://www.siasat.pk/forum/showthread.php?243647-Is-Pakistan-aiding-Syrian-rebels.

is not only providing military equipment to anti-Assad groups, it's also helping jihadists to go fight in Syria.

"We strongly reject the media speculation that Pakistan has changed its position on Syria or is supplying arms to Syrian rebels directly or indirectly. These impressions are totally baseless and misleading," Sartaj Aziz, told parliament. I would like to clarify that during the Saudi Crown Prince's visit, the two sides only mentioned the need to enhance bilateral cooperation in the field of Defense with an aim to have a mutually beneficial Defense and security cooperation," said Aziz.[1]

Pakistan's support to the Indian insurgents had been channelized through Bangladesh with the assistance of two premiere intelligence agencies of the country. The ISI maintained sustained links with Bangladesh through some of its repatriated Army officers. The ISI also maintained close links with the ULFA since 1988, when ULFA leader Paresh Barua visited Karachi for the first time.[2] The country provides financial and logistic support to ULFA from Dhaka since then. The ULFA cadres were trained not only in camps, in North West Frontier Province (NWFP) but also in Afghanistan. Paresh Barua visited Pakistan on a number of occasions on Bangladeshi passport.

Pakistan has two reasons to support the so-called mujahedeen; first, the Pakistani military is determined to pay India back for allegedly fomenting separatism in what was once East Pakistan and in 1971 became Bangladesh, and second, India dwarfs Pakistan in population, economic strength, and military might. In 2011, Pakistan had helped Bahrain quell an uprising against the monarchy by sending security personnel recruited through military's welfare wings—Fauji Foundation and Bahria Foundation. Fauji foundation is also sending retired army officers to Kashmir. A retired army officer once told me in Lahore that officers registered with Fauji Foundation are fighting Indian army, and train Mujahedeen for Kashmir jihad.

Former President Asif Ali Zardari signed an agreement with King Hamad bin Isa during his visit to Bahrain, as Pakistan army already receive millions dollars from Bahrain in exchange of thousands members of blackwater (Fauji Foundation) recruited for the gulf state. In June 2009, the Bahrain center for Human Rights expressed deep concern regarding the recruitment of young Balochs by Bahrani

---

1 "ULFA thrived with ISI backing during BNP-Jamaat rule." *Dhaka Times*, 18 Feb 2014.
2 "Bahrain king to visit JSHQ today," Baqir Sajjad Syed, 19 March 2014, *Express Tribune*, 11 March 2011, *United Press International*, 7 November 2013,

security forces, in Makran district of Baluchistan province. Recently, Shia clerics of Bahrain issued fatwas to kill Pakistanis wherever they are found in Bahrain.

On 08 April 2011, Hindustan Times reported the strained diplomatic relations between Pakistan and Iran, after the Iranian government protested recruiting of retired Pakistani military officers into the Bahrain police forces. Pakistan's charge d'affairs in Tehran was summoned to Foreign Ministry. "More than a hundred retired army men are now on their way to Bahrain to serve in that country's riot police and Defense force. Plans are also being finalized to send regular Pakistan army contingents to Saudi Arabia and possible Bahrain," the newspaper reported.[1]

The involvement of Pakistani Blackwater in the Sunni-Shia conflict in Middle East, Kashmir, Afghanistan, and the Gulf region raised many questions. The presence of Pakistan's private militias in Bahrain, Yemen, India, Afghanistan, and Saudi Arabia, and their fight against the local Shia population has diverted the attention of international community towards the new concept of the country's international jihadist culture, in the name of sectarian Islam. Intelligence reports confirm that there are militias including retired Pakistani military officers, and other Jihadi groups in Bahrain and Yemen, involved in target killing, and daylight assassination of prominent Shia leaders.

These reports about the presence of these militias were confirmed when several Pakistanis Blackwater members were killed or injured by Shia protesters in Bahrain. Recently, Bahrain's Foreign Minister, Sheikh Khaled bin Ahmed Al-Khalifa discussed the role of these militias with Islamabad, where the two sides agreed to increase in the number of private militias in the country. Pakistan's "Ex-Servicemen Society," like Blackwater (Ex. Services LLC) is now fully involved in sectarian fight in the Middle East, India and Afghanistan. Pakistani Blackwater also claimed that it had established a private militia in 2008, under the leadership of Lt.-Gen. (retired) Faiz Ali Chishti, the man who tortured Pakistan's Prime Minister, Zulfiqar Ali Bhutto.[2]

There are speculations in Islamabad and Kabul, that some retired Pakistani generals support Islamic State in Iraq, Syria, Afghanistan and Pakistan. The controversial role of the militia increased in the concern of Pakistani politicians over the Ex Services militia concept of Deobandi Jihad in South Asia and Middle East. Pakistani media

---

1 *The Express Tribune*, October 2013
2 "No soldiers for sale," Rafia Zakaria, 16 August, 2013, http://www.dawn.com/news/1036256.

recently reported that Fauji Foundation and Bahria Foundation are believed to be working in close cooperation with the Pakistani military and ISI. Bahria Foundation was established in 1982, under the chairmanship of the then Navy Chief, and Fuji Foundation was established in 1954.

Both the militias played vital role in the Afghan Jihad, the killing business of Taliban in 1990s and the recent Taliban insurgencies in Pakistan and Afghanistan. Some recent reports confirm that the Fauji Foundation, Ex Services men Society have close contacts with both Pakistani and Afghan Taliban and playing a leading role in recruiting Taliban fighters in Waziristan and FATA region. The society also sends jihadists to Afghanistan to destabilize the elected government.

A newspaper in Pakistan warned that by allowing these private militias to fight in Bahrain, the country has dangerously taken sides. Having expressed concern about the killing business of Pakistani Blackwater in Bahrain, Iranian government conveyed its resentment to Islamabad, and condemned the continuing recruitment of Ex Pakistani military officers to bolster the strength of the security forces of Bahrain. Bahrain National Guard has already advertised this new recruitment in Pakistan's Urdu newspaper, inviting Pakistani youth to join the sectarian conflict in the in Bahrain.

Media reports say that the Saudis would buy small arms from Pakistan's arms industry, and that it would recruit more Pakistani retired soldiers and policemen for the Gulf state of Bahrain, which has been facing long months of unrest, as Shia protests against the Sunni ruling family have escalated. The Sharifs government denied these reports, but western diplomats say the shift in Pakistan's policy is real. Islamabad maintains a policy of interference in the internal affairs of Muslim countries, and the intervention in Syrian conflict on the side of Saudi Arabia is hugely controversial.

Gulf States mostly rely on Pakistan army. In the case of Bahrain, for example, Bahraini Shi'a complain that, while they are effectively barred from joining their own security forces based on their religion, the government employs Deobandis and Takfiri Salafis from Pakistan to repress them. On 16 August 2013, Writer Rafia Zakria revealed in her article about the presence of Pakistani soldiers in Bahrain: "News of Pakistani soldiers being shipped to Bahrain first came almost two years ago, when the uprising had only just begun".[1]

According to a news report, from July 2011, Pakistani soldiers were front and center in the crackdown on pro-democracy protesters. The

1 *The News*, July 2011

report noted nearly 2500 Pakistani soldiers, including former army drill instructors, military police and riot police were all supplied, following several visits to Islamabad by Bahraini and Saudi officials. Recruited into the Special Forces Units of the Bahraini National Guard, Pakistani soldiers for hire were put in charge of suppressing the country's majority Shia protesters against the country's minority Sunni monarchy."[1]

In August, 2013, Pakistani soldiers were deployed in Manama. On 07 May, 2014, APP reported, Prime Minister Nawaz Sharif met with Khalifa Bin Ahmed Al-Dhahrani, Chairman of the Council of Representative of Kingdom of Bahrain at PM House in Islamabad. The Prime Minister said that recent visit of King Shaikh Hamad bin Isa Al Khalifa to Pakistan was a testament to the fact that the two countries enjoyed close and cordial relations based on mutual trust and understanding, which were deep rooted in culture and history:

> "Our two countries have always stood by each other in testing times and we deeply appreciate the assistance extended by the Kingdom of Bahrain following natural calamities in Pakistan over the years," the premier said.[2]

Mr. Sharif said that his government had introduced investor-friendly policies, due to which several foreign companies and governments had invested in many projects. He said Pakistan would welcome Bahraini investments in projects in the field of energy, downstream oil industry, port development, mining and minerals, infrastructure, education, banking, engineering and manufacturing sectors.

On 11 April 2014, the News International reported the Kuwait government to open its Defense office in Islamabad. Thus Kuwait became the fourth country of the six Gulf Cooperation Council (GCC) member countries that is opening its Defense Wing in Islamabad. Saudi Arabia, the United Arab Emirates and Oman have their Defense Attaches in Pakistan, while Bahrain and Qatar are without Defense wings in Pakistan. Kuwait announced to engage the services of military experts for imparting training to its army consisting of more than 11,000 personnel. The Defense wing of the embassy will greatly help in picking suitable experts from retired officers/trainers.[3]

---

1 *The News*, 11 April 2014
2 *The News*, 11 April 2014
3 "In too deep," Raza Rumi, *Himal South Asian*, 04 April 2014, *Himal Southasian* http://himalmag.com/in-too-deep/

Pakistan is a bankrupt state with a perpetual begging bowl held out to the rest of the world. The Americans fill the begging bowl with arms and the Saudis with money, in exchange for using Pakistan as a military pawn. One day, after the Taliban have taken Pakistan over, they will regret that such an unstable, nuclear-armed state was given so many weapons.

Journalist Raza Rumi noted Pakistan's interference in Afghanistan and the strategic importance of Afghanistan for Pakistan. In the past Pakistan army viewed Afghanistan as its strategic backyard, calculating that in case of war with India, Pakistan's army could withdraw into Afghanistan regroups and then mounts counter-attacks on Indian forces:

"Pakistan's security climate is linked with the situation in Afghanistan, and continuing instability in the neighborhood is a major concern. Pakistan's military in the past viewed Afghanistan as its strategic backyard, calculating that in case of war with India, Pakistan's army could withdraw into Afghanistan, regroups and then mounts counter-attacks on Indian forces. Growing relations between India and Afghanistan have alarmed an already suspicious Pakistan, and India seems willing to take over the US role in training Afghan security forces, at least to a limited extent. India aims to expand its footprint in Afghanistan beyond development aid but is constrained by its geography."[1]

On 12 March 2011, Saba Imtiaz reported an interesting story of Pakistani Blackwater in the Daily Express Tribune, which diverted the attention of international community towards Pakistan's new business of killing in the Middle East:

> The practice of exporting Pakistani security personnel to Bahrain has been going on for over 20 years, said a source, who named former Special Services Group officer Javed Latif Kahlon as the man responsible. "Kahlon is based in Bahrain and enjoys strong ties with its military. He serves as a senior adviser," said the source. "He left the Pakistan Army after being implicated in the Attock Conspiracy case. He has recruited at least 2,000 Pakistanis to serve in Bahrain's security forces, and they were the ones who shot at protestors in Manama's Pearl Square," the source said, referring to a crackdown in the Bahraini city last month in which seven protestors were killed and hundreds injured.[2]

---

1 "Ex-servicemen 'export' mercenaries to the Middle East." Saba Imtiaz, *The Express Tribune*, March 12, 2011, http://tribune.com.pk/story/131455/ex-servicemen-export-mercenaries-to-the-middle-east/.
2 *Express Tribune*, 11 March 2011

This involvement resulted in Iranian-sponsored agitators in Bahrain, killing several Pakistani workers for "collaborating with the Sunni rulers of Bahrain." Pakistani media reported that a private militia, Fauji Security Services (Pvt) Limited, which is run by the Fauji Foundation, is deeply involved in recruiting retired army soldiers from navy, air force the police, on war footing basis, who will be getting jobs in Middle East, Afghanistan, India, and Gulf region. Recent reports confirm Pakistan Blackwater is killing innocent Shia protesters while Protesters are targeting Pakistani militia members in their houses and on roads. Bahrain national army recruits people from across Pakistan. There are many Baloch in the Bahrain army. Pakistanis, particularly from Baluchistan along the Makran coast, are favored recruits.

On 11 March 2011, Express Tribune reported Pakistan's army backed Fauji Foundation advertisement for recruiting retired army officer for the Bahrain army. An Urdu language advertisement displayed on Overseas Employment website stated that retired army officers are immediately required for the security forces of Bahrain. According the Fauji Foundation statement, 7,000 people applied for 800 vacancies. Fauji Foundation has been exporting mercenaries to Middle East, Afghanistan and India for fight against their national security forces.[1]

In Bahrain, Pakistan's embassy reported the killing of two Pakistani policemen and three soldiers. In this unwanted sectarian war, forty Pakistani injured. Sectarian divide in the Middle East, and Pakistani involvement caused serious conflicts in the past, and continues to have its toll. Sunni regimes in both Bahrain and Saudi Arabia have monopolized power while the Shia population is marginalized from public influence and control. In Saudi Arabia, Shia has been oppressed due to the fear of Iranian political influence in the country. Pakistan is seriously beset with sectarian divides not only between Sunnis and Shias but also sects within each of them. Insurgencies in Baluchistan, Swat, Malakand, Waziristan and FATA are still very much active and with its geographical contiguity to Iran may emerge even hotter to handle.

Pakistan's own sectarian conflict since 1980s, left thousands people dead and dilapidated the country's relations with neighboring states. The recent sectarian conflict in the Middle East and Pakistan's involvement in it can cause countrywide sectarian war. The reaction of Pakistani Shia and their fight against the Salafi forces can anytime

---

1 *United Press International*, 7 November 2013

ignite the fire of sectarian war in the country. The sectarian framing in Bahrain is a deliberate regime strategy.

Shia groups in Bahrain explicitly reject sectarianism and seek democratic reform and national unity, but the involvement of Pakistani Blackwater in the country's internal conflict, the struggle for democracy seems to have become sectarian conflict or Saudi-Iranian war. The impact of sectarian war in Bahrain is causing disastrous consequences for regional states. Sectarian divide among Iraqi politicians is a new issue as some politicians slamming the Saudi-UAE intervention in Bahrain as unacceptable.

The involvement of Pakistani sectarian groups in the Sunni-Shia conflict in Yemen has recently become a major news item in print and electronic media. Al Arabia news recently reported that Yemen's Houthi rebels have Pakistani fighters in their ranks. Pakistani sectarian elements are helping Yemeni Shias in their war against Saudi Arabia, Al Arabiya TV reported, Yemen's Foreign Minister as saying that the way militants fight and the money they spend make the involvement of foreign powers almost a certainty.

On 07 November 2013, United Press International reported Saudi leader's disillusionment with the failure of the US and its allies to take effective military action against the Bashar Assad regime. Carnegie Endowment for International Peace scholar Yazid Savigh claimed that Saudi Arabia want to create a force of 50,000 mercenaries to undermine the Assad regime.[1]

Thus, Pakistan is playing a double role; on one hand, it supports Saudi Arabia in oppressing Shia groups in Bahrain, and it fights against Saudi Arabian forces in Yemen, on the other. Strong regional implications are likely to be generated by Pakistan's intrusiveness in the Gulf region. Pakistan seems to have now taken the first tentative steps to reassert its intrusive military presence in the Gulf region, as earlier visible in the 1970s but later diminished. Some media reports indicate that after the democratic movements emerge in Tunisia and Egypt, Pakistan Army started contingency planning for earmarking its two divisions for Saudi Arabia.

On October 2013, Express Tribune reported Pakistan's Ex-Servicemen Association (PESA) and Ex-Servicemen Society (PESS) decided to form a single organization to mobilize over two million former military servicemen and create awareness among the masses for defending national interest of Pakistan.[2]

---

1 *The Express Tribune*, October 2013
2 *Pakistan Observer*, 14 October 2014

On 14 October 2013, Pakistan Observer reported the meeting of Executive Council of PESA which was chaired by Lt Gen Ali Kuli Khan. Admiral Fasih Bukhari, Vice Admiral Ahmad Tasnim, Lt Gen Karamat, Lt Gen Naeem Akbar, Major General Niazi, and Mr. Saleem Nawaz Gandapur. Major Qaiser Nawaz Gandapur, Brig Riaz Ahmad, Brig Mian Mahmud, Major Farooq Hamid Khan, Major Babur Zaheeruddin, Brig Simon Sharaf, Brig Masud ul Hassan, Lt General Hamid Gul President of PESS and other members participated in the meeting.18[1]

Fuji Foundation has established 115 medical facilities, 100 schools, 65 vocational training centers and 9 technical training centers. Fuji Foundation own the following projects and industries: Fuji Cereals, Foundation Gas, Overseas Employment Services, Fuji Foundation Experimental and Seed Multiplication Farm, Fuji Fertilizer Company Limited, Fuji Fertilizer Bin Qasim Limited, Fuji Cement Company Limited, Fuji Kabirwala Power Company Limited, Foundation Power Company Daharki Limited, Mari Petroleum Company Limited, Fuji Akbar Fortia Marine Terminal Limited, Fuji Oil Terminal and distribution Company Limited, Pakistan Maroc Phosphore. S.A Morocco, Foundation Securities Limited and Askari Bank Limited.

---

1 *Ibid,* 14 October 2014.

CHAPTER 16. ARMED FORCES, CORRUPTION AND THE BLACK MARKET

The involvement of on duty and retired military generals of Pakistan army in illegal narco smuggling, and export of jihadists to Middle East, Afghanistan and India raised serious questions. On 08 December 2013, Dr. Lal Khan raised important question about the un-professional activities of the generals, and criticized military establishment for its personal business:

> The financial interests of military elite have greatly influenced the politics of the armed forces and have veered into adventures and an operation like the Afghan jihad of the 1980s that were prodigiously lucrative in this primitive accumulation of capital that has become a hallmark of today's military. However, this was not the only reason for the successive military takeovers in spite of the condemnations so much in vogue today. The army intervened not just to control the unraveling economy and political chaos that the bourgeois civilian government brought about but also to crush and curb the mass discontent morphing into a social revolt, threatening the whole system.[1]

The Army has the biggest share in stock exchange; operates banks, airlines; run factories, petroleum, and energy institutions; receive huge profit from their own schools, drug smuggling, colleges and hospitals. A Pakistani newspaper in 2011 reported, the country's Defense Ministry unearthed an alleged involvement of almost 100 army officials in billions dollar corruption. Moreover, in 2011, the Lahore High Court faced a legal and practical dilemma when a charge sheet about the corruption of armed

---

1 *Daily Times,* 08 December 2013

forces was filed in the court by a lawyer. From weapon smuggling to human trafficking, and forcefully disappearance, the army is now under fire for its business of extra-judicially killing of innocent Pashtuns, and Balochs in Swat, FATA, and Waziristan. Pakistani Defense analyst, Dr. Ayesha Siddiqa unearthed the illegal business of the army in her recent book:

> Pakistan's military runs a huge commercial empire with an estimated value of billions of dollars. Milbus in Pakistan involves: (1) the varied business ventures of four welfare foundations (small business such as farms, schools and private security firms, and corporate enterprises such as commercial banks and insurance companies, radio and television channels and manufacturing plants); (2) direct institutional military involvement in enterprise such as tolling collating, shopping centers and patrol stations; and (3) benefit given to retire personnel such as state land or business openings.[1]

In his analysis of Pakistan army business politics, Elliot Wilson argued that the army has dominated Pakistan's economy. The army owns bakeries, factories, farmland, and golf courses. Largest corporations in the country are also controlled by the army. Fuji Foundation, Shaheen Foundation and Bahria Foundation supply jihadists, and mercenaries to the Middle East, Afghanistan, and India. In Dubai, according to some reports, these foundations are involved with Blackwater in preparing a rogue army against Iran.

These foundations maintain an army of two million retired soldiers and officers. These biggest private militia members are fighting in India, Afghanistan, Bahrain, Qatar, Yemen, Iranian Baluchistan and Kashmir. In Kasur, Okara, Lahore, Karachi, Peshawar, Quetta, Islamabad, Rawalpindi, Jehlum and Multan, the army controls thousands acres of land. The army welfare trust also control several business firms like Askari Bank, the largest commercial bank of Pakistan. It also owns insurance companies, saving schemes and power supply companies.

There are numerous stories about the corrupt practices of Pakistan army in print and electronic media across the world. Pakistani newspapers are under deep pressure for the stories of armed forces criminal businesses, they often publish. According to the 2011 annual report of the Auditor General of Pakistan, there were massive financial irregularities totaling 60 billion Rupees. The report revealed

---

1 *Military Inc -Inside Pakistan's Military Economy*, Ayesha Siddiqa, 2007, Pluto Press, London

that Pakistani armed forces received millions dollars from more than 300 contracts signed from 2008 to 2010.[1]

The report found that armed forces retained and blocked 3 billion rupees funds due to inappropriate storage of 1,385 new vehicles at the Central Ordinance Depot in Karachi city. Irregularities have also been noted by the report, when the army transferred funds to Frontier Works Organization (FWO) for purveying bullet-proof jackets. According to the report, in Kharian, Lahore, and Sialkot districts, the army mismanaged more than 6 million rupees. In Kamra complex, more than 92 million rupees corruption surfaced.

According to the report of Indian intelligence, more than 30,000 Pakistani fighters in India depends on money, a staggering amount, which is generated through illegal animal skin trade and drug trafficking. Corruption cases against generals, air marshals and admirals are in increase. In 8 December 2009, Asian Human Rights Commission in its report criticized judiciary for not opening corruption cases against Pakistan's rogue army:

> Successive governments and courts, conspicuously avoiding investigating corruption cases against the top hierarchy of the armed forces. The concept of National Security has been misused by the authorities who perhaps unintentionally, made it possible for the officers to make huge amount of money through illegal methods.[2]

On 6 December 2009, the News International published a list of Pakistani generals involved in corruption cases. During the last 30 years, army officers and generals were running private businesses and received huge loans from banks. Moreover, pkpolitics.com also published a list of Pakistani generals involved in corruption cases:

> Air Chief Marshal Abbas Khattak (retired) had received Rupees 180 million as kickbacks in the purchase of 40 old Mirage Fighters. Air Chief Marshal Farooq Feroz Khan was suspecting of receiving five percent commission in purchase of 40 F-7 planes worth $271 million.[3]

However, in 1996, armed forces purchased 1047 GS 90s Jeeps at a cost of $20,889 per unit, while the market value of jeeps was $13,000. Asian Human Right Commission in its report revealed more case of corruption in the armed forces: "One hundred and eleven army men received 400 plots in Bahawalpur and Rahim Yar Khan Districts of

---

1 "Annual Report of the Auditor General of Pakistan," 2011
2 *Asian Human Rights Commission*, 8 December 2009
3 *The News International*, 6 December 2009

Punjab province, at throwaway prices of Rupees 47.50 per canal (600 Sq Yards), as against the actual price of Rupees 15,000 to 20,000."

Asia Human Rights Commission also reported some corrupt generals who received millions dollar in purchase of weapons: Army Chief General Jahangir Karamat received 20 million dollar as a bribe from a Ukraine tank company in a purchase of 300 tanks. Generals and their cronies have also written off their loans. Army Welfare Trust (AWT) written off its 15 million Rupees. General Ali Kuli Khan written off his loan in 1990s, while he had received millions from various banks and industries. Asian Human Rights Commission reported the following army generals and officer who written of their loans:

> Lt General (retired) K.M Azhar who later active in politics, of Rex Breen Batteries got Rupees 16 million written off by the agricultural Development Bank. Lt General (retired) S.A Burki and Lt General (retired) Safdar Butt also figure among the happy generals benefiting from the state institutions generously. Another prominent man on the list is Air Marshal (retired) A Rahim Khan; Air Marshal (retired) Waqar Azeem also got Rupees 15 million written off from Pakistan Kuwait Investment Co. Lt General (retired) S.A Burki, Major General Zahid Ali Akbar, Brigadier M.M Mahmood, Begum Omar Mahmood, Saeed Ahmad also got loan written off.[1]

Asian Human Rights also reported some civilians and military generals like, Gohar Ayub Khan, Mr. Reza Kuli Khan, and brother of General Ali Kuli Khan also got a loan of Rupees 7.2 million written off against Rehana Woolen Mills. The loan was written off by the financial institution, SAPICO. Major General (retired) M. Mumtaz from Abbotabad, Lt. Colonel (retired) Shaukat and Major General (retired) Tajuddin written off the loan of Rupees 1.2 million, Major General (retired) Ghaziuddin are also in the list. Major General (retired) G. Umar also got 8.5 million written off from the Agricultural Bank. Lt. General (retired) Safdar Butt, Major General (retired) Abdullah Malik, Brigdier (retired) M.M Mahmood, Col. (retired) M. Zafar Khan, Muhammad Afzal Khan and Mrs. Hamida Farhat also got benefit from the UBL. General (retired) Abdullah had resigned after the military coup of General Zia and opposed the military takeover of July 1977.[2]

Terrorism is just one part of the problem, there are ethnic and sectarian violence dancing in the streets of the country. Kidnapping

---

1 *Asian Human Rights*, 08 December 2009
2 *Ibid,08 December 2009.*

and murder is now a profitable business of the army generals and officers. According to a newspaper report, a senior officer from Pakistan Armed Services Board, official of PIA, and Air Defense faced corruption charges.

The scam regarding ISAF's 11,000 weapons-loaded missing containers raised many questions. Were these missing containers offloaded in Karachi, or diverted to the headquarters of the Punjabi Taliban in Bahawalpur, southern Punjab? These questions have become very irksome for the law enforcement agencies and the military establishment, fighting insurgencies across the country. The biggest scam of Pakistan's history and the missing of such a huge number of containers containing weapons, whisky, military uniforms and other prohibited and non-prohibited luggage, created a climate of fear and harassment across the country lest these lethal weapons fall into the hands of the Punjabi Taliban or the invisible terror army in Karachi.

In March 2015, a heavy contingent of Rangers raided Nine Zero, the headquarters of Muttahida Qaumi Movement (MQM), in Karachi's Azizabad neighborhood. A number of party workers, including member of MQM's Rabita Committee Amir Khan, were detained during the raid. Rabita Committee is MQM's central coordination cell. The operation was managed and executed by members of the paramilitary force alone and there was no sign of local police in the area. Jamaat-e-Islami Secretary General Liaquat Baloch said that recovery of NATO arms from Nine Zero proved that MQM was involved in acts of terrorism in Karachi. Giving his reaction over the situation arising out of the raid at the MQM headquarters, the JI leader asked the national security institutions to take serious notice of the activities of MQM. He said all the signs about the killing of leaders of political parties and workers, doctors, traders and common citizens lead to Nine Zero. He said there should be thorough investigation as to why all the convicts in heinous crimes were present at the Nine Zero. He said the statement by Altaf Hussain was admission of involvement in terrorism. Liaquat Baloch also questioned how the heavy weapons and long range guns with silencers of NATO origin reached the MQM headquarters.

The Federation of American Scientists (FAS) released a detailed report and identified important factors that gave rise to the threat of the jihadist Taliban inside the country. Military-grade weapons, the FAS say, are available to them in major towns and cities in all parts of FATA and Khyber Pakhtunkhwa. This means that the so-called

Pakistani nuclear threat is only a pretext; Pakistan is the real target—owing to its role in the complex US-China geopolitical relations. Writing in the Cutting Edge Magazine (June 22, 2011) Shoshana Bryen revealed that the CIA has been using drones in Pakistan from bases in Afghanistan because the US does not want to wage a war in Pakistan from Pakistan; the CIA wants to wage Pakistan's war from Afghanistan.[1]

On 19 November 2014, Pakistani journalist, Sardar Sikander Shaheen quoted the Auditor General of Pakistan (AGP) report on serious financial irregularities exceeding Rs 30 billion, including embezzlements, violation of rules, unauthorized occupation of public land and related malpractices, in the report for 2013-2014. The AGP found that unauthorized expenditures exceeding Rs 25 billion were incurred by the PAF authorities in terms of awarding an illegal consultancy contract to a private firm to execute a highly classified project.

Moreover, there are signals indicating that failure to win the war against the Taliban could prompt NATO to broaden the theatre of war into Pakistan. The danger is real. Notwithstanding President Obama's assurance about friendly ties with Pakistan; the US is changing its stance on partnership with Pakistan, and creates a new issue of distrust every week. In case of a NATO military operation in Pakistan, in addition to the Afghan and Pakistani Taliban, the alliance would be facing 725,000 professional personnel of a well organized army. The recent threat by General Petraeus to undertake unilateral military operations inside Pakistan was followed by NATO violations of Pakistan's airspace in North Waziristan. All these challenges faced by Pakistan are linked with the availability of military-grade weapons to insurgents and terrorist groups.

In 2011, I came across a report of Pakistan's Federal Tax Ombudsman on the issue of ISAF's missing containers. This is a comprehensive report, which gives readers a lot of information but only represents the government of Pakistan's standpoint. In my telephone conversation with one of the senior advisors of the Federal Tax Ombudsman in Islamabad, he told me that since ISAF's forward mounting base in Karachi was shifted to Kabul, the coordination mechanism between the customs authorities and ISAF representative were undermined. He told me that this is the biggest scam of customs reported in the country's history worth over Rs 220 billion. After NLC, Hajj, Steel Mills, Rental Power Plants, Railways, PIA, KESC,

---

1 *Cutting Edge Magazine*, June 22, 2011

and hundred other scandals, this scandal joins the series of high level corruption in Pakistan.[1]

According to Pakistan's Federal Board of Revenue (FBR) and customs intelligence sources in Lahore, these missing containers were imported to supply weapons to NATO in Afghanistan but they disappeared abruptly. Who received these containers and lethal weapons, who sold them to whom, nobody knows. But the question is: why has Pakistan's over 50 intelligence agencies so far failed in recovering this huge number of weapons-loaded containers or why they have not carried out a thorough investigation into the scam?

Counterterrorism authorities in Islamabad said these missing containers might cause more violence across the country, if they fall into the hands of the Punjabi Taliban or the invisible armies in Karachi, it would create more problems. Counter-insurgency experts said it will take Pakistan at least a decade tackling multi-faceted insurgencies across the country. Some military experts in Islamabad understand that the disappearance of these containers has put national security in constant danger. On 8 February 2011, Daily Times reported parliament's standing committee's serious reservations and pressure on the Defense minister and chairman FBR to explain the government's stance.[2]

The committee was told that only 7,000 containers were missing, which is not true. The committee asked about the agreement between Pakistan and the NATO alliance, which allowed NATO-ISAF containers to pass through Pakistan without scrutiny. In response to the Supreme Court and public allegations, the Federal Tax Ombudsman prepared a detailed report on the missing containers. The report accepts the inabilities of the customs officials. Moreover, following the report's revelations, the government of Pakistan suspended 22 officials of the Pakistan Customs Service for their involvement in the container scandal. According to a Pakistani think tank report, since the commencement of Operation Enduring Freedom in Afghanistan, Pakistan allowed more than 300,000 NATO containers to pass from Karachi to Afghanistan through the Chaman or Torkham border. During the Musharraf regime, Pakistani officials had no authority to even scan the containers.

The main hurdle here is that US military cargos carry Radio Frequency Identification Devices, which give the sole right of monitoring to American Homeland Security. No Pakistani agency or

---

1 "Pakistan's Federal Tax Ombudsman Report," 2011
2 Daily Times, 8 February 2011,

institution has access to these containers. The US government does not share this with other partners. More importantly, more than 80 percent of military cargos are being handled by ISAF- and NATO-hired private companies. The suspected threat arises from the delay of these containers.

For example, NATO containers need a certificate of the Afghan embassy to cross the border and this may take 15 days. Pakistani officials are of the opinion that in this relatively long space of time, most of the containers are changed, altered or emptied. The biggest problem faced by Pakistan is the smuggling of arms within the country through these suspect containers. Media reports have already highlighted the suspect movement of these containers carrying arms through false declaration or fake documents. Military experts in Islamabad say these containers are enough for sustaining the Taliban insurgents for a decade.

The presence of the Taliban in the Persian Gulf and the Middle East will bring more harm to the region as al Qaeda and the Taliban have made inroads into Libya and are now trying to enter Syria. Their long-term strategy is to conquer all Arab states and Pakistan step by step. They defeated Dictator Gaddafi; they will defeat Syria, Yemen, Jordan, and the whole of the Arab world. The Arab world comprises 22 states and territories of the Arab League stretching from the Atlantic Ocean in the west to the Arabian Sea in the east. An American author and journalist revealed in his recent interview that the Taliban of Afghanistan and Pakistan are going to be part of the government in Libya.

In FATA and Waziristan, Taliban terrorists kill and kidnap innocent people. 15 Pakistani soldiers, who were kidnapped near North Waziristan, were then killed ruthlessly. The Tehrik-i-Taliban Pakistan (TTP), according to Muhammad Yusuf Musa Khel, has also established its network in both Karachi and Mohmand Agency. Moreover, the Punjabi Taliban, Al Mukhtar network, Kharooj and Jandullah groups are playing on ethnic lines. Mr. Yusuf Musa Khel understands these groups are involved in kidnapping for ransom and target killings.

The Taliban insurgents are trying to re-establish their networks in Mohmand and Swat agencies. Member peace committee of Mohmand Agency, Muhammad Yusuf Musa Khel once told me that the Afghan Taliban and Mullah Fazlullah's terrorist groups are recruiting younger people for a fresh war with changing guerrilla strategies, against the Pakistan Army in Swat and Mohmand agencies. He mentioned that the Shura-e-Muraqiba (consisting of four major Taliban groups), a joint shura of Pak–Afghan Taliban, along the border region wants to carry out attacks with new style against Pakistan security forces.

In Kurram Agency, sectarian war left thousands dead notwithstanding that several agreements were negotiated under the auspices of the Pakistan Army from 2007-2011. No agreement will work unless border infiltration is stopped. The Afghan warlords and war criminals are fighting on both Sunni and Shia sides in the Kurram Agency, destroying and looting the houses of the local population. On 03 July 2012, in Russia & India Report, Rakesh Krishnan Simha quoted a survey (2012) of the United States based Pew Research Center which suggested Pakistan is not only a universally dislike country but the Pakistanis themselves have learnt nothing from their history.[1]

No single 'good' Taliban commander has so for been arrested in the military operation in North Waziristan and FATA. Yes, the army has arrested a good number of innocent Pashtuns and continues to prosecute them in military courts. The inclusion of a few inactive Taliban in the Afghan cabinet cannot stabilize the country, as all active forces have joined Islamic State (ISIS). The Taliban leaders Pakistan advocates have no active role in any anti-Afghan insurgency. The Pakistan army has painted an ugly picture of its country by recruiting jihadists from around the world. Its neighbors now openly criticize the country's policies of jihadism and sectarian Islamism. All wars Pakistan fought against India failed and the country generals lost their credibility. The report clearly describes the attitude of neighboring states toward Pakistan:

> It is a measure of Pakistan's penchant for exporting terrorism, counterfeit currency and drug that India has constructed a 2043km long steel fence across its border with its wayward Western neighbor. The floodlit fence is so bright it can be seen from space as a bright orange line snaking from the Arabian Sea to Kashmir. Now Iran is building a 700km steel and concrete security fence along its border with Pakistan "to prevent border crossing by terrorists and drug traffickers." When complete it will make the most fenced-in country in the world.[2]

---

1 "Russia & India Report," Rakesh Krishnan Simha, 03 July 2012
2 "Terrorist Islamic Republic of Pakistan," *May 13, 2013, Bharat Rakshak,* Consortium of Indian Defense Websites, http://forums.bharat-rakshak.com/viewtopic.php?p=1488817.

Postscript

A document on Pakistan's Internal Security Policy (2014–2018) categorically states, that the country faces the threat of nuclear terrorism. That threat comes as an addition to the possibility of chemical and biological terrorism. As the fatal war against terrorism entered crucial phase, another powerful extremist militant group (ISIS) emerged with a strong and well-trained army in Afghanistan, and parts of Pakistan. They are purportedly seeking to establish an Islamic state. The massacre of 100 innocent civilians, and the ANA soldiers in the Ajristan district of Ghazni province in Afghanistan, by the ISIS forces, and the brutal killings of children in the army school in Peshawar, raised serious questions about the future of security and stability in South Asia. The Tehreek-e-Taliban Pakistan (TTP) claimed responsibility, and called it a revenge attack for the Pakistan Army's Operation Zarb-e-Azb in North Waziristan and FATA regions.

The organization is focusing on Waziristan and Swat to train its fighters in TTP training centers. The Times of India reported that Islamic State wants to expand its influence in Pakistan. Journalist Kiran Nazish also reported the presence of ISIS in Pakistan: "Local sources in Peshawar and KPK say ISIS started recruitment in Pakistan two years ago—even before they emerged as ISIS themselves," a member of the jihadist group Lashkar-e-Jhangvi said, on condition of anonymity. "More than 200 fighters have left from Pakistan to join what is now called the Islamic State." With the establishment of ISIS networks in Pakistan and Afghanistan, the whole Shia population might come under attack. Shias (Hazara) are under attack in Afghanistan. There would be an unending war between Sunni and Shia sects from Mazar-e-Sharif to Karachi, and Gilgit and Baltistan, and the possible participation of Pakistan and Afghan armies in this sectarian war would cause huge destruction in the region.

Given the Islamic State (ISIS) attacks in Syria and Iraq, and its secret networks and propaganda campaign in Pakistan and Afghanistan, the international community has now focused on the proliferation and smuggling of chemical and biological weapons in the region. The recent debate in Europe-based think tanks suggest that as the groups retrieved nuclear and biological material from the Mosul University in Iraq, it can possibly make nuclear explosive devices, with an amount of plutonium considerably smaller than eight kilograms. The debate about bioterrorism and bio-defense is not entirely new in military circles of South Asia; the involvement of Islamic State in using biological weapons against the Kurdish army in Kobani is a stark lesson for Pakistan and Afghanistan.

The TTP, Afghan Taliban, Hezb-e-Islami and Punjabi Taliban have supported Islamic State (ISIS) in their statements. A salafi group operating in Nuristan, Kunar, Jalalabad, and Laghman provinces declared allegiance to the Islamic state, while two leaders of the group (Abdul Rahim Muslim Dost and Mullah Abdul Kahar) openly supported Abu Bakr al-Baghdadi.

The ISIS, now calling itself the Islamic State, holds control of vast areas of Iraq. The group established close contacts with Afghan warlords whose private militias challenged the authority of the government of Afghanistan. In the 1980s and 1990s, militants of the Islamic State received military training in Pakistan; therefore, Islamic State wants to reinvent its previous relationship in the region.

A former Mujahedeen commander of the Hezb-e-Islami group, Mr. Mirwais, told BBC that his party can join the forces of Islamic State. He also said that the group plan to fight Afghan army, beyond 2014. 'Great mujahedeen,' "we know Daish, and we have links with some Daish members. We are waiting to see if they meet the requirements for an Islamic caliphate," Mr. Mirwais told BBC.

In Afghanistan, the army is fighting on various fronts but so far has failed to defeat the insurgents. In Northern Afghanistan, the Taliban captured several districts and established their government, along the borders of Central Asia. Hezb-e-Islami forces are fighting in Pul-e-Khumri under the command of Mr. Mirwais.

The Jerusalem Center for Public Affairs in its report noted that 1,000 Chinese jihadists received military training at a military base in Pakistan. What makes the existence of a training camp in North Waziristan in Pakistan even more interesting, from a Chinese perspective, is that China and Pakistan are allies?

Pakistani anger at the US is matched by more quiet US anger with Pakistan and by a near total lack of real world tolerance for Pakistani rhetoric about its role in counterterrorism, sacrifices, and the lack of continued US support. Barring radical shifts in Pakistan's conduct, the US will not be seen as a real strategic partner, and Pakistan's failures to develop tensions with India will be seen as an unfortunate, but fully acceptable risk. Pakistan has been on the brink for some years.

Prominent Indian scholar Rana Banerji, in one of his books noted that Pakistan has become a hyper national-security state. Mr. Banerji urged that the State's long term policies have neither focused on economic development, nor shown political cohesion. Despite the impact of the internet revolution, enabled by a reasonably free media, the younger generation has not been allowed to globalize or benefit from economic liberalization. The education, science and technology sectors have languished or remained bound under old narratives of insecurity. Mr. Banerji understands that the real political power is today diffused and spread among several actors. The center-right politicians, who received an overwhelming popular mandate in the 2013 general elections, have built their own patronage and connections with radical Islamic actors; and the latter too have emerged with increasing clout in civil society, Banerji argued.

Afghanistan and Kashmir are other regions where Islamic State wants to boost its influence. Pakistan's Fuji Foundation contribution in Islamic State may possibly endanger India and Afghanistan in the near future. Needless to say, both Pakistan and Afghanistan are shown as part of the Islamic caliphate, envisaged in the Islamic State's map. The group's propaganda pamphlets in Dari and Pashto appeared in eastern Afghanistan, and in Afghan refugee camps in Khyber Pakhtunkhwa. The new group, which calls itself Jamatul Ahrar, is led by a man called Omar Khalid Khorasani. He is the one who appears sporting a black turban and beard in various Taliban videos.

It is said that, in their unerring commitment to uniformity, all the Taliban love to look like all the other Taliban. The religious groups think that Pakistan has to function as a country solely to protect and promote Islam, and anything else should be secondary in the priority of governance. This attitude has cost the country dearly, as people with independent and progressive outlook and without excessive commitment to religious sentiments, cannot have decision making authority in the government. To this extent, the talent available to the government has become restricted.

Among many factors, the Pakistani state's protracted apathy and inaction on the issue of security has provided non-state actors the spaces, to grow and expand their influence. They used these spaces not only to propagate their ideologies and narratives, but also to establish 'state within the state' in Pakistan's tribal areas. Even as counteraction is now underway, the sudden rise of Islamic State (IS) has threatened to make matters worse for us.

The militants are jubilant over the success of the Islamic State of Iraq and Syria (IS), which has established a 'caliphate' or 'Islamic state' in parts of Syria and Iraq. This is not the first time militants have captured some territory, and established their so-called Islamic writ. Writer Gupta suggests that India informed the US that the Pakistan-based proscribed groups, including Lashkar-e-Taiba (LeT) and Jaish-e-Mohammed (JeM), were sending recruits to Syria and Iraq via Saudi Arabia and Turkey, to join the Islamic State in Iraq. In a shocking development a National Investigation Agency dossier retrieved, alleged that more than 300 Indian youth have been recruited by Pakistan-based Tehreek-e-Taliban which has joined hands with Islamic State (ISS). Pakistani army now secretly planned to develop contacts between ISIS and Thripura Mujahedeen and Assam separatists.

According to a Times Now report, the NIA dossier noted that the youth are being recruited from Kerala, Tamil Nadu, Maharashtra and Karnataka. They are being trained in Pakistan, Iraq and Syria to be Fidayeen. The jihadist army of the Islamic State, formerly known as ISIS, had taken over large swaths of Iraq, and declared the establishment of a caliphate, governed by Islamic law, or Shariah, that also includes north-eastern Syria. American author Michael Spangler revealed some important aspects of Pakistan's counter terrorism policy:

> Pakistan apparently calculates that by fighting the Tehrik-e-Taliban but providing tacit support to other groups such as the Haqqani Network, Pakistan (1) stays close to a bloc that could emerge as a key power-broker in Afghanistan; (2) sustains asymmetric proxies harassing an Indian presence in Afghanistan and Kashmir; and (3) secures Pakistan's north-western border by restraining some Taliban groups from coalescing with others to oppose Pakistan's secular authorities. Accepting this objection, however, boxes the

United States into maintaining a middle-of-the-road foreign policy with Pakistan that neither accomplishes nor risks much.[1]

In July 2014, senior Afghan officials claimed that Pakistani forces and militants were fighting alongside Afghan insurgents in the Sangin district of Southern Helmand province. Pajhwok news reported government officials that Afghan government considered the involvement of Pakistani forces and insurgents in the ongoing clashes in Sangin as "a clear invasion of Afghanistan." The four-day clashes in Sangin resulted in heavy casualties among civilians, security forces and insurgents and the displacement of thousands of families. The unrest on its third day spread to four more districts—Musa Qala, Kajaki, Nawzad and Marja—in Helmand.

Senior interior and Defense Ministry officials told reporters in Kabul that Pakistan Army soldiers were among those fighting against Afghan forces. Defense Ministry spokesman Gen. Zahir Azimi said that hundreds of fighters associated with Pakistan-based Lashkar-e-Taiba (LeT) and Pakistani security personnel had joined the Afghan Taliban in carrying out attacks in Sangin. "We will not let our enemies reach their strategic plans in our country. Our enemies through their strategic plans have been trying to control our big towns and provinces, but they have always been defeated," Azimi said.

On 04 August 2014, Khaama Press reported Afghan Foreign Ministry spokesman Ahmad Shekib Mostaghni told reporters, that three memos revealing three violations by Pakistani side in Afghanistan, were handed over to Pakistani ambassador Abrar Hussain. However, he was summoned by the Ministry of Foreign Affairs of Afghanistan, a day after the National Security Council (NSC) accused the Pakistani military, of increasing its military presence among the terrorist groups in Afghanistan.

Mr. Mostaghni said the government of Pakistan was taking seriously its commitment to fight against terrorism, and the Pakistani military personnel and advisers increased their presence among the terrorist groups in Afghanistan. He said, other issues including cross-border shelling by Pakistani military in Dangam and Shegal districts of Kunar province, and coordinated attacks by nearly one thousand militants in Hesarak district of Nangarhar province, shows the obvious violation by Pakistan on Afghan soil.

---

1 Spangler: Strategic Studies Institute: "Pakistan's Changing Counter-terrorism Strategy: A Window of Opportunity?" http://www.strategicstudiesinstitute.army.mil/pubs/Parameters/issues/Spring_2014/4_Spangler.pdf

The presence of ISIS in parts of Pakistan prompted concern about the exponential network of the group. Analysts in Pakistan believe that if the country's army failed to undermine the threat of Islamic State network, the terrorist groups might inflict more fatalities, after the US military operations in Iraq and Syria. The sudden jump of ISIS into the battle field to support TTP war against Pakistan army is considered a bigger security challenge.

The Islamic State is now planning to join the TTP fight against Pakistan army in North Waziristan and FATA region, therefore it started distributing jihadist literature, titled "victory," in Pashtu and Persian languages, which can easily be read by Afghan and Pakistani citizens as well. Wall chalking in Waziristan, Khyber Pakhtunkhawa and parts of Afghanistan started, asking the people of both the states to join and support Islamic State. This is a new challenge to the military establishment in Pakistan, which is deeply embroiled in the fights against the TTP terrorist group in Waziristan and FATA regions.

Now, with the establishment of the Islamic State in Pakistan and Afghanistan, the threat of nuclear and biological terrorism deserves special attention from the governments of Pakistan and Afghanistan, because the army of the Islamic State can develop a "dirty bomb," in which explosives can be combined with a radioactive source like those commonly used in hospitals or extractive industries. Such a weapon could cause more disruption than destruction, as it would affect the health of the population in various ways. Political and military circles in Pakistan fear that as the IS has already seized chemical weapons in Al Muthanna, in Northern Iraq, some disgruntled retired military officers, or experts in nuclear explosive devices might help the Pakistan chapter of the group to deploy biological and chemical weapons. A letter from the Iraqi government to the United Nations warned that the militant captured chemical weapon site, which contains 2,500 chemical rockets filled with the nerve agent Sarin.

In Europe, there is a general perception that as the Islamic State already used some dangerous gases in Iraq, it could use biological weapons against civilian populations in Pakistan. If control over these weapons is weak, and they become available in the open market, there would be huge destruction in the region. In July 2014, the government of Iraq announced that nuclear material was seized by the ISIS army from Mosul University: a laptop containing a 19-page document in Arabic on how to develop biological weapons, and a 26 page religious Fatwa which allows the use of weapons of Mass Destruction. "If

Muslims cannot defeat the kafir (unbelievers) in a different way, it is permissible to use weapons of mass destruction," warns the Fatwa.

The effects of chemical weapons are worse as it causes death or incapacitation, while biological weapons cause death or disease in humans, animals or plants. We have two international treaties, which interdict the use of such weapons. Notwithstanding of all these preventive measures, the threat of chemical or biological warfare persists. In 2011 and 2013, there were complaints and allegations that some states wanted to target Pakistan with biological weapons. The country has been trying to counter biological attacks, but has so far failed due to the limited funds and medical advancement. As Pakistan noted in its statement to the meeting of states parties in December 2013, the country ratified the BTWC in 1974 as a non-possessor state and remains fully committed to implementing all provisions of the Convention.

Fatalities due to Dengue and Ebola viruses in Pakistan, and West Africa are grave forms of bioterrorism. In 2011, the Pakistan Medical Association called on ISI to investigate fears that the deadly disease was deliberate spread in Punjab. There are speculations that in the future, measles, dengue, polio and the Ebola viruses can be used as a weapon of bioterrorism in Pakistan. Some states might use drones for the purposes of bio-war against their rival states. In 2013, writing in Global Policy Journal, Amanda M. Teckman warned that Islamic State might possibly use Ebola as a weapon against civilian populations. Groups like IS, which has demonstrated a willingness to engage in large scale mass murder, including the uninhibited murder of civilians, has the capability to produce a weaponized version of Ebola.

The University of Birmingham Policy Commission Report warned that terrorists could also turn the remotely-piloted aircraft into flying bombs by hooking them up to improvised explosive devices. Sir David, a former British intelligence researcher, warned that the drones had gained a reputation as unaccountable killing machines because of their widespread used in America's controversial anti-terrorist campaigns in Pakistan, Yemen and Somalia.

On 26 September 2014, TOLO News reported several insurgent groups actively engaged in crossfire with the Afghan National Security Forces (ANSF) throughout the country, but according to security officials signs of the Islamic State surfaced near central Ghazni province. According to Ghazni security officials, more than 300 Arab and Pakistani insurgents, Haqqani network, Afghan Taliban and what officials believe to be the Islamic State fighters are currently active in Andar district of Ghazni province. Officials emphasized that 13 Turkish female suicide attackers were operating alongside the insurgent groups in Andar. "They wave their black flags in the air, speaking in Arabic, Punjabi and Farsi," the Head of Ghazni's Provincial Council, Abdul Jami said. "They have arrived to Ghazni with strong and aggressive forces."

Ghazni's Deputy Governor Mohammad Ali Ahmadi said that these militants are on the rise in the province, causing greater threat to the people of the province and the nation. "These terrorists have revised their leadership in Ghazni," "This means that these militants have chosen their shadow governor, shadow district governor and commanders in Ghazni. They will be directed by foreign citizens and will activate their fight very violently and brutally." Ahmadi said.

On 27 September 2014, Daily Outlook reported around 100 civilians was brutally killed by militants in Ajristan district of south-eastern Ghazni province. According to local government officials, around 800 Taliban militants including 200 foreign fighters staged coordinated attacks in Ajristan district. Provincial council chief, Abdul Jami, said clashes intensified and major transport routes were closed by the Taliban fighters. Mr. Jami further added that Taliban militants brutally shot dead and burnt civilians in Ajristan district. On 26 September 2014, Zabihullah Tamanna reported from Kabul that more than 100 Afghan civilians were killed in five days of brutal fighting in eastern Afghanistan. A senior local official in Ghazni province, south-east of Kabul, claimed there was evidence that the influence of the Islamic State is spreading to the region with militants using more vicious methods.

Upon the change of the government in Afghanistan, ISIS launched terrorist attacks. No one could have thought of Daesh or ISIS launching an offensive in Afghanistan alongside the Taliban, but now people in Ghazni said they saw masked men wearing camouflage who carried the black flag of the IS. Locals said that none of the militants spoke any local language. Their flag shows they were members of Daesh. Al-Qaeda had picked Afghanistan for its global jihad because at that time it had no opportunity to wage its jihad against the West from Arab soil, but why would Daesh do the same when it has been already engaged in Syria and Iraq and capturing city after city?

Deputy Provincial Governor Mohammad Ali Ahmadi said the violence in Ajristan district had been marked by beheadings, torched homes and slaughtered livestock with at least 50 police killed and around 250 homes set ablaze. He said Taliban fighters linked to

ISIS were active in the province and raised its flag in certain areas, campaigning in support of the Syria and Iraq-based group. On 23 September 2014, Dawn reported the farewell speech of the former Afghan President Hamid Karzai. Mr. Karzai blamed both the United States and neighboring Pakistan for the continuing war with the Taliban-led insurgency and warned the new government to be extra cautious in relations with the US and the West.

Yet, Pakistan's strategic objectives in Afghanistan remain largely unchanged, and there are few reasons to believe that the shift is anything more than a tactical adjustment to meet new regional and international realities. Pakistan's reaching out to the former Northern Alliance—an expansion from its traditional Pashtun focus–is primarily a response to India's successful use of development programs, to enhance its influence with every Afghan ethnic group since 2002. Pakistan, systematically blamed in Afghanistan for whatever goes wrong in the country, cannot expect to generate the same level of sympathy. Pakistan's real motive in seeking to dominate Afghanistan is the fear of its own dismemberment. Until the Soviet invasion of Afghanistan in 1979, Islamabad's main agenda was to prevent Kabul-supported Pashtun and Baloch nationalism from escalating into full-blown movements for independence.

Advisor to the Prime Minister on National Security and Foreign Affairs, Sartaj Aziz called on countries like India and Iran, to emulate Pakistan's stated policy of non-interference in Afghanistan, and not to fight proxy wars. Speaking at the Conference on Pakistan–Afghanistan and the International Security Assistance Force (ISAF) withdrawal, organized by the South Asian Free Media Association (SAFMA) in Islamabad, he said that Pakistan has no favorites in Afghanistan and its policy of non-interference in Afghanistan affairs has helped improve bilateral relations.

The combination of a long-term Western commitment towards Afghanistan coupled with an increasing focus on Pakistan gave the latter leverage against India; in January 2010, under Pakistani pressure, India was excluded from the International Conference on Afghanistan held in Istanbul. But within 18 months, in June 2011, President Barack Obama announced that Western troops would transfer responsibility for security to Afghan forces by 2014. Such policy changes led many in India to conclude that their parallel engagement both at community and government level has been vindicated.

The same day, American ambassador to Afghanistan, James B. Cunningham, responded quickly and publicly to the Afghan president's remarks. "They were ungracious," he said. "It makes me kind of sad. I think his remarks, which were uncalled-for, do a disservice to the American people and dishonor the sacrifices that Americans have made here—the huge sacrifices that Americans have made here and continue to make here" Mr. Cunningham, who had planned to leave Afghanistan after the election was completed, was unusually frank. He had been ambassador for three years, but the relationship between Mr. Karzai and American officials became increasingly hostile. New York Times reported,

> "...not recognizing the many contributions that Americans have made, and our partners, that's the part that's ungracious and ungrateful," Mr. Cunningham said. "The good news, however, is that I am absolutely confident in reassuring Americans that Afghans themselves absolutely value and are grateful for the sacrifice and the commitment of the United States to the future of this country."[1]

On 18 September, 2014, Daily Times editorial noted cross border skirmishes between Pakistan and Afghanistan. On 16 September 2014, a group of militants from Afghanistan attacked a Frontier Constabulary (FC) border post in North Waziristan (NW). Reports said 11 militants were killed and one captured, while three FC men died. On the same day the military said it had killed 23 terrorists in airstrikes in Khyber Agency. The nature of these and other attacks over the summer indicate militant attempts to probe defensive preparedness. They are getting ready to go on the offensive when NATO leaves.

On 19 September 2014, Daily Times reported Pakistan advised Afghan authorities to take appropriate steps to eliminate safe havens of terrorists from its soil. In her weekly press briefing, Foreign Office spokesperson Tasnim Aslam said, that the terrorists carry out attacks on Pakistani side from such safe havens present in Afghanistan. About 90 to 100 terrorists attacked a check post inside Pakistan on September 17, she said, adding that Islamabad lodged strong protest with Kabul over the incident. Referring to allegations from the Afghan side, the spokesperson said that Pakistan was an important and mature country and does not feel necessary to respond to every baseless allegation. She said that Pakistan was pursuing developments related to one of its journalists, Faizullah, who was detained in Afghanistan.

Among other things, on 19 June 2014, the New Yorker reported, Pakistan's generals fear the "reverse sanctuary" problem—that is, rather than Pakistan providing sanctuary for anti-Afghan fighters,

---

1 *Boston Globe*, "In farewell speech, Karzai lashes out at US 'agenda'."

as it has done for several decades, Afghanistan might become a durable sanctuary for anti-Pakistan groups. Indeed, the current chief of the Pakistani Taliban, Mullah Fazlullah, is said to be hiding out in northeastern Afghanistan, along with other armed radicals. Pakistan's sponsorship of religious extremist proxy groups is an open secret. After its use of proxies was exposed, it destroyed whatever diplomatic credibility and capital the country had.

There is no guarantee that proxies used today will not do the same if they achieve success in Afghanistan. Pakistan Army frequently denies links with the Taliban fighting in Afghanistan, and said its recent operation against militants in North Waziristan was indiscriminate. On 18 September, 2014, Dawn reported violence on Pak–Afghan border. The Foreign Ministries of the two countries sparred over the implications of Punjabi Taliban leader Asmatullah Muawiya's announcement that his group would no longer commit violence inside Pakistan, while they continued to believe in jihad elsewhere; Pakistani security personnel came under attack from Afghan-based anti-Pakistan militants.

"The Punjabi Taliban's recent message clearly indicated that the Pakistani military was preparing to interfere in Afghanistan's affairs again," Faizi told Radio Free Europe. "We have evidences that Punjabi Taliban were leading the recent attacks in Kandahar and Helmand provinces." In Pakistan, meanwhile, the political crisis further put on the defensive a government that had very limited input on the Afghan policy anyway. Pakistan worries about an Afghanistan where regional rivals gain ground and about a porous border from which trouble can be exported to Pakistan.

On 17 September 2014, TOLO News reported that Afghan Minister of Defense, Bismillah Mohammadi, Minister of Interior Umer Daudzai, and the National Directorate of Security (NDS) Deputy Hasamuddin Hassam, were summoned to the Senate to answer for their inability to counter Taliban insurgency. The officials stated that Taliban insurgents conducted about 700 offensives in different parts of the country, with the cooperation of their foreign and domestic counterparts in 2014. "This year has been the deadliest year in the past 13 years. The Taliban have conducted 691 offensives this year with the cooperation of their domestic and foreign counterparts," Minister of Defense Bismillah Khan Mohammadi said. "We had the cooperation of the NATO forces in the past; but we fought alone this year." Minister of Interior Umer Daudzai stated that 2014 was worse for the Afghan police.

"There were many foreign Taliban this year; they were not speaking Dari or Pashto [Afghanistan's official languages]; they were speaking Urdu [Pakistan's official language]," Mr. Daudzai said. He stated that in the first six months of 2014, 955 civilians and 1,523 police officers were killed and another 2,394 civilians and 2,506 police officers were injured. The Taliban too, suffered casualties. Moreover, 5,503 Taliban insurgents were killed and another 2,370 were wounded in 2014. The ANSF tackles the unprecedented rates of insurgent attacks as the forces get ready to take on the full security responsibility after the foreign troops withdraw from the country at the end of the current year.

On 21 August 2014, Daily Outlook Afghanistan reported rocket shelling from across the Pakistani border into the Afghan soil. As usual, government done nothings more than condemning these attacks on media and the poor people of Kunar were left on the mercy of these rockets. Members of civil society also condemned attacks that resulted in the casualties of dozens of innocent and neutral citizens of Kunar province. Once again, the tensions between the two neighboring countries soared, and the ties between them are touching the lowest point in the recent years.

However, in June 2014, former Afghan President Hamid Karzai said that foreign elements were behind the attacks in southern Helmand province, which caused a number of civilian casualties. A statement issued by Presidential Palace said the attacks were orchestrated by intelligence agency of the neighboring country, in an indirect reference to Pakistan.

Tribal elders from Helmand, Farah and Nimroz provinces expressed grave concern over terrorist attacks in Helmand province. "Foreigners interfere here; their fighters are fighting in our provinces," former President Hamid Karzai said.

Appendix 1. Urgent Petition: Stop Pakistan Army's Crimes Against Humanity

Petition by: A global citizen
Appeal to the International Court of Justice, International Criminal Court, United Nations Human Rights Council, United Nations Security Council and other international human rights groups

Stop Crimes against Humanity: Petition against Senior Generals of Pakistan Army

Given the ongoing patronage of Jihadi-sectarian networks by Pakistan army and its various agencies (Inter Services Intelligence, Military Intelligence etc), in the light of the ongoing human rights abuses and massacres of the Baloch, Pashtun, Shia Muslims, Barelvis, Ahmadis, Christians, human Rights activists, political workers, students, lawyers and journalists by Pakistan army and its various proxy groups spread all over Pakistan. Numerous reports by Human Rights Watch, Amnesty International, Media and other material is available as a proof of the atrocities committed by Pakistan army, its Intelligence Agencies and Jihadi-sectarian proxy groups.

We the people of Pakistan, Afghanistan and diasporas living in the US, Canada, Europe and other countries appeal to the United Nations and international human rights and legal authorities to take concrete steps, not against the people of Pakistan or the civilian government, but against Pakistan army generals (all Major Generals and above) and commanders of its various agencies.

Such steps may include but not be limited to:

1. Their trial in the International Court of Justice and International Criminal Tribunal to investigate into their crimes against humanity and to award exemplary punishment to those found guilty;

2. We also appeal to the United States, Canada, Australia, UK and other European countries to impose visa restrictions on officials of Pakistan army and other individuals who are a part of the Jihadi-Sectarian Complex in Pakistan. The Pakistan army and allies subject to this visa ban may include uniformed officers as well as non-uniformed proxies and affiliates of the terror network. Such travel restrictions must also apply to a broader class of individuals who have played a role in the ongoing persecution and murders of religious and ethnic minorities.

3. All financial and non-financial assets, bank accounts, properties etc of senior officers of Pakistan army and its various agencies may be frozen in USA, Canada, Europe and other parts of the world.

Such action would demonstrate a commitment to express solidarity with victims of torture, persecution, murder and arbitrary detention; urge respect for the rule of law, UN resolutions and universal rights in Pakistan and entire region, and hold officials accountable for terrorism and human rights abuses committed against their own people. We recommend that a Terror Black List is compiled and publicized comprising all senior officers of Pakistan army, rank Major General and above, and heads and directors of its various institutions and agencies.

We believe it is time for action. Mere rhetoric has failed to save the people of Pakistan, including democracy in Pakistan, and the entire region from the brutal clutches of Pakistan army and its Jihad-sectarian Enterprise. It is time to hold the mentors of terrorism and human rights abusers accountable for their crimes. Change.org is the world's largest petition platform, empowering people everywhere to create the change they want to see. http://www.change.org/petitions/urgent-petition-stop-pakistan-army-s-crimes-against-humanity.

APPENDIX 2. FAUJI FOUNDATION OR MILITARY BUSINESS ENTERPRISE

This milbuss was established in 1954 to provide mercenaries to the Arab world and promote the personal business of Pakistan's corrupt generals. Fauji Foundation is running the following industries:

1. Fauji Cereals
2. Foundation Gas
3. Fauji Fertilizer Company Limited
4. Fauji Fertilizer Bin Qasim Limited
5. Fauji Cement Company Limited
6. Fauji Kabirwala Power Company Limited
7. Foundation Power Company Daharki Limited
8. Mari Petroleum Company Limited
9. Fauji Akbar Portia Marine Terminal Limited
10. Fauji Oil Terminal and Distribution Company Limited
11. Pakistan Maroc Phosphore, S.A., Morocco
12. Foundation Securities private limited
13. Askari Bank Limited
14. Askari Cement Company
15. Fauji Sugar Mills Tando Mohammad Khan.
16. Fauji Sugar Mills Khoski.
17. Fauji Sugar Mills Sangla Hill.
18. Fauji Corn Complex.
19. Fauji Polypropylene Products Foundation Gas.

Appendix 3. Pakistan's Nuclear Facilities

Nuclear Conversion
Chemical Plant Complex
Chemical Processing Plant (CPP)
Islamabad Conversion Facility
Nuclear Education and Training
Chasnupp Centre for Nuclear Training
Karachi Institute of Power Engineering
Pakistan Institute of Engineering and Applied Sciences
Nuclear Enrichment
Chaklala Enrichment Plant
Gadwal Uranium Enrichment Plant
Golra Sharif Enrichment Plant
Kahuta Research Laboratories
Sihala Enrichment Plant
Nuclear Exploration and Mining
Baghalchure
Nanganai
Qabul Khel
Shanawa Uranium Mine Project
Taunsa
Nuclear Fuel Fabrication
Kundian Nuclear Complex 1 (KNC 1)
Nuclear-Heavy Water Production
Khushab Complex
Multan Heavy Water Production Facility

Nuclear Milling
BC-1 Uranium Mill
Issa Khel Uranium Mill
Nuclear-Plutonium Production Reactors
Khushab Complex
Nuclear Power Reactors
Chasnupp 1
Chasnupp 2
Kanupp
Nuclear Regulatory
Pakistan Atomic Energy Commission (PAEC)
Pakistan Nuclear Regulatory Authority (PNRA)
Nuclear Reprocessing
Experimental Reprocessing Facility
Kundian Nuclear Complex 2 (KNC-2)
New Laboratories Reprocessing Facility
Nuclear Research Reactors
PARR-1
PARR-2
Nuclear Research and Development
Pakistan Institute of Nuclear Science and Technology (PINSTECH)
Nuclear Testing
Ras Koh Test Site
Wazir Khan Khosa Test Site
Nuclear Weaponization
Khushab Tritium Production Facility
Wah Cantonment Ordnance Complex

APPENDIX 4. MISSILES FACILITIES

Missile Base
Jinnah Naval Base (JNB)
PAF Base Mushaf
Missile Education and Training
Air University
Ghulam Ishaq Khan Institute of Engineering Sciences and Technology (GIKI)
National University of Sciences and Technology (NUST)
Missile Production
Air Weapons Complex (AWC)
Defense Science and Technology Organization (DESTO)
Khan Research Laboratories (KRL)
National Defense Complex (NDC)
Pakistan Atomic Energy Commission (PAEC)
Pakistan Ordnance Factories (POF)
Space and Upper Atmosphere Research Commission (SUPARCO)
Missile Regulatory
National Command Authority (NCA)
National Engineering and Scientific Commission (NESCOM)
National Security Council of Pakistan (NSC)
Strategic Plans Division (SPD)
Missile Testing
Mashhood Test Firing Range (MTFR)
Sonmiani Flight Test Range (FTR)

Appendix 5. National Counterterrorism Authority (NACTA)

The Authority shall have the following functions, namely:

(a) to receive and collate data or information or intelligence, and disseminate and coordinate between all relevant stakeholders to formulate threat assessments with periodical reviews to be presented to the Federal Government for making adequate and timely efforts to counter terrorism and extremism;

(b) to coordinate and prepare comprehensive National counter terrorism and counter extremism strategies, and reviews them on periodical basis;

(c) to develop action plans against terrorism and extremism and report to the Federal Government about implementation of these plans, on periodical basis;

(d) to carry out research on topics relevant to terrorism and extremism and to prepare and circulate documents;

(e) to carry out liaison with international entities for facilitating cooperation in areas relating to terrorism and extremism;

f) to review relevant laws and suggest amendments to the Federal Government; and

g) to appoint committee of experts from Government and non-Government organizations for deliberations in areas related to the mandate and functions of the Authority.

Board of Governors

The Authority shall have a Board of Governors comprising:

(a) Prime Minister Chairman
(b) Minister for Interior—Member
(c) Chief Ministers of Provinces—Members

(d) Chief Minister of Gilgit Baltistan—Member

(e) Minister for Law and Justice—Member

(f) Minister for Finance—Member

(g) Minister for Defense—Member

(h) Prime Minister of Azad Jammu and Kashmir—Member

(i) One Senator to be recommended by—Member Chairman Senate)

(j) One MNA to be recommended by—Member Speaker National Assembly)

(k) Secretary, Ministry of Interior—Member

(l) DG Inter Services Intelligence—Member

(m) DG Intelligence Bureau—Member

(n) DG Military Intelligences—Member

(o) National Coordinator—Member

(p) Chief Secretaries of the Provinces,—Members Gilgit Baltistan and Azad Jammu and Kashmir

(q) DG Federal Investigation Agency—Member, and

(r) Inspector General of Police of Provinces,—Members Azad Jammu and Kashmir and Gilgit Baltistan

(2) The National Coordinator shall act as the Secretary to the Board.

(3) The Board may invite any person to the meeting on special invitation.

National Coordinator

The National Coordinator shall have the following powers, namely:

(a) to execute the policies and plans approved by the board and instructions issued by the Federal Government:

(b) to prescribe terms and conditions of the employees and grant additional allowances or any other incentives;

(c) to have full financial and administrative power for effective administration of the Authority, as approved by the Board;

(d) to engage any person or entity on contract basis to carry out assignments for the consultancy in accordance with acclaimed best practices;

(e) to establish administrative structures at the field level for efficient implementation and accessibility of the Authority;

(f) to submit quarterly progress reports to the Board on the Financial and functional aspects of the Authority;

(g) to perform such other functions as may be delegated by the Board;

(h) to undertake any other assignments given by the Board in the respective fields; and

(i) produce periodical journals relating to counter terrorism and counter extremism issues.

Bibliography

Abbas Hassan. 2004. *Pakistan's Drift into Extremism: Allah, the Army and America's War on Terror*. M.E Sharp Inc.

Abid, Abdur Rehman, 22 April, 2009, "Buner Falls into the Hands of Swat Taliban," *Dawn*

Karachi.

Abrams Herbert L. 1991, "Human Reliability and Safety in the Handling of Nuclear Weapons," *Science and Global security*.

Abrahamson, James L and Paul H. Carew, 2002, *Vanguard of American Atomic Deterrence, the Sandia Pioneers*, Westport, Praeger.

Abrams, Herbert L., 1991, *Human Reliability and Safety in the Handling of Nuclear Weapons*, Science & Global Security

Abu Zahab Mariam. March 19, 2009. "Sectarianism in Pakistan's Kurram Agency," *Terrorism Monitor*

Ackland Len. 1999. *Making a real killing: Rocky Flats and the Nuclear West*. Mexico Press

Acton James, 2010, *Deterring During Disarmament: Deep Nuclear Reduction and International Security*. Routledge, New York, USA.

Ahmad Khaled. 2011. *Sectarian War: Pakistan's Sunni Shia Violence and its Links to the Middle East*, Oxford University Press.

Albright David, 2002, "Al Qaeda's nuclear program: Through the Window of Seized Documents." *Policy Forum on Line, No. 47, November, 6*, Nautilus Institute Berkeley. USA.

Allen James S. 1952. *Atomic Imperialism, International Publisher*, New York, USA

Alley, William M and Rosemary Alley, 2013, *Too Hot to Touch, the Problem of High Level Nuclear Waste*, Cambridge University Press

Arnold, Lorna and Mark Smith, 2006, *Britain, Australia and the Bomb: The Nuclear Tests and Their Aftermath*. New York: Palgrave Macmillan.

Aron, Raymond. 1965. *The Great Debate: Theories of Nuclear Strategy*. Garden City, New York.

Ayson, Robert. 2004. *Thomas Schelling and the Nuclear Age: Strategy as Social Science*. New York. Frank Cass.

Albright, David, 2002, "Al Qaeda's Nuclear Program: Through the Window of Seized Documents," *Policy Forum On-line, Special Forum No. 47, November 6*, Nautilus Institute, Berkeley, CA

Basrur, Rajesh, October 2002, "Kargil, Terrorism, and India's Strategic Shift," *India Review*

Basrur, Rajesh, "September 2003, Nuclear India at the Crossroads," *Arms Control Today*

Badash, Lawrence. 1994. *Scientists and the Development of Nuclear Weapons*. Atlantic Highlands, NJ: Humanities Press.

Badash, Lawrence. 2009. *A Nuclear Winter's Tale: Science and Politics in the 1980s*. Cambridge, MIT Press.

Bashkar Roy. 2008, "China Unmasked—What Next"? South Asian Analysis group Paper No. 2840.

Basrur Rajesh and Rizvi Hassan Askari. 2003, "Nuclear Terrorism and South Asia." *Occasional Paper 25*. Cooperating Monitoring Centre

Badash Lawrence, 1994. *Scientists and the Development of Nuclear Weapons*, Atlantics Highlands, Humanitarian Press.

Bellany Lan. 2007. *Terrorism and Weapons of Mass Destruction: Responding to the Challenge*. Routledge Global Security Studies.

Brachman. Jarret M and William F. McCant, 2006. *Stealing al Qaeda's Playbook*, West Point, US Military Academy, Combating Terrorism Center.

Byman Daniel. 2008. *The Five Fronts War: The Better Way to Fight Global Jihad*, Hoboken, Wiley.

Bellamy Alex J. 2008. *Fighting Terror: Ethical Dilemmas*, Zed Books, USA and UK.

Cameron Gavin. 1999. *Nuclear Terrorism: A Threat Assessment for the 21st Century*. St. Martin's Press New York.

Bailes, J. 2013. *Weapon of the strong: conversations on U.S. state terrorism.* London: Pluto Press.

Burt, Richard R. 1982. "Use of Chemical Weapons in Asia: Laos, Cambodia, and Afghanistan." *US Department of State Bulletin*

Burgess, Lisa. 1998. "Initiative Expands Guard's Role in Bio-Chem Defense." *Army Times*, April 6.

Caldicott, Helen. 2002, *The New Nuclear Danger: George W. Bush's Military–Industrial Complex.* New York: The New Press.

Carlotta Gall, 2014. *The Wrong Enemy: America in Afghanistan 2001–2014.* Houghton Mifflin Harcourt, New York.

Chalmers Malcolm. 2012. *Less is Better: Nuclear Restraint at Low Numbers.* Royal United Services Institute for Strategic Studies London.

Clarke, J. W. 2007. *Defining danger: American assassins and the new domestic terrorists*, New Brunswick, N.J.: Transaction Publishers.

Clarke, R. A., & Knake, R. K. 2010. *Cyber war: The next threat to national security and what to do about it.* New York: Ecco.

Carruthers S. 2000. *The Media at War: Communication and Conflict in the 21st Century.* St. Martin's Press. New York.

Crenshaw P. 1981, *Psychology of Terrorism: An Agenda for the 21st Century.* Wesleyan University.

Carey Schofield. 2010. *Inside Pakistan army: A Women Experience in the Frontline of the War on Terror.* Biteback.

Cole, B, 2011, *the changing face of terrorism: How real is the threat from biological, chemical and nuclear weapons?* London: I.B. Tauris.

Chandran D. Suba 2008, "Violence against Women in Swat, Why Blame only Taliban"? IPCS Issue Brief, No. 97, India

Clarke Richard. 2004. "Against All Enemies: America's War on Terror," Free Press, New York, USA.

Coll Steve. 2004. *Ghost Wars: The Secret History of the CIA, Afghanistan and Bin Laden, from the Soviet Invasion to September 10, 2001,* Penguin Publishers. USA.

Dahl Robert, 1985, *Controlling Nuclear Weapons: Democracy versus Guardianship.* Syracuse University Press, New York.

Dando Malcolm. 2001. *The New Biological Weapons: Threat, Proliferation and Control.* Lynne Rienner Publishers, London.

Dark Sun. 1995, *the Making of the Hydrogen Bomb, by Richard Rhodes,* Simon & Schuster, New York.

Davies Philip H. J and Gustafson Kristian C. 2013. *Intelligence Elsewhere: Spies and Espionage Outside the Anglosphere.* Georgetown University Press, Washington DC. USA.

Eager Paige Whaley, 2008, *From Freedom Fighters to Terrorists: Women and Political Violence*, Ashgate, Hampshire

Editorial *Dawn*, "Deployment of Troops Begins in South Waziristan." 21 February, 2004.

Editorial *the Nation*, 21 February, 2004. Troops Moved Towards Angoor Adda.

Falk Richard and David Krieger, 2008, *At the Nuclear Precipice: Catastrophe or Transformation?* Palgrave MaCmillan, USA.

Farmelo Graham. 2009. *The Strangest Man: The Hidden Face of Paul Dirac, Mystic of the Atom.* Basic Books, New York. USA.

Faruqui Ahmad, 2001. *The Complex Dynamics of Pakistan Relationship with China*, Policy Research, Islamabad

Farmelo Graham. 2013. *Churchill's Bomb: How the United States Overtook Britain in the First Nuclear Arms Race.* Basic Books, New York, USA.

Ferguson Charles D, William C. Potter. 2004. *The Four Faces of Nuclear Terrorism*, Monterey Institute of International Studies.

Frank P. Harvey. 2008. *The Homeland Security Dilemma: Fear, Failure and the Future of American Insecurity.* Routledge, London.

Frederic Volpi, 2008. *Transnational Islam and Regional Security*, Routledge, London.

Freedman Lawrence. 2003. *The Evolution of Nuclear Strategy.* Palgrave. UK.

Freedman Lawrence. 2013. "Disarmament and Other Nuclear Norms," *Washington Quarterly.* USA.

Fair C. Christine. 2007. "Militant Recruitment in Pakistan: A New Look at the Militancy–Madrasa Connection," *Asian Policy.*

Fresch Hillel & Inbar Efraim. 2008. *Radical Islam and International Security.* Routledge,

First, Brian. 2009. *Terrorism, crime, and public policy*, Cambridge: Cambridge University Press.

Frost, Robin M. 2005. *Nuclear terrorism after 9/11, Abingdon*: Routledge for the International Institute for Strategic Studies.

Gerstein, Daniel M. 2009. *Bioterrorism in the 21st century: emerging threats in a new global environment.* Annapolis, Md.: Naval Institute Press.

Fuhrmann, Matthew. 2012. *Atomic assistance: how "atoms for peace" programs cause nuclear insecurity*. Ithaca: Cornell University Press.

Gavin, Francis J. 2012. *Nuclear statecraft: history and strategy in America's atomic age*. Cornell University Press.

Gibson, David R. 2012. *Talk at the brink: deliberation and decision during the Cuban Missile Crisis*. Princeton: Princeton University Press.

Graham, Allison T. and Philip Zelikow, 1999, *Essence of Decision: Explaining the Cuban Missile Crisis*, Longman, New York

Graham, Allison T. 2004. *Nuclear Terrorism: The Ultimate Preventable Catastrophe*. Henry Holt & Co, New York

Guhar Altaf, 1996, Ayub Khan: *Pakistan's First Military Ruler*, Oxford University Press.

Gulati Col. M.N.2000. *Military Plight of Pakistan*, Manas Publication, India.

Ganguli Sumit and Devin T. Hagerty. 2006. *Fearful Symmetry: India–Pakistan Crisis in the Shadow of Nuclear Weapons*. Seattle, W.A, University of Washington Press.

Ganguli Sumit and S. Paul Kapur. 2009. *Nuclear Proliferation in South Asia: Crisis Behaviour and the Bomb*. Routledge, New York.

Harvey, Frank P. 2008. *The Homeland Security Dilemma: Fear, Failure, and the Future of American Insecurity*. Contemporary Security Studies.

Howie, Luke. 2012. *Witnesses to terror: understanding the meanings and consequences of terrorism*. Basingstoke: Palgrave Macmillan.

Howitt, Arnold M. 2003. *Countering terrorism: dimensions of preparedness*. Cambridge, Mass.: MIT Press.

Han Henry Hyunwook. 1993. *Terrorism & Political Violence: Limits & Possibilities of Legal Control*, Oceana Publications, New York, USA.

Hoffman Bruce. 1998. *Inside Terrorism*, Columbia University Press. New York.

Husband Mark. 1998. *Warriors of the Prophet: The Struggle for Islam*. Westview Press.

Hurley Jennifer A. 1999. *Weapons of Mass Destruction: Opposing Viewpoints*. San Diego, Greenhaven Press.

Ikram S.M. 1965. *Modern Muslim India and the Birth of Pakistan*. Ashraf, Lahore, Pakistan.

Ikle Fred Charles. 1958. *The Social Impact of Bomb Destruction*. Norman, OK: University of Oklahoma Press.

Ikle Fred Charles. 2006. *Annihilation from Within: The Ultimate Threat to Nations*. Columbia University Press, 2006.

Itty, Abraham. 2009, *South Asian Cultures of the Bomb: Atomic Publics and the State in India and Pakistan*, Indiana University Press.

Iversen, Kristen. 2013. *Full Body Burden: Growing Up in the Nuclear Shadow of Rocky Flats*. New York: Random House, 2013.

Jahan Rounaq. 1972. *Pakistan: Failure and National Integration*, Columbia University Press. New York.

Jalal Ayesha, 2011. *The Past and Present in Pakistan: Beyond the Crisis State*, Columbia University Press, New York.

Jenkins Brian Michael. 2008. *Will Terrorist Go Nuclear?* Promethus Book. New York.

Jaspal Zafar Nawaz. 2009. "Threat of Extremism and Terrorist syndicate Beyond FATA." *Journal of Political Studies*.

Jeremy Bernstein. 2008, *Nuclear Weapons: What You Need to Know*. Cambridge University Press

Kellman Barry. 2007. *Bioviolence: Preventing Biological Terror and Crime*. Cambridge University Press, New York.

Kenneth N. Luongo and Naeem Salik. December, 1, 2007. "Building Confidence in Pakistan's Nuclear Security," *Arms Control Today*.

Kenneth D. Bergeron. 2002, *Tritium on Ice: The Dangerous New Alliance of Nuclear Weapons and Nuclear Power*. Cambridge, MIT Press.

Khan Saira. 2009. *Nuclear Weapons and Conflict Transformation (The Case of India–Pakistan)*. Routledge (Taylor and Francis Group), London.

Krepton Michael. 2009. *Better Safe than Sorry: The Ironies of Living with the Bomb*. Stanford University Press, USA.

Krotz Ulrich and Schild Joachim. 2013. *Shaping Europe: France, Germany, and Embedded Bilateralism from the Elysee Treaty to Twenty-First Century Politics*. Oxford University Press, UK.

Lan Bellany. 2007. *Terrorism and Weapons of Mass Destruction: Responding to the Challenge*. Routledge, London

Lian W. 2010. "Talibanization in the Tribal Area of Pakistan," Journal of Middle Eastern and Islamic Studies.

Lewis, Jeffrey. 2014. *Paper Tiger: China's Nuclear Posture*. International Institute for Strategic Studies, London.

Lichbach M.I. 1989. "An Evaluation of "Does Economic Inequality Breed Political Conflict"? *A Quarterly Journal of International Relations*.

Lindholm C. 1986 Jan. 1. "Leadership Categories and Social Process in Islam: The Case of Dir and Swat." *Journal of anthropological Research.*

Martinage Robert C. 2008. *The Global War on Terrorism: An Assessment. Centre for Strategic and Budgetary Assessments.* Washington DC.

Mehra Parshotam. 1998. *The North West Frontiers Drama, 1945–47: A Re-Assessment.* Manohar Publisher, New Delhi, India.

Mir Amir. 2009. *Talibanization in Pakistan, Pentagon Security International,* Publisher, India.

Nawaz Shuja. 2009. *FATA: The Most Dangerous Place,* Centre for Strategic and International Studies. USA.

Omand David. 2010. *Securing the State.* Hurst & Company, London.

Osama W.M. 2002, *The Case of US Leadership in Rebuilding of Afghanistan,* Analysis from East West Centre.

Perez Margaret Gonzalez. 2008. *Women and Terrorism: Female activities in Domestic and International Terror Groups,* Routledge, London and New York.

Pape R.A. 2003. "The Strategic Logic of Suicide Terrorism," *American Political science Review.*

Philip H. J. Davies and Kristian C. Gustafson, 2013. *Intelligence Elsewhere: Spies and Espionage outside the Anglosphere.* Georgetown University Press, USA

Pinault D. 2003. "Shia–Sunni Relations in Contemporary Pakistan." *Journal of South Asian and Middle Eastern Studies*

Raza Rumi. 2010–2011. *The rise of Violent Extremism. Extremism Watch. Mapping Conflict trends in Pakistan,* Jinnah Institute Islamabad.

Rhodes, Richard, 1986. *The Making of the Atomic Bomb,* Simon & Schuster, New York.

Rid, Thomas. 2013. *Cyber War Will Not Take Place.* Hurts & Company London.

Satu Limaye, Robert Wirsing & Mohan Malik. 2004. *Religious Radicalization and Security in South Asia.* Honolulu Asia Pacific Centre for Security Studies.

Saima Afzal, Iqba Hamid l, Inayat Mavara. 2012. *Sectarianism and its implication for Pakistan's Security. Policy Recommendations using exploratory study.* Department of Peace and Conflict Studies, National Defense University Islamabad.

Shulsky Abram N. and Schmitt. Gary J. 2002. *Silent Warfare: Understanding the World of Intelligence.* Potomac Books Washington, USA.

Siddiqa Ayesha, Military Inc.: *Inside Pakistan's Military Economy*, Pluto Press 20 Apr 2007.

Taj Farhat. 2012. *Taliban and Anti Taliban*, Cambridge Scholars Publishing.

Weller George. 2006. *First into Nagasaki: The Censored Eyewitness Dispatches on Post-Atomic Japan and its Prisoners of War*, Crown, New York.

Wellock Thomas R. 1998. *Opposition to Nuclear Power in California, 1958–1978*. Madison, University of Wisconsin Press.

Wenger, Andreas, and Reto Wollenmann, 2007, *Bioterrorism: Confronting a Complex Threat*, Lynne Rienner, London.

Whitney Craig R. 2005. "The WMD Mirage: Iraq's Decade of Deception and America's False Premises for War," *Journal of Public Affairs*, New York.

Yoshihara Toshi and James R. Holmes. 2012. *Strategy in the Second Nuclear Age: Power Ambitions and the Ultimate Weapon.* Georgetown University Washington DC.

Younger Stephen M. 2010. *The Bomb: A New History.* ECCO, New York.

Yusafzai Hamid Iqbal. 2011. *The US Factor in Pak–Afghan Relations Post 9/11*. Lambert Academic Publishing, Germany.

Yusufzai, Rahimullah, "Fall of the Last Frontier?" *Monthly Newline Magazine* (Karachi), June 2002.

Zaeef, Abdul Salam, *My Life with the Taliban, London*: Hurst and Company, 2009.

Zahab, Mariam Abu, and Olivier Roy, *Islamist Networks: The Afghan–Pakistan Connection*, London: C. Hurst, 2004.